FALSE BODIES, TRUE SELVES

FALSE BODIES, TRUE SELVES

Moving Beyond Appearance-Focused Identity Struggles and Returning to the True Self

Nicole Schnackenberg

Routledge
Taylor & Francis Group

LONDON AND NEW YORK

First published 2016 by
Karnac Books Ltd.

Published 2018 by Routledge
2 Park Square, Milton Park, Abingdon, Oxon OX14 4RN
711 Third Avenue, New York, NY 10017, USA

Routledge is an imprint of the Taylor & Francis Group, an informa business

British Library Cataloguing in Publication Data

A C.I.P. for this book is available from the British Library

  ISBN 9781782203964 (pbk)

Edited, designed and produced by The Studio Publishing Services Ltd
www.publishingservicesuk.co.uk
email: studio@publishingservicesuk.co.uk

CONTENTS

ACKNOWLEDGEMENTS and PERMISSIONS

A book never emerges solely through one person but through the hearts of all those who encourage, support, and offer their love along the way. Every person in my life is responsible for this book in some way and, as such, I am a co-author or, more truthfully, a scribe. If our paths in this life have crossed, I wish to thank you. Every encounter makes us who we are and what we write.

Thank you to Maria Escribano for creating the spellbinding patchwork doll on the front cover and to Ingrid Sanchez for photographing it with such sensitivity and for re-working some of the images in Chapter Nine. You are exquisite artists and exquisite friends.

Thank you to everyone at Karnac for your astonishing patience and expertise. Particular thanks to Rod Tweedy for this amazing opportunity and for your guidance and support throughout every fascinating step of the publishing process. Our tea and chats have been some of my most favourite of times over the past year. A special thank you also goes to Cecily Blench, Kate Pearce, and Alex Massey, and all the team at The Studio, with grateful mention also to Heather Allan at *PCCS* and Richard Cox at T!M FREKE Publications.

Thank you to so many dear friends for your encouragement and advice. It is impossible to name you all but I trust you know who you are. Special thanks to Mandy Scott, Heather Mobbs, Amoreena Campbell, Minnie Iris, Sergio Petro, Sara and Lucio Angeli, Paula Taylor, Rebecca Bennett, Georgie Winn, Emma Sharman, Rachel Turnball, Carly Travers, Gemma Creek, Jenny "Wren" White, Suzanne Engelen, Senait Debesay, Jonathan and Emma Gadsby, and Karin Hildebrandt.

Huge gratitude is warmly extended to Jo Manuel and everyone at *Special Yoga Foundation*. Finding you was truly a homecoming and I still cannot get over how blessed I am to be working with you all. A very special thank you also to Sonia Sumar, founder of *Yoga for the Special Child* and to Heather Mason, founder of the *Minded Institute*.

Sincere appreciation goes out to and every one of you beautiful and brave women in my cohort for the *Eat Breathe Thrive* training with the indomitable Chelsea Roff and Sam Child. Special acknowledgement goes to the lovely Malin Johansson. Let's bring *Eat Breathe Thrive* to London ladies!

A million heartfelt thanks to the trustees of the *BDD Foundation*, headed by Rob Willson and David Veale. You are changing the world with your passion and refusal to engage only with the surface level of body image distress. This book and my life are richer because you are around.

Immeasurable thanks to Professor Bryan Lask of Great Ormond Street Hospital, who passed away late last year. Thank you also to David Petro and to Sally Geeson. Your inspiration will far outstay your time with us. You are deeply missed.

Thank you to my wonderful extended family in both England and Germany. Forgive me for not mentioning you all by name (there are so many of you!) but please know how deeply grateful I am for your unwavering support and love. Special thanks go to Nanny Betty, Dave Jesson, Nanny Liz, Uncle Ernie, Sandra Kennedy, Eddie Kennedy, Kelly Bartlett, Dave Bartlett, Roxie Bartlett, Mia Bartlett, Phoebe Bartlett, Florence Bartlett, Dean Kennedy, Kelly Jenner, George Kafatos, Terri Peake, Peter Cooper, Laura Cooper, Sophie Cooper, Sheldon Cooper, Marlon Cooper, Marie Bragg, Lee Finch, Grady O'Brien, Christa Schnackenberg, Georg Schnackenberg, Katrin Schnackenberg, Margrit Schnackenberg, Christoph Schnackenberg, Sonja Bucher, and Hanna Schröder. Deep gratitude in particular go to Nanny Joan and Granddad Johnson whose influence stretches far beyond their earthly lives.

Thank you from the very bottom of my heart to my parents, Michael Peake and Pauline Cooper and to my sister and brother, Jordana Peake and Michael Peake. Without you I simply would not have been around to write this. Thank you for refusing to give up on me and for running after me no matter how far I went. Your courage and determination reach beyond words. I love you so much.

Finally, this book is permeated with your incredible love and fearless influence Joachim Schnackenberg. *Alles ist gut, meine Liebe.*

Every effort has been made to obtain permission for any quote or extract by another writer or artist contained within this book. If an extract appears for which you are the copyright holder and do not wish to give permission for its use, please inform the author or publisher in writing and it shall be removed from any future edition of this book.

A Bright Red Scream by Marilee Strong, published by Penguin; reprinted by Virago. Reproduced with permission of Penguin Group: USA.

A Straight Talking Introduction to Psychiatric Diagnosis by Lucy Johnstone, published by PCCS. Reproduced with permission of PCCS.

A Straight Talking Introduction to Psychiatric Drugs by Joanna Moncrieff, published by PCCS. Reproduced with permission of PCCS.

A Way of Being by Carl Rogers, published by Houghton Mifflin. Reproduced with permission of Houghton Mifflin.

Beautiful by Katie Piper, published by Ebury Press. Reproduced with permission of The Random House Group.

Before I Am by Mooji, published by Mooji Media. Reproduced with permission of Mooji Media. Permission also granted for video transcripts.

Be As You Are by Sri Ramana Maharshi, edited by David Godman, published by Penguin. Reproduced with permission of The Penguin Group.

Body of Truth: How Science, History and Culture Drive our Obsession with Weight – and What We Can Do About It by Harriet Brown, copyright

2015. Reprinted with permission of Da Capo Lifelong Books, a member of The Perseus Books Group.

'Burst of Light' from the collection 'I Am Your Sister' by Audre Lorde. Published by Oxford University Press. Reproduced with permission of the Charlotte Sheedy Literary Agency.

C.G. Jung and Herman Hesse: A Record of Two Friendships edited by Miguel Serrano. Published by Routledge. Reproduced with permission of Routledge.

Closer to Home: Bi-Sexuality and Feminism edited by Elizabeth Reba Weise. Published by Seal Press. Address of author obtained from Perseus Group; no known rights held.

Critique of Pure Reason by Immanuel Kant. Published by Penguin Classics. Reproduced with permission of the Random House Group.

Eat Fat by Richard Klein, published by Macmillian. Reproduced with permission of Macmillan.

Emptiness Dancing by Adyashanti, published by Sounds True Inc. Reproduced with permission of Sounds True Inc.

Gaining: The Truth about Life after Eating Disorders by Aimee Liu. Reproduced with direct permission of the author.

How to Know God, by Deepak Chopra, published by Penguin. Reproduced with permission of Penguin Random House.

Hunger Strike: Starving Amidst Plenty by Susie Orbach. Published by Karnac. Reproduced with permission of Karnac.

Maturational Processes and the Facilitating Environment: Ego Distortion in Terms of True and False Self by Donald Winnicott. Published by Hogarth. Reproduced with permission of The Random House Group.

Phenomenology of Perception by Maurice Merleau-Ponty. Published by Routledge. Reproduced with permission of Routledge.

Poems that Make Grown Men Cry: Love after Love by Derek Wallcott. Reproduced with permission of Faber and Faber.

Saint Francis and the Sow in Mortal Acts, Mortal Words by Galway Kinnell, published by Houghtom Mifflin. Reproduced with permission of Houghton Mifflin.

Selected Poems: Rainer Maria Rilke translated by Ranson and Sutherland, published by Oxford University Press. Reproduced with permission of Oxford University Press.

Social and Ethical Interpretations in Mental Development by James Mark Baldwin, published by Macmillan. Reproduced with permission of Macmillan.

Sylvia Plath by Linda Wagner, published by Taylor and Francis Group. Reproduced with permission of Routledge.

The Beauty Myth by Naomi Wolf, published by Penguin. Reproduced with permission of Penguin Random House.

The Black Sun: The Alchemy and the Art of Darkness by Stanton Marlon, published by A &M University Press. Reproduced with permission of Texas A & M University Press.

The Body Keeps the Score by Bessel van der Kolk, published by Penguin. Reproduced with permission of Penguin Random House.

The Broken Mirror by Katharine Phillips, published by Oxford University Press. Reproduced with permission of Oxford University Press USA.

The Essential Rumi by Rumi and Coleman Barks (translator), published by HarperCollins. Reproduced with permission of HarperCollins.

The Gospel of Thomas translated by Richard Valantasis. Reproduced with permission of Routledge.

The Hero with a Thousand Faces by Joseph Campbell, published by New World Library. Reproduced with permission of The Joseph Campbell Foundation (JCF).

The Language of Emotions: What your Feelings are Trying to Tell You by Karla McLaren, published by Sounds True Inc. Reproduced with permission of Sounds True Inc.

The Latino Male by David Abalos, published by Lynne Rienner. Reproduced with permission of Lynne Reinner.

The New Individualism by Charles Lemert, published by Taylor and Francis. Reproduced with permission of Routledge.

The Prophet by Kahlil Gibran, published by Pan Reprints. Reproduced with permission of Penguin Random House.

The Origin of Consciousness in the Breakdown of the Bicameral Mind by Julian Jaynes, Copyright © 1967, 1990. Used by permission of Houghton Mifflin Harcourt Publishing Company. All rights reserved.

The Velveteen Rabbit by Margery Williams, published by Penguin. Reproduced on the advice of The Penguin Group (out of copyright and in the public domain, therefore no official permission required).

Thin by Grace Bowman, published by Penguin. Reproduced with permission of Penguin Random House.

T.S. Eliot, The Poems. Edited by Martin Scofield, published by Cambridge University Press. Reproduced with permission of Faber and Faber, holders of the T. S. Eliot estate.

Waking: A Passage into Body by Matthew Sanford, published by Rodale. Reproduced with permission of Rodale.

Wasted by Marya Hornbacher, published by HarperCollins. Reproduced with permission of Harper Collins.

Why Love Matters by Sue Gerhardt, published by Taylor and Francis. Reproduced with permission of Routledge.

Nicole Schnackenberg is a psychotherapist, teacher, and therapeutic yoga practitioner based in Woking, Surrey. She currently divides her time between her role as a school counsellor in Guildford, her position as a yoga therapist at Special Yoga Foundation in London, and her trusteeship with the Body Dysmorphic Disorder Foundation. She is also working towards full accreditation in systemic family therapy and educational psychology. This is her first book.

It is an honour to write a Foreword for this book. This is a timely manuscript and much needed in a world in which we are increasingly defined by our image and appearance and, partially due to the rise of social media, are bombarded with a daily onslaught of ideas, images, and representations of what constitutes beauty and perfection. It is becoming ever more difficult, even with a strong sense of self, to ascertain what is real and what is superimposed upon us by both the media and our own, often damaged, interior vision of who we are. These struggles are not helped at all by Western standards of beauty, which seem to have become largely centred on the "thin ideal" and other notions of restricting and altering the body.

False Bodies, True Selves is a beautifully written, thoughtfully presented treatise on the schism between our external image and internal realities. Nicole Schnackenberg draws upon her experiences as a psychotherapist and yoga practitioner as she skilfully blends academic research and psychoanalytical theory with Eastern philosophy and ideas of embodiment.

The book is a must, and not only for those afflicted by clinical conditions such as body dysmorphic disorder and disordered eating, but for anyone who battles with general anxiety about their appearance or any kind of negative body image. I believe there is much comfort to be found in this book's non-dogmatic approach, which can serve to open our eyes to the societal and cultural norms that seem to encourage a hyper-vigilance around the way we look.

False Bodies, True Selves is a timely reminder of the need to return to the body—and how practices such as meditation, mindfulness, and yoga can serve to mend severed and faulty connections from body to brain and vice versa. The observations made in this book are grounded in current neuroscientific research, which has shed so much light on how our minds and bodies are inextricably connected.

Nicole also writes eloquently and beautifully about her own painful struggles with anorexia and body dysmorphic disorder, which resonate with some aspects of my experience. As a former dancer now working in the field of dance training and education, I am painfully aware of the tendency for young women in particular to seek self-esteem and self-worth in low body weights. It is not uncommon in my field, for example, for women to be clinically underweight in a bid to get work. High levels of perfectionism often correlate with high levels of anxiety, depression, and eating disorders. I hope to be able to share some of the insights this book offers both with my students and trainee yoga teachers and know it will be of enormous help to those working in the field as counsellors, therapists, and educators.

False Bodies, True Selves has made a groundbreaking contribution to the frontiers of self-acceptance and healing in appearance-focused distress.

Dr Abby Hoffmann
Founder of Embodied Dancer Yoga and
Head of Studies at Rambert School of Ballet and Contemporary Dance

INTRODUCTION

Albert Camus once beautifully said, "In the depths of winter, I finally learned that within me there lay an invincible summer" (Sparks, 1962, p. 112). The practice of embracing the darkness in our lives and discovering our luminous Selves within this darkness is at the heart, I shall argue throughout this book, of the human experience. Such an understanding, however, seems rarely to be at the forefront of psychological theory, treatment, and literature. The emphasis, instead, would appear to be on escaping the winter, annihilating the cold, and banishing the icy parts within us.

I have read many stunning books and engaged in many fascinating discussions with specialists in the field of appearance-focused identity struggles. In the main, there is a genuine appreciation of the utter devastation caused by appearance battles in their many forms to the individual, their families, and their wider communities. There is also some understanding that the surface-level battle with the body is only ever that, a superficial smoke screen that simultaneously serves both to cover up and express a person's deeper pain and need for healing.

Throughout my own treatment for intentional starvation and self-loathing, however, the main agendum brought to the table was the obliteration of the so-depicted demonic force most regularly referred to as anorexia. For almost two decades, therefore, I ploughed all of my energies into fighting my insatiable hunger for starvation and self-harm. It never really got me very far.

This book has been written largely in response to the dearth of literature expounding a true appreciation of the underlying metaphor beneath our appearance battles. It is my deep conviction that until our story is heard, our anguish recognised and assimilated, and the deeper metaphor underpinning our self-destruction understood, we have little hope of truly moving beyond the vicious circles we become entrenched in. I would also argue that we are unlikely to find peace by fighting against our pain but, rather, by entering into our emotions and seeking the *invincible summer* within us.

The focus of this book is not on psychiatric diagnoses or mental health labels, but on experiences, on people's stories. Every single behaviour, however seemingly aberrant, is understandable when contextualised.

You will also come across terms such as "appearance distress", "appearance struggles", and "appearance battles" used interchangeably. It is a seemingly impossible task to come up with a neat phrase to encapsulate the full range of experiences related to appearance and identity. My ideal phrase would probably read something like, "displaced distress on the physical body due to living life as a false self"; a bit too lengthy and clunky an encapsulation to use throughout the book. I have used "appearance distress" and so on, therefore, for ease of reading, hoping that the reader will keep in mind the truth of such experiences, which have nothing to do with appearances at their heart and everything to do with the pain of living a life in opposition to who you truly are.

We begin our journey together by looking at some of the myths, superstitions, and fairy tales related to mirrors before moving on to society's current obsession with appearance, which would seem to have been compounded by the mass media. After looking at some of the most common manifestations of appearance-focused identity struggles, we begin to unpick the possible underlying meanings beneath them with a particular emphasis on difficult childhood experiences in their many forms and on wider issues of a systemic nature. We then take a brief moratorium to explore some of the processes of visual perception in the Interlude. In Part II, we begin a conversation about the spiritual aspects of psychological distress, including the benefits of addressing our appearance anguish through a transpersonal lens.

The true Self, as described by Donald Winnicott, would appear to become manifest through the acceptance and assimilation of our shadow side, which involves a journey of an existential nature. You will notice that many times throughout this book, the Self is referred to as a proper noun. This is deliberate and sympathetic towards Jungian psychology within which the Self signifies the part of us that is whole and integrated. Jung's Self is the transcendent, unchanging part of ourselves, in stark contrast to our undulating ego, shadow, and complexes. I argue that we are enabled to emerge from our appearance struggles when we return to this Self, to the true Self, and move away from the pseudo, false selves we have created in an attempt to please the world around us. When you come across a "Self" with a capital "S", therefore, I implore you to call to mind your deeper truth and authenticity. This is the true Self written about by Jung and Winnicott and is the Self which transcends any identification we might have with our physical bodies.

This book has been written with the distinct understanding that what is helpful for some us will not be useful to us all. The focus of the latter part of this book on mindfulness and matters of a transpersonal nature springs from my own experience of what helped me the most. Appendices I and II, in particular, then, focus on how we can address appearance distress within our families and societies. It is my firm belief that appearance struggles are best addressed, where possible, within the context through which they emerged.

There have been many books written about other ways of addressing appearance battles. If you feel drawn to more behavioural methods of confronting your inner pain, you might find that this book does not cover your desired content at the current time, although you will find cognitive behavioural therapy (CBT) related references throughout this book. Another publisher I approached with a proposal for this manuscript told me that it did not make sense to have CBT citations in a book primarily focused on transpersonal avenues of healing. I beg to differ. My hope is that we can begin to move beyond these closed-box delineations. I also hope we can increasingly appreciate that the therapeutic actions we feel the most comfortable with might not be the most useful to us. Change, after all, only really happens outside of our comfort zone.

The pretending game, day and night.
Each seeking, fearing, voiceless scene,
a fortress in the bedroom of our journey,
silent and white,
pressing against the dawning light.

Selves split and spirits aching,
a twisting, grating, reckless play.
A prison in the labyrinth of our being,
capricious and black,
throbbing against the passage back.

Curtains lift as emotions surface.
Little puppet, wake up,
find your flesh and your bones.
The phoenix is rising,
each denial known
is pulsing amidst the ache to
come home.

Love ends the circling
and tears down the theatre,
our place to hide.
Space blown open wide
for us to dance in.

N. Schnackenberg

Sometimes it is necessary to re-teach a thing its loveliness. (Galway Kinnell, from *Saint Francis and the Sow*, 1980, p. 9)

PART I
MIRRORS AND MYTHS

CHAPTER ONE

Mirrors and misplaced identities

"The greatest healing is to know who you are"

(Mooji, 2011)

A dear friend of mine, whose beautiful artistry appears on the front cover of this book, once gave me a homemade patchwork doll. I was instantly mesmerised by it. It had been lovingly and painstakingly sewn together by hand using old, discarded pieces of scrap material and loose cuttings of thread. It looked haphazard, captivating, strangely beautiful. The more I looked at my quirky little gift the more I recognised myself in those sewn together pieces of cloth. For most of my life I had been a patchwork person, a marionette made up of gathered scraps of other people's ideas and expectations. Painfully unable to placate or to please, I had squirrelled away other people's perceptions and desires about who I should be as a child, sewn them together and made a person out of them, a person other people called "Nicole'", a person I could barely even recognise. The shreds of my true Self were left in rejected tatters. The Germans have a beautifully onomatopoeic word for this: *Zerrissenheit*, meaning "torn-to-pieces-hood".

The patchwork doll.

I had become, as Donald Winnicott, the pioneering English paediatrician and psychoanalyst, called it, a false self (Winnicott, 1965). And
I was certainly not alone. As I began to scan my periphery, I observed
the tragic annihilation of people's true needs and desires in almost
every direction I looked. I began to see, beneath so many smiles, a
deep brokenness, a gaping void, a tragic loss of Self.

It is this move away from the true Self, in the context of appearance-focused identity battles, which will concern our discussion for
the entirety of this book. It is my firm conviction that appearance
struggles arise out of the pain of living as a false self and can, therefore, reach a resolution by allowing the true Self to re-emerge.

Many of us begin our day by looking into the mirror. We assume
that what we see there is our self. Yet, it continues to remain unclear as
to how we recognise our own image, known in scientific circles as
visual self-recognition. Jacques Lacan believed that human infants
recognise themselves in a mirror from the age of about six months old
and from then on view themselves as an object that can be viewed from
outside of themselves (apperception). He called this the "mirror stage"
(Lacan, 1977). More recent research suggests, however, that we only
begin to recognise our own reflection between the ages of eighteen and

twenty-four months (Nielsen et al., 2003). We are not alone in this ability to recognise our own image. In a classic experiment, Gallup (1970) found that chimpanzees are also capable of self-recognition, since they are able to use mirrors to direct their behaviour towards an otherwise unseen novel mark placed upon their face. More recent studies have found that the only other primates who share this capacity are the apes (Posada & Colell, 2007).

While Lacan initially proposed that the mirror stage was simply part of an infant's development, his theory later evolved. He no longer believed the mirror stage to be a singular pivot in the life of a small child, but, rather, viewed it as a permanent structure of subjectivity, as something he termed the *paradigm of the imaginary order*. The basis of the imaginary order is that the ego is formed in the mirror stage, which occurs through identification with the viewed image. Our ability to recognise ourselves and identify with the recognised image is thought to be especially fundamental to the awareness of being a self among others like us. We can then build more complex forms of self-identity on to this awareness, such as a diachronic (over time) sense of self. Our bodies change significantly over the course of our lives, with each life stage altering multiple facets of our appearance. As we age and our appearance changes, we must adapt to the altered reflection in the mirror in order to sustain recognition of the changing face and body that we see there.

There are many reasons why we might look into the mirror. Perhaps we are checking our hair or deciding if our shoes look as if they are having an argument with the rest of our attire. These are trivialities, yet looking into the mirror can also be anything but a trifling experience. Perhaps we are looking to derive our sense of self-worth from the reflection we see. Perhaps we are checking whether we actually exist at all. The human body and its appearance are heavily value laden and imbued with meaning. The body is a

> site of birth, growth, ageing, and death, of pleasure, pain and many things . . . an object of desires . . . a bearer of features . . . a biological machine that provides the material preconditions for subjectivity, thought, emotion and language. (Cromby & Nightingale, 1999, p. 10)

When we look into the mirror we are seeing a rich web of experience, overlaid with our current ideas and notions about who we have been and who we think we now are.

Mirrors have featured heavily in myths and legends and in children's literature across time. They also abound in superstitious thinking across the ages. In some ancient cultures, it was considered necessary to cover all the mirrors in the house when a loved one died under difficult circumstances, since people believed that the spirit of the dead person would linger on, looking for a body to possess in order to complete any unfinished business. Breaking a mirror, as many of us will know, is said to carry bad luck for seven years, a superstition traceable to the Romans, who were actually the first to create glass mirrors. The Romans, along with the Greek, Chinese, African, and Indian cultures, believed that a mirror had the power to take away part of the gazer's soul. Some cultures have long exclaimed that if you look into a mirror often enough you will see the devil, perhaps by way of warning people against the so-called sins of vanity and self-obsession.

In Greek mythology, one person who might have done well to heed this advice was Narcissus. Narcissus was an exceptionally handsome young man who constantly spurned the affection of the adulating nymphs. One day, desiring a drink, Narcissus took himself to a clear pool of water wherein he saw his reflection and promptly fell in love with it. Since he could not gain the love he felt, he remained pining at the pool and died there. When the nymphs heard of his tragic fate, they went down to the pool and found no body, but a flower at the spot where Narcissus died, the flower that now bears his name. Another Greek myth famously featuring a mirror reflection is that of Perseus, one of the first heroes of Greek mythology. To avoid looking into Medusa's eyes and, thus, being turned into stone, Perseus viewed Medusa through a reflection in the mirror and was, thereby, able to cut off her head and defeat her.

The fauna of mirrors is a rather interesting superstition, springing from an ancient Chinese myth, which claims that behind every mirror there is a completely different world, first described in a story by Jorge Luis Borges entitled "Fauna of mirrors" (Borges, 2006). Such thinking has also been adopted by more modern writers, including Lewis Carroll in *Alice through the Looking Glass*, the sequel to *Alice's Adventures in Wonderland*. Alice, while pondering what the world is like on the other side of a mirror's reflection, climbs on to the fireplace mantel and pokes at the wall-hung mirror there. To her immense surprise and delight, Alice finds that she is able to step through the mirror and into an alternative reality, into a world in which she is adoringly crowned as a queen before waking up to the realisation that it has all been nothing more than a dream.

In Snow White, we also find the legend of the mirror possessing other-worldly abilities, with the wicked step-mother summoning the spirit in the mirror to tell her who is the "fairest one of all" in order to reassure herself of her own good looks. This legend is based on scrying, which, in its basic form, is the belief that a young woman will see her future husband if she applies focused concentration and asks who "is the fairest one of all?" while combing her hair by candlelight at midnight in front of the mirror. Mirrors have long been used as a means of divination, an art known as catoptromancy. In this ancient practice, it is said to be possible to divine the past, present, and future by gazing into the surface of a mirror, usually positioned to reflect the moonlight. Catoptromancy was practised for many centuries and is the origin of much folklore. Père Cotton, confessor to King Henry IV of France, reputedly used a mirror to reveal plots against the King. It is also known that Pythagoras, the famous Greek mathematician, frequently practised catoptromancy during a full moon.

In my favourite fairy-tale, *The Snow Queen*, by Hans Christian Andersen, an evil troll makes a magic mirror that has the power to distort the appearance of anything reflected in it. While failing to reflect all the good and beautiful aspects of the gazer, it nevertheless magnifies all the dark and ugly qualities, making people seem far worse than they actually are. The trolls are so delighted with their creation that they wish to carry the mirror into heaven to make fools of the angels. As they lift the mirror higher and higher, it begins to shake, eventually shattering into millions of tiny pieces and falling back down to earth. The splinters are blown asunder by the wind, entering into people's hearts and eyes, freezing their hearts over like ice and rendering their eyes blinkered like the troll-mirror itself; they are now only able to see the dark and ugly in everything.

Looking into the mirror and perceiving only the dark and ugly aspects of the self is sadly not an occurrence restricted to the realm of fairy tales. For growing numbers of people all over the world, the mirror can become such a window into self-loathing, abandoned self-worth, and disintegrating self-respect. A report by the All Party Parliamentary Group on Body Image (2012) found that girls as young as five are worrying about their size and appearance, and that one in four seven-year-old girls have tried to lose weight at least once. Heartbreakingly, 34% of adolescent boys and 49% of girls surveyed were found to have been on a diet to change their body shape or lose weight and 60% of participating British adults reported feeling ashamed of the way they look. These figures are hardly surprising given that, according to the British Social Attitudes Survey conducted in October 2014, almost half of all adults (47%) think that "how you look affects what you can achieve in life", and one third (32%) agree with the statement "your value as a person depends on how you look" (Government Equalities Office, 2014). Such messages permeate our media, with 75% of those surveyed by the All Party Parliamentary Group viewing media, advertising, and celebrity culture as being the main social influences on body image.

Western culture would appear to be providing the ideal conditions for difficult life experiences to seek resolution in appearance battles. By the end of the twentieth century, popular culture had begun to identify bodies as sites of commodified forms of health and beauty, offering glamorous identities and powerful sexuality, though at a price. Since then, we have been increasingly drip-fed the myth that happiness can be constructed via the manipulation of our physical appearance. Many of us, subsequently, have dabbled or thrown ourselves headlong into our beauty projects, hoping to soothe and negate any emotional pain, most likely rooted in our childhood, through the modulation of our flesh. As we lose weight, increase our musculature, clear our skin, and increase our cup size, Western culture takes a standing ovation, thus legitimising further action. It is amazing, for some of us, just how deep the rabbit hole can go.

It is disadvantageous to their perpetuation for capitalist societies to extol the acceptability and beauty of our bodies, since this would negate any need for the purchase of goods. It is far more lucrative to sell the "you must look a certain way in order to be happy" myth, and to encourage us to change and "enhance" our bodies through diets, cosmetics, surgery, and other such means. Notably, cosmetic surgery rates in the UK have increased by almost 20% since 2008 to an estimated value of £2.3 billion, an upsurge that has been largely attributed by researchers to advertising and irresponsible marketing ploys. By insidiously fostering the belief that we can become better, more acceptable, and increasingly loveable by altering our physical form and appearance, we are persuaded to buy into the multiple industries whose survival depends on us spending money on their products and signing up for their programmes.

Too many of us have decided that if we are seemingly imperfect it must be our fault. If we are too large by society's standards, it is because we have not dieted enough; if our hair is too frizzy, it is because we have not searched earnestly enough for the right products to smooth it down; if we have dark rings under eyes we should be ashamed for not covering them up with one of the plethora of concealers sitting expectantly on the chemist's shelf. We have heedlessly and tragically swallowed the cultural myth that it is not only our business to make ourselves look good, but also our *obligation* to be beautiful. As Martina Cvajner writes, having interviewed Italian women about their perceptions of their appearance,

> For my informants, to "take care of their appearance" did not necessarily mean pursuing one's natural physical beauty. Rather, beauty was something to be constructed. The body, in other words, is a canvas that counts—to define if and whether a person is a woman—not for its intrinsic qualities but for the degree of effort and creativity of what is being painted on it. If you take care of yourself, you are a woman. (Cvajner, 2011, p. 364)

This sense of being agents of our own beauty is tangled up in our experience of our body image. Such body image develops partly as a function of culture in response to cultural aesthetic ideals (Rudd & Lennon, 2001). We cannot really talk about body image, therefore, without considering the society within which a person is situated. In current Western culture, thinness and attractiveness are seen to be highly desirable physical traits for women, while men are lauded for being muscular and handsome. These notions of attractiveness are intrinsically wrapped up in experiences of self-worth. Such perceptions are reinforced through evaluations of, and comparisons to, others, including family members, peers, and media images. Comparison to idealised images in the mass media, for example, has been shown to create and reinforce a preoccupation with physical attractiveness (Groesz et al., 2002).

Western culture's current standard of attractiveness for women, as portrayed in the media, is slimmer than it has been in the past and, hence, is unattainable by most women (Hausenblas et al., 2002). Many women, however, subliminally absorb the thin ideal and could come to berate themselves for any failure to morph into it. Such ideation wreaks havoc, as one might imagine, on self-esteem and self-worth. Ninety-five per cent of women are estimated to diet at least once in their lifetime (Grogan, 2008), a practice which has become a cultural norm in many Western societies and yet is life-threatening at worst and painful to some degree at best. The body reacts very strongly to a shortage of food, as we shall see in Chapter Three, which can result in significant compromises to the person's physical, emotional, and psychological health. Comparisons to media images have been shown by Heinberg and Thompson (1995), among others, to trigger depression, anger, and distortions related to body image. In terms of media images of men, research has found that men are now portrayed as more muscular than in the past (Leit et al., 2001), with almost one third of British men wanting to look like the models they see in magazines (Diedrichs et al., 2011).

While some advertising does portray relatively "ordinary" or "average" people in everyday situations, most advertising presents an unrealistic or idealised picture of people and their lives (Richins, 1995). Sadly, the level of beauty and physical attractiveness presented in media images is characteristic of only a tiny proportion of the population. Yet, the message we are perpetually sold is that this level of beauty and attractiveness is the norm, or, at least, something towards which we can realistically strive. The digital manipulation, or "airbrushing", of such media images is likely to further exacerbate this reality gap.

Cultivation theory posits that consistent media representations construct an alternative reality: in this case, a reality in which the world is populated by slim, attractive women and handsome, toned men. Due to the pervasiveness of these images, an upward shift of people's personal image expectations can occur (Blowers et al., 2003). In an innovative study by Hargreaves and Tiggeman (2003), the effects of appearance-related television commercials and non-appearance-related television commercials on body dissatisfaction among adolescent girls were analysed. The girls exposed to appearance-related commercials became more dissatisfied with their own appearance than those who were exposed to non-appearance-related commercials. Overall, findings indicated associations between greater body dissatisfaction and more frequent television viewing. In another study, Myers and Biocca found that women's perceptions of their bodies changed after watching less than thirty minutes of programming or advertising, a finding which suggests that our body image is highly elastic and susceptible to outside influence. They concluded,

> Television images that are fixated on the representation of the ideal female body immediately led the female subjects to thoughts about their own bodies. This in turn led to the measurable fluctuations and disturbances in their body image. In their mind's eye, their body shape had changed. (Myers & Biocca, 1992, p. 126)

These influences can be understood within the concept of social comparison theory, as outlined by Leon Festinger (1954). Social comparison theory postulates that people are driven to acquire a precise assessment of themselves by discerning their abilities and opinions in comparison to the individuals around them. According to Festinger, people obtain a sense of validity and clarity by comparing themselves in specific domains against an objective benchmark provided by the people with whom they are comparing themselves. Comparing ourselves with someone similar produces more accurate appraisals, while comparing ourselves to more dissimilar others creates less accurate assessments. Due to the overwhelming societal preference for thin, beautiful women and handsome, muscular men, most of us, therefore, are comparing ourselves with people highly dissimilar to ourselves, resulting in less accurate appraisals of our own attractiveness and body shape. Indeed, it has been estimated that less than 5% of the population could ever realistically attain to the body image ideals presented in the media.

While media attention and societal discussion focus primarily on the health risks of being overweight, the health risks of being underweight (which are considerable) receive far less attention. Research conducted by Flegal and colleagues (2005), for example, found that being underweight was associated with an estimated 33,746 excess deaths (above the usual mortality rate) in the year 2000 in the United States, despite the very small percentage (2.7%) of the subject pool in this category. Conversely, many people classed as being overweight live longer and healthier lives than people categorised as normal weight (Flegal et al., 2013) and around 19% of people classed as obese are metabolically healthy (Hankinson et al., 2013). With the exception of osteoarthritis and cancer, causal links between body fat (adiposity) and disease remain largely hypothetical (Campos et al., 2006). Despite this, an overweight body continues to be culturally unacceptable in many societies and often comes laden with an oppressive burden of stigma and discrimination. Overweight individuals have been found to be regularly negatively stereotyped as lazy, weak-willed, and self-indulgent and are frequently devalued and discriminated against by classmates, parents, co-workers, and other overweight individuals in Western society (Latner et al., 2005). Since weight is widely perceived as being controllable, it is increasingly seen as acceptable to make sweeping judgements about a person based solely on their size and shape. This is all despite the fact that efforts to lose weight are unsuccessful in the long term for most people.

A huge amount of fear-mongering around being overweight is causing increasing numbers of us to obsess and tremble over body mass index (BMI) charts, which are highly inaccurate predictors of health and all too readily tell us that we are obese. In 2014, the National Obesity Forum, an extremely influential lobbying group in the UK working on behalf of a host of pharmaceutical companies, admitted to lying. As Harriet Brown explains, the authors had warned that obesity in Britain was continuing to rise when, in actuality, rates of obesity in the UK have plateaued or diminished slightly (Brown, 2015). Tam Fry, the National Obesity Forum spokesperson, confessed that the group had knowingly misinterpreted the facts in order to reach a wider public (Stones, 2014). Reports such as these only serve to heighten fearful and confused relationships with food and pose the question as to whether we can trust any of the "experts" on weight and shape at all. Encouragingly, the Foresight Report recently acknowledged that BMI needs careful interpretation on an individual basis and that other measures, such as waist circumference and waist-to-hip ratio, may be more accurate predictors of health-compromising body weights. This recognition pleasingly echoes the recent update to the obesity guidelines made by the National Institute for Clinical Excellence (NICE) in 2014.

The current cult of thinness is also combined in today's Western culture with the imperative of health (Lupton, 1995). Society's current health promotion obsession advances health as an issue of individual responsibility. Health, alongside attractiveness, is, therefore, located in the domain of personal agency. Health and beauty projects would appear to have become moral virtues. People pervasively equate being larger than the cultural ideal with being unhealthy in current Western culture. Wright and colleagues found that young women most commonly understand health in relation to body shape and weight as requiring constant work on their appearance and a close monitoring of eating and exercising, while, for young men, health and fitness signify the capacity for physical action (Wright et al., 2006). It would also seem that many people prefer to present themselves as healthy while resisting health ideals. This might be due to the fact that Western culture values both attractive, healthy bodies *and* individualism and independence. A typically esteemed individual by Western standards, therefore, has an attractive and healthy body while displaying some independence in relation to the cultural expectations of health and beauty (Crossley, 2003). Many of us, therefore, would ideally like to be attractive and healthy but not so focused on these things as to seem self-obsessed. We want to be beautiful without being seen to be forgoing our own individuality, independence, and personal autonomy.

In addition to the issues of health and beauty is the matter of sexuality. Many feminist writers have identified the ways in which girls and women are taught to relate to themselves as objects of the male gaze, with their worth and potential for happiness being bound up in their ability to be found desirable by men (e.g., Jeffreys, 2005). Objectification theory, for example, states that women's and girls' bodies are treated as though they exist for the use and pleasure of others (Fredrickson & Roberts, 1997). The observer's perspective may then be assumed, with women consequently regarding themselves as objects to be appraised on the basis of their appearance (Tylka & Hill, 2004). Objectification theory suggests that the sexual objectification of females is likely to contribute to mental health labels that are disproportionately given to women, such as eating disorders and depression. This can be via two main pathways. The first pathway is overt, direct, and involves sexual objectification experiences. The second is indirect, subtle, and involves women's internalisation of sexual objectification experiences or self-objectification. Self-objectification manifests in a greater emphasis being placed on one's appearance and in how frequently a woman self-evaluates her appearance and body according to how it looks. Fredrickson and Roberts (1997) have demonstrated that self-objectification can increase a woman's anxiety about her physical appearance, reduce opportunities for peak motivation states, diminish awareness of internal bodily sensations, and increase opportunities for body shame.

This notion of women as objects is not difficult to find in the mass media. This can be either overt (such as an advert for female underwear which puts the male's pleasure centre stage) or more covert (such as an advert equating female happiness with sexual attractiveness). The American Psychological Association's review of studies (2007) examined depictions of women in the media and found that women more often than men are depicted in sexualised and objectified manners (e.g., wearing provocative clothing, portrayed in ways that emphasise their body parts and sexual readiness, serving as decorative objects, and so on). Women are also more frequently portrayed as the target of men's sexist comments, remarks, and behaviours. This research also indicated that the media often depicts narrow and unattainable standards of female beauty and links these standards to a woman's perceived sexiness and level of worth.

In addition to these media forms of sexual objectification, many women also experience more extreme manifestations such as sexual harassment and sexual assault. Figures suggest that one in four women have been the victims of sexual assault of some kind and that more than half of all college women have experienced some form of sexual victimisation. Such experiences of sexual victimisation and/or sexual abuse have been related to more body shame (Kearney-Cooke & Striegel-Moore, 1994) and adverse psychological outcomes, including extreme emotional distress (Kendall-Tackett et al., 1993). Women are also more likely to work in environments whose main purpose is to offer them as explicit objectification targets: for example, in exotic dancing and cocktail waitressing. As we shall see in Chapter Five, however, despite the fact that sexual victimisation and sexual objectification are more common in the female population, men are also increasingly exposed to such distressing treatment and experiences.

The message continually disseminated in Western society, therefore, would appear to be that we must be beautiful in order to be desirable and that desirability is an intrinsic necessity of what it is to be a human being. Throughout the course of Western history, philosophers have argued for the importance and centrality of beauty. Interestingly, ratings of facial attractiveness have a high degree of consistency between cultures (Perrett et al., 1994). Attributes found to contribute to perceived facial attractiveness include symmetry and conformity to an average prototype: in males, the prototype consists of thick brow ridges and a large jaw structure, and in females, corresponds to a small lower face, full lips, and high cheekbones.

This notion of symmetry's equation with beauty is long held and often cited. This, it has been claimed, links with our desire for perfection, with symmetrical faces and objects being viewed as somehow more seamless. Researchers have also found that symmetry can ignite a feeling of oneness. Rank (1932), for example, explained that an appreciation of symmetrical forms promotes an experience of intimate relationship with an ideal other. As a result of this, the enjoyer feels whole, vital, and enriched by the experience. Beauty, in fact, can even be defined numerically, with 1.6180339887 being the golden ratio. This was first described by the Pythagorean mathematicians, as they kept seeing this particular ratio in things regarded to be beautiful, and can be expressed either as a linear relationship or as a shape, within which ratio we can also expect to find balance and symmetry.

It has been suggested that an attractive face functions as a reward. Studies have shown that one brain region involved in representing the reward value of various stimuli is the orbitofrontal cortex (OFC). The OFC is involved in representing the reward value of taste, sounds, smells, and other sensory stimuli and is also sensitive to abstract reinforcers such as praise or criticism. As Edmund Burke writes, "beauty is, for the greater part, some quality in bodies acting mechanically upon the human mind by the intervention of the senses" (Burke, 1757, p. 191). For example, activity has been observed to be activated in the OFC when male subjects are exposed to attractive female faces (Aharon et al., 2001). Female subjects have also been tested and no significant gender differences have been found.

The OFC is also involved in processing at least some emotion-related facial expressions (Blair et al., 1999). The degree of pleasure experienced seeing an attractive face is modulated, therefore, by the extent to which people perceive the presence of a positive facial expression, such as a smile (O'Doherty et al., 2003). Attractive faces that are more consistently rated as displaying a happy expression produce a stronger reaction in the OFC compared to faces displaying a neutral expression. While there are clear male and female preferences, therefore, in relation to perceived beauty, it is certainly the case that physical attractiveness ratings can be increased by facial expressions and shared emotions.

Freud believed that the enjoyment of beauty was a sublimation of sexual attraction (Freud, 1905d). For many people, facial attractiveness appears to play at least some part in selecting a potential mate. In one study, Johnston and Franklin (1993) developed a computer pro-gramme that allowed individuals to evolve their most attractive facial composite. They found that evolved attractive female faces are judged to be about twenty-five years of age but possess features and propor-tions that are systematically different from an average face of that age. Specifically, the lower jaw region was smaller and the lips fuller than average. These nuances, perhaps unsurprisingly, would seem to be strongly related to hormones.

Both sexes enter puberty with very similar proportions of muscle, fat, and bone but exit puberty with completely different ratios. These changes are primarily as a result of steroid hormones. The high oestro-gen levels in young females cause an average gain of thirty-five pounds in weight, as the ladies among us might, perhaps fondly or not so fondly, remember. This additional weight would have changed the shape of our breasts, hips, thighs, and even our lips. Conversely, a young male acquires around one-and-a-half times as much muscle and bone mass, controlled primarily by the action of androgens. The average adult male, therefore, has a longer and broader lower jaw than that of a female and more sunken eyes as a result of brow ridge growth.

Female faces displaying physical features indicative of higher levels of oestrogen, therefore, are frequently perceived as more attrac-tive by their male counterparts. Alterations in perceived physical attractiveness during ovulation have also been observed (Roberts, 2004). In a similar way, male faces displaying features promoted by higher levels of androgens are often identified as more attractive by females. The preferred age of twenty-five can also be explained in terms of hormones. Female fertility reaches its maximum in the mid-twenties and declines by about 20% in the mid-thirties and by a further 60% during the forties. Interestingly, these changes are paral-leled by the thinning of the female lips. It is, perhaps, not surprising under the current societal pressures, therefore, that women choose to use lipstick, and, increasingly, collagen, to counteract these changes.

From a biological perspective, it is beneficial for females to select males with robust immune systems, given that the major threat to our health comes in the form of bacteria and viruses. While immuno-competence genes are not directly visible, visual clues are available via a male's secondary sexual traits. A male's body must choose between the demands of parasite resistance and the display of secondary sexual characteristics, and only the male physiologies with the strongest genetic resistance have the luxury of choosing the latter. Testosterone-dependent displays, therefore, can serve as reliable proxies for robust genes, as they are simply beyond the means of weaker immune systems.

The competition for social status also plays into humanity's preoccupation with beauty. There are many complex, evolved mechanisms for monitoring the self in relation to others by social comparison. Monitoring our attractiveness in comparison to others has been referred to as *social attention holding power*; in other words, our ability to evaluate and monitor the kinds of attention we can elicit from others and hold (Price, 1988). Displays of attractiveness are one way in which we vie for social attention and, thus, a means of competing for social rank and status. Just as the peacock can elaborately splay his illustrious feathers for the pleasure of any potential mates, so, too, can we don carefully selected clothes, apply our lipstick, flex our muscles, and flash our smile as a way of getting the attention of those around us.

Whether male or female, research repeatedly indicates that people perceived as being attractive are attributed other, unrelated, positive characteristics as a result of their attractiveness (Eagly et al., 1991). Physically attractive people are seen as more likely to achieve success and more hireable as managers and management trainees. Research by Drogosz and Levy (1996) has also shown that physically attractive individuals frequently receive higher offers for starting salaries and higher performance evaluations. Furthermore, such individuals receive higher ratings for admissions to academic programmes, better offers in bargaining, and more favourable judgements in criminal trials.

If this all seems rather disheartening, it is useful to remember that visual cues such as smiling, gaze, hand movements, and body orientation have also been related to interviewer and performance ratings (DeGroot & Motowidlo, 1999). The perception of physical attractiveness is modulated, as we have seen, by social cues which then feed into employability ratings and so on. It is not clear, therefore, whether higher starting salaries and other similar phenomena are due to subjective appraisals of physical beauty or, rather, attributable to other, non-appearance related phenomena such as a warm smile, sociable eye contact, and a friendly attitude.

The English art historian, Clive Bell, believed that the starting point of aesthetics is always the personal experience of a particular emotion and that aesthetics, therefore, by their very nature, can never be objective (Bell, 1914). Such a sentiment is aptly captured in the phrase, "beauty is in the eye of the beholder". Many of us have had the experience of a previously "beautiful" face seemingly morphing before our very eyes at the utterance of an unkind word or a previously "plain" face blossoming under the spell of a smile. Ishizu and Zeki (2011) propose that everything which appears beautiful to a subject has a single brain-based characteristic, which is a change in the strength of activity within the OFC, as we have previously explored, but specifically in field A1 within it. Activity in the A1 section of the OFC is proportional to the intensity of beauty experienced, regardless of any objective measure of beauty. Such a proposal shifts the definition of beauty in favour of the perceiving subject and away from the characteristics of the apprehended object, upholding the exclamation of Confucius who said, "everything has its beauty, but not everyone sees it".

It is not only the adults among us with appearance preferences. A penchant for attractive faces is also found in the very young, with infants naturally gravitating towards more attractive faces (Langlois et al., 1990). Children have also been shown to relate to others using stereotypical concepts of attractiveness (Langlois et al., 2000). Children are more likely to attribute positive social behaviours and traits to attractive children and ascribe negative behaviours and qualities to unattractive children. In an early study by Dion (1973), 3–6-year-olds were found to believe that attractive children were more friendly, less likely to fight and shout, and less likely to hit another child, even if the other child hit them first. Young children have also been found to prefer attractive children as friends and to consider them more intelligent than less attractive children. Researchers have dubbed this stereotype the "beauty is good" stereotype and it can be found in children whether they know the judged subject or not. In a study by Langlois and colleagues, twelve-month-old babies were more willing to approach and play with an attractive stranger than with an unattractive one (Langlois et al., 1990).

Deny it as we may, every one of us lives our lives somehow influenced by a range of stereotypes. It has been suggested that these stereotypes exist as cognitive structures known as schemata, which include organised knowledge or understanding of the stereotype and also beliefs and expectations about individuals who belong to the stereotyped group. Such schemata can affect attention and perception on account of the expectations and beliefs attached to them. The "beauty is good" stereotype, therefore, might affect the processing of information related to attractive and less attractive individuals via corresponding schemata. Research with children by Bigler and Liben (1993) indicates favouring towards stereotype-consistent information. In other words, children are more likely to pay more attention to information which upholds the "beauty is good" stereotype and ignore any information that might refute it. Such a bias is not helped at all by popular media, in which the "goodie" is most frequently displayed as beautiful and the "baddie" as disfigured or "ugly". Children in current Western culture frequently watch a considerable amount of television from an extremely young age. I am yet to come across a children's programme or film in which negative character traits are not equated with undesirable physical features. Characters with positive personality traits, on the other hand, are typically displayed as colourful and/or with symmetrical, conventionally attractive faces. As Lucy Ryan, a pupil from Maria Fidelis School in London, explained, "The media is constantly bombarding kids with unrealistic images . . . pretty people look like this, ugly people look like this" (All Party Parliamentary Group on Body Image, 2012, p. 28).

Unfortunately, exposure to attractive and unattractive people behaving in counter-stereotypical ways will do little to alter our skewed perceptions if we fail to accurately encode information on account of our existing schemata. The distortion of stereotype-incon-sistent information, both in children and in adults, could be one reason why so many of us appear to retain the "beauty is good" stereotype throughout our lives. Accurate information processing, outside of the constraints of our current schemata, therefore, might be our greatest hope of escaping the stereotypes in which we have become entrenched. As we shall see as we move through this book, one way to step outside of these cognitive constraints can be through practices of a mindfulness nature.

> Beauty is eternity gazing at itself in a mirror.
> But you are eternity and you are the mirror.
>
> (Gibran, 1991, p 102)

CHAPTER TWO

Embodiment and perceived ugliness

"My face I know not. One day ugly as a frog the mirror blurts it back: thick-pored skin, coarse as a sieve, exuding soft spots of pus, points of dirt, hard kernels of impurity—a coarse grating. No milk-drawn silk . . . I shiver, chilled, the grave-chill against the simple heat of my flesh: how did I get to be this big, complete self, with the long-boned span of arm and leg, the scarred imperfect skin?"

(Sylvia Plath, 1958, cited in Wagner-Martin, 1997, p. 302)

"I have no knowledge of myself as I am, but merely as I appear to myself"

(Kant, 2007[1781], p. 121)

When we look into the mirror, we believe that what we see there is the self. We identify with the visual image and have a sense of ourselves within a body, which belongs to us. Winnicott referred to this sense as "corporization", denoting the fact that we each have a body in which we live and can make our own (Winnicott, 1945, p. 139). This notion of embodiment has gained much interest in recent literature. Embodiment is the subjective experience of having and using a body, the sense of the self as located in the body, and the body as experienced both objectively and subjectively as my body. We usually experience ourselves as being located within the body that we experience as our own. This has been frequently referred to as embodied self-location: in the words of the well-known psychologist and philosopher William James, we normally experience "the feeling of the same old body always there" (James, 1890, p. 149).

Researchers and philosophers who view the self as embodied suggest that we have knowledge of our bodies *from the inside*, believing ourselves to be distinct from other physical objects and psychological subjects (Bermúdez, 2009). A particularly succinct definition of a sense of a biological self is offered by Blanke and Metzinger (2009) as "the experience of being a whole, distinctive entity, capable of global self-control and attention, possessing a body and a location in space and time" (p. 7). Most of us hold the intrinsic belief that our bodies belong to us, and not to anybody else. Our current culture, however, is deeply embedded in a technological age, which builds on radically new concepts of identity and embodiment. Our human identity has been translated into information patterns, leaving some of us, arguably, with completely new notions of human identity and, indeed, of whom we actually are.

It is certainly the case that bodies have long been used for classification and identification, with skin colour, gender, appearance, and so on having been used for many a century. The new biometric surveillance of the body (e.g., iris-scanning, finger-printing), however, takes such identification and classification to a completely new level, reducing the body to "a binary language of ones and zeroes which radically reduces possibilities for negotiation and therefore also resistance" (Aas, 2006, p. 150). Instead of being a person of a certain gender, with an age, an ethnic origin, a specific eye colour and, most importantly, a story, we are now numbers and codes held on mass databases. Where, then, does this leave us as people with thoughts, life experiences, and emotions? As Katja Franko Aas, Professor of Criminology at the University of Oslo, explains,

> Biometrics gives the body unprecedented relevance over the mind. Now, the body itself becomes the source of information. The coded body can "talk" . . . A talking individual, who owns the body, is in fact seen as unnecessary. (Aas, 2006, p. 154)

With such blurred lines between a body that is ours and a body that belongs to the technological world in which it is situated, it is hardly surprising that growing numbers of us are experiencing vast changes in our relationships to our bodies and to our sense of self within these bodies. Incidences of body disownership, for example, have increased dramatically in recent decades. Such manifestations involve a person experiencing a general alteration of their relation to the self, with a common belief being that their body does not belong to them or has disappeared. This can lead to compulsive touching of the body, as though to check it is still there, or even self-harm related behaviours, such as pouring hot water over the skin, as a reassurance of the body's existence (Sierra et al., 2005).

There have also been many reports of people who experience an overwhelming desire to have one or more of their perfectly healthy limbs amputated on account of it feeling alien, even going as far as performing the amputation themselves if a surgeon fails to consent to their wishes. The desire for amputation of a healthy limb was first reported in 1785 (cited by Johnston and Elliot, 2002), with such incidences increasing exponentially since this time. People with such desires usually describe their feelings as developing early in life, usually before puberty and most commonly before the age of eight years (First, 2005), with most emphasising that they are primarily seeking a sense of wholeness or completeness, or attempting to correct a mismatch between their bodies and sense of self.

One poignant case is that of a fifty-one-year-old civil servant, whom we shall call Sam, who arrived by ambulance at the Accident and Emergency department of his local hospital after having amputated his own left hand (Sorene et al., 2006). He had bound an elastic stocking tightly over his forearm as a tourniquet before severing his hand with an axe. On arrival at the hospital, Sam expressed a desire for surgery to fashion the stump for the future fitting of a prosthetic hand. On taking a psychiatric history, Sam reported feelings and urges to have his body modified since his pre-adolescent years, after seeing an amputee. He had already undergone an over-knee amputation of his right leg ten years previously following a minor injury of the lower leg that had failed to heal due to Sam tampering with the wound. In addition, Sam had also already self-amputated his right little finger and left ring finger, explaining that he had done so in order to quell his overwhelming desire to amputate his whole hand. Each of these actions were undertaken by Sam in the desperate hope of creating a body that physically conformed to an idealised image he had of himself.

The persistent urge to have a part of the body amputated can lead to high levels of anxiety and depression and even suicide. Shame and guilt are also common correlates. People with these experiences are often shrugged aside as being attention seeking or masochistic and in pursuit of pain. Conversely, people with these experiences are known to commonly shrink away from attention and have no desire for or any enjoyment of pain. There has been some debate as to whether surgeons should be permitted to amputate healthy limbs if people are experiencing extreme distress and are at an increased risk of lethal attempts at self-amputation, with those on the "for" side of the debate commonly believing that body disownership is an illness which is curable through amputation. Indeed, elective amputations of healthy limbs were carried out in the UK in 1997 and 1999 (Dyer, 2000; Fisher & Smith, 2000), although, after heavy publicity, such surgery has now been banned on the NHS.

It is, in my opinion, preposterous to blame incidences of body disownership on a so-called disease process. It would appear more likely, rather, to be a response to the societal and social milieu within which one lives, within the context of difficult and perhaps traumatic life experiences. Is it really so surprising that a person should wish to dismember the body in a society which systematically and meticulously promotes the dissection of the body at every turn?

It is also possible to experience a disconnect between ourselves and our entire bodies, temporarily, in what are known as out of body experiences (OBEs). While such experiences can also be distressing, they are more commonly experienced positively and typically occur without negative psychological ramifications. An OBE is defined as the experience in which a person seems to be awake and can see his body and the world from a location outside of the physical body. Autoscopic hallucinations are closely related to OBEs and are characterised by the experience of seeing one's body in extra-personal space. During an OBE the sense of spatial unity between the self and the body is outside of normal experience, since the self is not experienced as residing within the limits of one's body. Often, the self seems to be located in a second body, which characteristically hovers above the physical body, in a phenomenon often referred to as abnormal self-location. Fascinatingly, many blind individuals have reported being able to "see" during such OBEs, such as the case cited by Dossey (1989) of Sarah, blind from birth, who had a detailed visual perception during surgery when her heart had stopped. The following is the account of another young lady, named Vicki, who is congenitally blind. She experienced an OBE in the hospital after a road traffic accident left her with multiple, life-threatening injuries:

> "I knew it was me . . . I was pretty thin then. I was quite tall and thin at that point. And I recognised at first that it was a body, but I didn't even know that it was mine initially. Then I perceived that I was up on the ceiling, and I thought, 'Well, that's kind of weird. What am I doing up here?' I thought, 'Well, this must be me. Am I dead? . . .' I just briefly saw this body, and . . . I knew that it was mine because I wasn't in mine. Then I was just away from it. It was that quick." (Ring & Cooper, 1997, p. 110)

OBEs are not only found in clinical populations, but also occur in around 5% of the general population worldwide (Irwin, 1985). It has been proposed by Mohr and Blanke (2005) that such experiences spring from a failure to integrate sensory information in personal space (due to conflicting tactile, proprioceptive, kinaesthetic, and visual information) and a second disintegration between personal and extrapersonal space (on account of conflicting visual and vestibular information). It has, therefore, been postulated that the double disintegration of body-related information and vestibular information is the main causal factor in OBEs (Blanke et al., 2004). Compelling research conducted by Jane Aspell of Anglia Ruskin University, Cambridge in 2013 found that the visual projection of human heartbeats can be used to generate an OBE, which could provide some potentially helpful experiences for people with body image disturbances (Aspell & Heydrich, 2013). Volunteers in the study were fitted with a head-mounted display (HMD) and filmed in real-time by a video camera connected to the HMD, which allowed them to view their own body standing two metres in front of them. The volunteers' heartbeat signals were also recorded using electrodes, and the timing of the heartbeat was used to trigger a bright, flashing outline which was superimposed on to the virtual body shown via the HMD.

The subjects described experiencing a strong identification with the virtual body after watching their body outline flash on and off in synchronisation with their heartbeat for several minutes, explaining that it felt as if it was their own body. They also experienced themselves as being in a different location in the room to their physical body, reporting that they felt closer to their double than the elected two metres in addition to experiencing touch at a different location to their physical body. Aspell hopes that the use of this technique might help people experiencing body image issues, perhaps providing them with an opportunity to see their bodies in a truer light than the value-laden mirror affords them. I additionally harbour a strong hope that techniques such as this may provide an experience of being more than the body, of having a Self and a consciousness beyond the physical.

Our preconceptions of body ownership have been particularly heavily questioned since the discovery of the rubber hand illusion (Botvinick & Cohen, 1998). In the classical set-up, participants sit with one of their arms resting on a table hidden behind a screen. A rubber hand is then presented in front of them. The participant's attention is directed towards the rubber hand as the experimenter simultaneously strokes both the participant's hand and the rubber hand. Participants frequently report feeling as though they are being touched on the rubber hand, as if the rubber hand is a part of their body. Later research has found that healthy individuals believe they can control the movements of a virtual hand if they match their own bodily movements or motor imagery, regardless of the visual resemblance and the spatial proximity between the real hand and the virtual hand (Short & Ward, 2009). Similarly, amputees often experience the phenomenon of a phantom limb, particularly during the observation of virtual hand movements. Paralysed patients have also been reported to feel a movement of their paralysed limb after seeing a prosthetic limb moving (Fotopoulou et al., 2008).

Embodiment can also extend to a prosthetic limb, which somehow becomes integrated into the person's sense of self. The notion of a phantom limb has been much written about in the literature. It is interesting to note that generally, while using a prosthesis, many amputees' phenomenological bodily experience is one of being whole, with the amputee feeling that the prosthesis is a part of themselves and that they somehow, when wearing it, have an intact body. Furthermore, amputees who wear their prosthesis regularly tend to report that any presence of a phantom limb disappears when wearing the prosthesis, with others reporting that the prosthesis is embodied or "fleshed out" by the phantom limb (Melzack, 1990).

We not only experience our bodies as our own, but also experience ourselves as occupying a given location within a given perspective. In order for such an experience to occur, our bodily related inputs need to be somehow integrated with environmental information, thus signalling the position and orientation of the physical body in relation to the external environment. Vestibular signals are critical to this (which code the orientation and movement of the body with respect to gravity), as are visual signals (which code the orientation and movement of the body with respect to the environment). Some people struggle with signals of this kind. Francis Tustin, a child psychother-apist, wrote, for example, about children who have "bodily sensations of falling forever and spilling out into annihilation" (Tustin et al., 1992, p. 359). It would appear that some of us, both children and adults, experience difficulty in feeling our edges, and experience our body as "spilling out" beyond the confines of our skin. For some people, this is a terrifying experience, while for others it serves as a spiritual awak-ening, igniting a transpersonal understanding of intrinsic connection with others.

A further representation of the body many people struggle with is body image. This is a conscious representation thought to predomi-nantly rely on visual information and represents the sizes and shapes of body parts and their arrangement to form a whole. The term "body image" was originally defined by Paul Schilder in the 1920s and later articulated by him as "the picture of our own body which we form in our mind, that is to say, the way in which the body appears to our-selves" (Schilder, 1950, p. 11). This concept has since been expanded to include both attitudes and perceptions (Rudd & Lennon, 2000). To date, however, we know very little about the brain's conscious repre-sentation of the body as a physical object. The studies that do exist have mostly involved participants adjusting the size of an image to match their actual body size. Such tasks are limited in that they provide only an estimate of the perceived body image and fail to assess the various parts of the body individually.

It is not uncommon for us to possess a healthy body image in rela-tion to certain parts of our body and a less healthy body image in rela-tion to others. We might perceive our body as a whole in a positive light, for example, but experience intense dislike of a specific part. Some people are more able to see their bodies as a whole and, thus, are able to accept and assimilate any less esteemed parts, while others tend to home in on those specific, disliked body parts, thus marring the perception of the body as a complete entity. Research backs up these two propensities. Body checking has been found to be a normal experience, particularly among young women, but people who have significant shape concerns tend to use the mirror to scrutinise the parts of their bodies they dislike more than those whose level of shape concern is low (Farrell et al., 2004). Fairburn and colleagues propose that the frequent but brief checking of shape, while in a state of high arousal, magnifies perceived bodily imperfections (Fairburn et al., 1999), with such body checking often resulting in an over-evaluation of shape and weight. A more recent study however, found that the process of body checking only influences body dissatisfaction for a brief period, after which it returns to its baseline level (Shafran et al., 2007). This is consistent with findings that self-critical thoughts and feelings of body dissatisfaction fluctuate during the day, with it being probable that these fluctuations are secondary to body checking.

Why is it, then, that some of us feel compelled to check our image in the mirror on such a regular basis? Research suggests that repeated body checking is a way for us to regulate our emotions. Such checking might regulate our emotions negatively by confirming our fears, or positively by attenuating our fears and, thus, alleviate our previously invalidated concerns (De Berardis et al., 2007). According to experts, mirror gazing, while often undertaken in the hope of alleviating anxiety, most commonly serves only to increase self-consciousness and selective attention and could magnify a person's perception of any perceived defects (Veale et al., 1996). In one study, the most common reasons for looking into the mirror cited by people with appearance worries were:

"I have to know for certain how I appear in public".

"The hope that I can feel comfortable with my appearance".

"I have to make myself look my best".

"The hope that I might look different when I first look into the mirror". (Veale & Riley, 2001, p. 1385)

For some people, the mirror can truly become their nemesis. It is becoming increasingly commonplace for people to describe themselves as ugly and to experience extreme distress on account of this perceived ugliness. Such people can become preoccupied with perceived defects in their appearance, leading to significant distress and chronically low self-esteem. In her exceptionally insightful book, *The Broken Mirror*, Katharine Phillips describes a number of people deeply affected by the sense of their own ugliness, such as the tragic case of Jane:

> Jane was so tormented by her "huge" nose, "crooked lip", "big" jaw, "fat and round" buttocks and "tiny breasts" that she dropped out of school and couldn't keep a job. She stopped dating and seeing her friends. Because she thought she looked so monstrously ugly, she locked herself up in her house for five years, finally even trying to kill herself. (Phillips, 2005, p. 4)

If a person is extensively preoccupied with a perceived defect or defects in his appearance, which present to the outside eye as imperceptible or nothing more than a normal physical variation, and if he experiences related distress for more than an hour each day, he might be diagnosed with body dysmorphic disorder (BDD). BDD is most commonly focused around the face (especially the nose, facial skin, hair, eyes, mouth, jaw, and chin), although any body part can be involved, with the preoccupation often extending to more than one area of the body. One is almost equally likely to be diagnosed with BDD whether male or female, and such a diagnosis tragically equates to very high levels of distress and completed suicide. An increased sensitivity to disgust has been noted in people with this diagnosis (Neziroglu et al., 2010), including an acute anger directed at the self. Since self-disgust is part of the subjective experience of shame, frequent and even constant feelings of shame can gradually make up a large proportion of a person's life, which only feeds into cycles of self-hatred and suicidal ideation.

Perceived ugliness and imagined defects can bring with them a host of repetitive behaviours, aside from mirror-gazing. Other cyclical behaviours might include taking photos of oneself, touching disliked body parts or contours of the skin, questioning others about the physical appearance, changing and rearranging clothes, excessive exercise, extreme grooming and make-up application, the seeking of cosmetic and dermatological procedures, using clothing and other means as camouflage, and skin picking. Individuals might also avoid certain lighting for fear of their perceived abnormalities being accentuated.

There have been numerous reports of people avoiding going outside during daylight hours on account of being afraid of their perceived facial blemishes appearing to be more prominent.

Unsurprisingly, people diagnosed with BDD frequently avoid public situations and intimacy. Self-imposed social isolation is a common component of the lives of people experiencing such distress over their physical appearance. A significant proportion, in fact, become housebound, sometimes for many years. People might shut themselves away, fearful of being judged for their appearance and terrified of being the brunt of bullying and derision. Indeed, many of them would have experienced such bullying in the past, perhaps having been teased for the state of their skin or the size of their ears. A decision might have been made to keep oneself safe from rejection by isolating the self completely. One's appearance cannot be derided if there is nobody else around to scrutinise it.

In one case study, cited by Burrows and colleagues (2013), a young adolescent named Brittany was spending between five to nine hours per day tweezing her eyebrows and applying make-up, getting up at 1.00 a.m. in order to begin her make-up ritual. She felt unable to leave the house unless her perceived defects were sufficiently masked. She also engaged in constant mirror checking and exhibited depressed mood. Lack of sleep on account of her extensive make-up ritual was severely affecting her social life and schoolwork and putting a strain on her family relationships. Sadly, as can often be the case in such situations, Brittany unintentionally induced physical symptoms where none previously existed: her face broke out in a severe acne rash and she developed sores from continual washing and excessive make-up application.

It is not only over-the-counter products that might be used to excess by people who are acutely ashamed of their physical appearance. With cosmetic surgery becoming increasingly more common, it is perhaps not difficult to imagine how people diagnosed with BDD might seek out such surgery as a culturally acceptable way of alleviating their distress. Rather frighteningly, in one study by Phillips and colleagues (2001), of 250 adults given this diagnosis, approximately 75% had sought treatments such as plastic surgery and 66% had received them. Often, there is a belief that if the physical defect is somehow "fixed", the person's emotional state will be miraculously transformed and they will subsequently be able to get on with their lives. Due to this excessive focus on the perceived defect, family and friends could also come to believe that surgery or dermatological procedures could be beneficial in alleviating their loved one's distress. People diagnosed with BDD have also been found to frequently "doctor shop", hopping from one specialist to another in search of a practitioner willing to perform a desired procedure or dispense a certain drug (Cotterill, 1996).

People seeking surgery on account of perceived ugliness are rarely satisfied with any treatment received. The bulk of the scientific research suggests that people with intense feelings of dislike related to their physical appearance often experience the outcomes of any surgery as unsatisfactory, with one study reporting that only 4% of people diagnosed with BDD stated that their surgery had been of any help (Phillips et al., 1993). In another study, 16% of people cited a worsening of their distress after their cosmetic procedures, with nine of the twenty-five participants being so dissatisfied that they went on to perform do-it-yourself cosmetic procedures at home (Veale, 2000).

Rather worryingly, in a study by Sarwer (2002), more than 80% of cosmetic surgeons questioned indicated that they did not realise they were treating a patient with highly unrealistic appearance beliefs and goals until after the surgery was completed. Given the secretive nature of many appearance-related battles, this statistic is hardly surprising, alongside the fact that such worries are increasingly seen as the norm. Sadly, in the same study, 43% of surgeons reported that their patient was now preoccupied with a different perceived defect post surgery. Certainly, for some of us, therefore, it would seem that our appearance-related projects can be never-ending. As soon as we "improve" or "solve" one appearance-related problem, we find another upon which to focus. Clearly, the actual issue is not the perceived physical defect at all, but, rather, the underlying sense of not being good enough as one is, a sense that is not going to evaporate on account of a smaller nose or clearer skin.

Since perceived defects, while very real to the person herself, might not be detectable to the outside eye, people with extreme anxiety related to their perceived ugliness might be told they are imagining things and palmed off with medication for anxiety or depression without any accompanying psychosocial support. In a sensitively filmed documentary aired by the BBC in 2007, entitled *Too Ugly for Love*, important insights were given into the lives of three people who believed so strongly that they were ugly that every area of their lives were painfully affected. Tragically, Jolyon, a man who was plagued by the belief that he had large, dark circles under his eyes, has since taken his own life. At the first international conference for BDD held in central London by the BDD Foundation in May 2015, a number of families present had lost a loved one, who had been diagnosed with BDD, to suicide. The following was written by the brother of an intensely gentle and intelligent man named David who was a personal acquaintance of mine and a fellow trustee of the Body Dysmorphic Disorder Foundation.

> It was Thursday morning, 12 March 2015, when my father told me that David wasn't breathing on his own. Half-asleep, I assumed the staff at the hospital had placed him on to some sort of life-support machine. In a way, I was actually relieved. David had been in a psychiatric ward after being rescued from the edge of Beachy Head by the Chaplaincy Team that patrols the area. Since being admitted into the hospital, he'd been talking about how much he regretted not jumping, and how he'd find a way to end his life there instead. My immediate reaction to my father's news was that that would be impossible (even for him) if he was on some sort of machine, and so despite the seriousness of the situation, and how terrible it was that it had come to this, I was relieved– almost glad. I thought this would be both the lowest point and a turning point. It couldn't get any more extreme than this; he'd be shocked into taking positive steps to get better. It would force him to.

> A few minutes later, my father came back to tell me that he was dead. I remember asking him a stupid question about whether they'd phoned us or he'd phoned them. It seemed important to find out, since there must've been a miscommunication: my brother wasn't dead. And in those first few seconds of denial, there was a sudden realisation too, as if all my feelings towards him had crystallised, and were finally clear to me, only now at the exact moment when it was too late to tell him.

> About ten years ago, David started to fixate on what he considered to be unacceptable hair loss. He had a successful hair transplant—but not long afterwards he began to talk continually about other perceived flaws: his nose, his jawline, his forehead, the asymmetry (as he saw it) of his face . . . in all likelihood the seeds of being bullied as a child had finally started to take root; certainly the crippling insecurities had been pushed to the forefront of his mind. Combined with his Asperger

syndrome, and depression, David's body dysmorphic disorder would eat away at him for the rest of his life. It would consume him; eventually it was nearly all he could think or talk about.

David's story serves as an intensely tragic reminder of the seriousness and depth of pain associated with perceived defects in one's appearance. David is desperately missed and spent the last few years of his life working determinedly to raise awareness and offer support through the BDD Foundation. He was one of life's truly kind and genuine souls.

We now understand, through scientific research, that when people are confronted with an appearance-related trigger, such as their reflection in a mirror, a dysfunctional mode of processing may be activated (Neziroglu et al., 2008). Attention is shifted inwards and the person could begin to process themselves as an aesthetic object, as opposed to a human being with thoughts and emotions. The person then becomes involved in comparing an internalised, mostly negative, image of his appearance to the external reflection in the mirror and to an internal image of his desired appearance. The repeated comparison that occurs renders the internal image unstable and can cause the person to become uncertain about the way he or she looks. This model also proposes that the person pays selective attention to certain features within both the internal and external images, which serves to magnify any perceived defects. Many of us have probably experienced this to some degree; the more we selectively focus on a disliked aspect of our appearance, the more abhorrent it often appears to become. Processing the self as an aesthetic object in this way also can activate negative beliefs about the importance of appearance in terms of self-worth, which, in turn, can trigger negative feelings such as shame.

Further evidence upholds this propensity of people diagnosed with BDD to home in on specific aspects of their appearance. The "face inversion effect" is a phenomenon in which the recognition of inverted (upside-down) faces is less accurate and slower relative to recognition of upright faces, due to the absence of a holistic template for inverted faces (Farah et al., 1995). In a study of people diagnosed with BDD, the experimental group demonstrated a smaller inversion effect than controls during the longer duration stimuli (Feusner et al., 2010b). Such a finding would suggest an imbalance in global vs. local processing in people diagnosed with BDD, with an increased tendency to engage in highly detailed processing of faces, in contrast to controls who might primarily engage in holistic processing of faces. This would appear to become more pronounced the longer the time one spends in front of the mirror: people diagnosed with BDD have reported spending up to six hours at a time in front of the looking glass (Veale & Riley, 2001).

A sense of one's own ugliness is intrinsically intertwined with one's body image. Body image can be divided into three areas: body reality (the body as it really is), body ideal (the mental picture of how one believes one's body should be), and body presentation (how the body is presented to the outside environment) (Kraus, 1999). If there is a discrepancy between the real and the ideal, the person might feel pressured to re-model herself. The connection between identity and body can become particularly visible during life changes or crises, such as the commencement of menstruation and the growth of breasts in women and the increase in muscle mass and body hair in men. Changes occurring through child bearing, and illnesses necessitating structural changes to the body, such as the removal of a breast or testes in cancer patients, can also be triggers. As we shall see in Chapter Four, any change in the physical appearance can be challenging and traumatic, depending on the person, his previous life experiences, his sensitivities, his support network, and so on. Such alterations have the potential to raise fundamental and often existential questions about one's body and one's Self. This might, in part, explain why so many appearance battles first emerge in adolescence, when bodily changes are at their most dramatic.

Some theorists attempting to explain appearance-related distress point to the indisputable fact that human beings are intrinsically wired for survival. The fight or flight response is, thus, built into our make-up to ensure such survival, with a scanning for potential threats occurring continually in all of our lives. Other ways in which we avoid threats can include avoidance, freezing, and submissive behaviour. Threats may be linked to physical harm, but could also have their roots in potential rejection, humiliation, and social isolation. Safety-seeking behaviours are present in all human beings and, in our current appearance-obsessed society, can also pin themselves on to the physical body in terms of mirror checking, skin picking, and so on. It could be that some of us, at least in part, are looking into the mirror in order to feel safe and to alleviate concerns of having cause to be rejected by others. Previous threats of bears and lions have morphed into the physical body itself becoming the perceived enemy, a body perhaps associated with significant potential suffering and questionable self-worth.

When a threat is detected, such as the perceived threat of rejection, the mechanism that helps the individual to escape from the situation (the fight or flight response) is activated. Some people might flee the threat by entering into their own internal reality, perhaps by mirror checking or feeling their skin for blemishes. This is similar to the way in which some people might engage in repeated hand washing, for example, in order to undo the perceived threat (i.e. germs) by literally wiping it clean. Engaging in these behaviours can reduce the whole world into an internalised reality within which the person feels as though they are in some semblance of control and no longer need to concern themselves with the threats posed by the outside world. Sadly, when we engage in these behaviours and correlate decreased anxiety with them, we fortify the pattern and, thus, reinforce the underlying belief that *this is what I need to do in order to feel better.* Having strengthened such a message, we are unlikely to seek alternative ways of coping the next time we feel anxious unless we challenge or manage to break the cycle in some way.

In a classic study conducted by Cook and Mineka (1989), laboratory monkeys who had never before seen a snake seemed to lack the fear of snakes innate in monkeys within the wild population. If the laboratory monkeys, however, observed other monkeys reacting fearfully to snakes, they, too, began to develop this fear. It has been argued that there might be a specialist mechanism for the detection of aesthetic cues that could lead to feelings of disgust and rejection, but that it is possible that the threat detection systems require social learning to trigger them fully, as in the case of Cook and Mineka's monkeys. Veale and Gilbert (2012) propose that in people diagnosed with BDD, individuals may draw on both direct personal experiences of the threat to body appearance and functioning in the form of shame and on the observations of others' feelings of body dissatisfaction linked to shame. Such shame then drives self-disgust and self-hatred and can lead to an all-consuming and even fatal preoccupation.

Shame, indeed, appears to play a significant role in the incidence of perceived ugliness and supposed physical defects. It has been found that people diagnosed with BDD have frequently been deeply affected by social experiences of shame: for example, emotional neglect, poor attachment, bullying, and sexual abuse (Buhlmann et al., 2007). As Professor Thomas Fuchs explains, "the ashamed person doubles by perceiving herself from outside i.e., being the perceiver and the perceived at the same time. She looks with the eyes of the others at her embodied self" (Fuchs, 2003, p. 229). The mirror, in this way, represents the perspective of others on the body. Sartre (1943) explained this tension compellingly within his discussion of "the look", describing two very different kinds of looking: the me-who-looks (the voyeur) and the me-who-is-on-view (the spectacle). The sense that we are constantly exposed to the perspective of the other can lead to strong feelings of self-consciousness and vulnerability, particularly since we have absolutely no control over the perspective of the other and no way of truly knowing what they are thinking or feeling about us.

Shame most commonly arises in situations of disclosure or rejection and is immediately related to the other's gaze. Fuchs, in fact, believes that shame is the "the incorporated gaze of the other" (Fuchs, 2003, p. 228). For some, the shame which becomes manifest in the gaze of the other might be experienced as too much to withstand. The person's thinking might then become re-directed, introverted, and come to constantly revolve around the appearance of the body in an attempt to control outside perspectives on the self. In this way, an attempt to create the "ideal" body could be seen as an endeavour to ensure the other's accepting and loving gaze.

People with extreme anxiety related to their appearance often refrain from seeking treatment both on account of intense feelings of shame and out of fear of being seen as self-obsessed and vain. They might also worry about being judged and misunderstood. As one man explained to Katharine Phillips,

> This obsession is the perfect torture. I'd rather be blind or have my arms cut off. I'd be happy to have cancer, because that wouldn't isolate me the way this does, and people would believe that something was wrong with me. They wouldn't trivialise it. I could talk to people about it, and they'd understand. (Phillips, 2005, p. 4)

Perceived ugliness is a significant cause of distress in young people today and a great deal of further research into this area is desperately needed. Brushing people's anxieties aside on the basis of assumed vanity is incorrect at best and deadly at worst. On the contrary, people diagnosed with BDD frequently emphasise that BDD is the opposite of vanity: they are not attempting to make themselves beautiful by spending so many hours in front of the mirror, but, rather, believe their physical appearance to be so hideous that they are simply trying to achieve something akin to an "average" or acceptable appearance in order to feel able to leave the house.

Sadly, the social conditions which engender a greater emphasis on physical appearance seem only to be getting more pronounced, while there continues to be a massive dearth of support and acceptance available. Social media sites such as Facebook and Instagram reinforce a scenario within which young people are constantly being appraised on snapshots of their lives of a highly visual nature. Facebook has over one billion unique users, with research suggesting that young people's social networking site (SNS) use involves exploration and presentation of different facets of the self (Manago et al., 2008), the central task of which is identity construction. Self-esteem has been shown by Michikyan and colleagues (2014) to be an important predictor of whether emerging adults choose to display their true Self on social media sites or a false self, which attempts to either impress or deceive other users. A lack of knowledge about, and contact with, the real on such SNSs mean both that we cannot perhaps fully trust the other self we are communicating with or derive any sense of our own self if that which we are projecting is inauthentic. As Boon and Sinclair (2009) put it, "to some, these digital selves become fractured, confused reflections of a person, never wholly unreal, but never wholly real either— a seeming half-truth" (p. 103).

It has been argued that the very structure and functioning of Facebook encourages superficiality, with the meaningful laid aside in favour of the popular and novel. Integral elements of many SNSs, such as status updates, commentaries, feedback, conversations, images, and videos, are frequently gathered together on a single page as documentation, as Castells (2000) puts it, of every shift in identity. We are able, for example, to look at a friend's wall on Facebook and read a biography that is presented in reverse order, which comprises momentary slivers of a fragmentary self. Elements of this fragmentary self can then be revisited at a later date and deleted and manipulated at will. Nothing in the world of SNSs appears to be finite, in much the same way that our identities are not set in stone but, rather, constantly shifting in response to new ideas about who we think we are and who we wish to be. Danah Boyd describes how the users of SNSs write themselves into being through the use of statements on a profile page, thus creating a digital body (Boyd, 2006), which has the potentiality to be far removed from our true, authentic Self.

The explosion of social media also creates a scenario within which we are more frequently and easily able to experience our image as though from an observer's perspective, as we tend to do when looking at a photograph. Such a perspective is often associated with emotional memories, which have not been adequately processed (Osman et al., 2004). Such unprocessed memories are commonly rooted in a perceived threat, such as being bullied or emotionally neglected. The processing of such memories, therefore, would appear to be a necessary element in moving beyond our appearance struggles. Without this emotional processing, the brain may continue to ruminate on the appearance problem as if it is a conundrum to solve, as opposed to the person tackling the underlying fear. This, I believe, can be said of all obsessions: the fixation is developed as a form of self-soothing for an underlying fear and serves as the ultimate distraction technique. It is only when we face the root fear and enter into the underlying pain that any distress related to our physical appearance can begin to loosen its iron grip upon us.

> If I see another person, I perceive her essentially in her gaze which is directed towards the objects like a ray; I see her as the centre of a gaze. Now, if this roaming gaze turns on me, I am suddenly caught, as it were, in a force, in a suction that attracts me, or in a stream that floods me. I am torn out of the centrality of my lived-body and become an object inside another world. The other's gaze decentralizes my world. (Fuchs, 2003, p. 226)

CHAPTER THREE

Disturbed selves, disturbed eating

"'You must sit down' says Love, 'and taste my meat.'
So I did sit down and eat"

(Herbert, 1919, p. 286)

"He asked Siva, 'Whom then do I eat?' to which the
God replied, 'Well, let's see; why not eat yourself?'"

(Traditional Hindu tale)

O n 4 February 1983, Karen Carpenter, member of the successful musical brother and sister duo known as The Carpenters,
died of complications related to years of disordered eating.
She was thirty-two years old. Her death put a face on destructive
eating behaviours, paving the way for others, like Princess Diana, to
talk about their own disordered eating and the consequent havoc
wreaked on their lives. In modern Western society, disturbing
numbers of people die from voluntarily starving their bodies; a
phenomenon referred to in the psychiatric arena as anorexia. Figures
published by the National Institute for Clinical Excellence (NICE) in

2004 suggest that around 725,000 people in the UK alone have a diagnosable eating disorder (NICE, 2004). Around one in five people given a clinical diagnosis of anorexia will be chronically ill for the rest of their lives (Steinhausen, 2009), with death most often resulting from the effects of starvation or from suicide. Appearance struggles often go hand-in-hand with restrictive eating, including a preoccupation with bodily appearance and compulsive behaviours such as mirror checking as first described by Bruch (1962).

Extreme nutritional restriction is frequently a highly secretive practice with high levels of attached shame and self-loathing. People might avoid seeking help for fear of being coerced into eating more and gaining weight, or might even believe that their behaviours are "normal", given that dieting has become not only culturally acceptable but increasingly societally commendable. Many people, therefore, fail to ask for help despite feelings of despair and anxiety, which are frequently profound and life altering. In a recent survey conducted by B-EAT, the UK's leading charity for eating disorders, it was found that almost half of sufferers will wait longer than a year after recognising symptoms before seeking help (B-EAT, 2015), a decision which could have extreme psychological and physiological implications. Severe and multiple medical complications can occur as a result of self-starvation, including renal, liver, and cardiac failure and osteoporosis. Multiple visible differences can also emerge, which have the potential to further compound a negative view of one's body, including visible bones, wasted muscle, the presence of lanugo (downy hair), skin problems, loss of hair (alopecia), and rotten teeth.

Other anomalous eating behaviours include bingeing episodes followed by the intentional removal of calories from the body through self-induced vomiting, the use of laxatives, and excessive exercise, whilst commonly maintaining a safe weight; a constellation of symptoms typically diagnosed as bulimia, with lifetime prevalence rates ranging from 0.5% to 3% (Keski-Rahkonen et al., 2009). As is often the case with those who intentionally starve themselves, an extreme preoccupation with body weight and shape can be found in people with this diagnosis, with dissatisfaction with, and concerns about, weight and shape being significant risk factors for its development. Purging behaviours can often occur after a period of self-restriction, with the migration from the diagnostic category of anorexia to bulimia being a well-documented phenomenon. It has been recognised that up to 62% of people who excessively restrict their food intake will eventually become entrenched in binge–purge cycles (Tenconi et al., 2006), which was certainly the case for me. As Aimee Liu explains in *Gaining: The Truth About Life After Eating Disorders*,

> As I began to gain weight I'd become secretly and seriously bulimic. I also drank too much, slept with men I never intended to see a second time, and pretended not to care. It didn't occur to me that these 'bad behaviours', so common as to seem typical of my peers, might in my case constitute another face of anorexia. (Liu, 2007, p. 18)

Individuals who regularly purge have been found to overestimate their body size to a greater extent than controls when using image distortion methods (McKenzie et al., 1993). They also frequently have unrealistic expectations about what their ideal body shape should be, with researchers who used silhouette techniques finding that such individuals select a smaller ideal than that selected by controls (Williamson et al., 1990). Societal appearance standards transmitted through peers, parents, and the media seem to strongly contribute to the value placed on appearance in this population, particularly for young, adolescent women with low self-confidence and self-esteem, who might believe their looks to be responsible for any failures they have experienced.

While some people starve themselves and others purge away what they have eaten, others still consume large quantities of food without attempting to get rid of the calories. Such binge-eating episodes are typically characterised by a sense of a loss of control and feelings of distress associated with the food intake. One large-scale study concluded that binge-eating behaviours are more common than both self-starvation and purging and are at least as stable and chronic (Hudson et al., 2007). Increased levels of body dissatisfaction and a disturbed body image have been found to be serious problems associated with obesity, which is commonly related to regular episodes of binge-eating (Adami et al., 1998), with avoiding and checking behaviours also being present in this population. People who eat large quantities of food in short amounts of time have reported regularly checking their body by pinching layers of fat and avoiding wearing certain clothing. If such binge-eating episodes do indeed lead to obesity, there is likely to be an additional host of social and cultural difficulties to navigate, possibly including the endurance of stigmatism and bullying which have been found to relate, not unsurprisingly, to lower life satisfaction, low self-esteem, and depressive symptoms, including suicidal ideation (Eisenberg et al., 2003). Overweight people have also been found to be more likely to experience social isolation and to have peripheral social roles (Strauss & Pollack, 2003). As Shakespeare wrote in *King Henry IV*, "Thou seest that I have more flesh than another man and therefore more frailty" (Shakespeare, 2002 (reprint), p. 277).

Bingeing, as with behaviours related to other appearance struggles, has been postulated by Barnes and Tantleff-Dunn (2010) to be an escape tactic used to reduce, or distract from, difficult thoughts and emotions. Food, as in the case of hair-pulling, skin picking, starving, and so on is used in this way to block out painful thoughts and emotions; the person who binges becomes seemingly lost in her consumption of food in the same way in which the person who starves himself becomes lost in the white noise of his grinding hunger. Binge eating has been found by Heatherton and Baumeister (1991) to induce a trance-like state, which can serve to facilitate an escape from negative feelings. The bingeing, however, would appear only to serve as a distraction from unwanted emotions in the short term. The emotions typically come flooding back soon after the binge cycle is terminated, potentially prompting engagement in yet another cycle, thus perpetuating the behaviour. In addition, the act of bingeing can produce difficult emotions of its own, most commonly related to feelings of shame and guilt. To escape this shame and guilt, the person might again turn to food and the vicious cycle is compounded, becoming self-amplifying.

It is interesting to note that food has very strong associations with memory. It could even be argued that within our food choices we are attempting to remember something or attempting to interrupt and intercept that very memory. The foods that people choose to binge upon, therefore, might have something to say about the nature of the difficult emotions they are attempting to repress or the positive emotions they are aiming to re-ignite. When I think of the foods I chose to binge on in my early twenties, each and every one of them had a strong associated memory, such as the powder of instant malted drinks and their association with bedtimes in my family during happier times.

Obesity arising from binge eating can have far-reaching health implications in addition to any psychological distress. Studies have correlated obesity with diabetes, hypertension, heart disease, stroke, colon cancer, gallbladder disease, osteoarthritis, and sleep apnoea, among other chronic presentations. Unfortunately, many of these conditions can compromise energy levels, which can lead to less exercise and more time available and better conditions (such as simply being at home more often) for binge episodes to occur. Unsurprisingly, binge eating has been found to be more likely to occur when the individual is at home, alone, with large quantities of food present (McManus & Waller, 1995).

As we have seen, each of these atypical eating behaviours has been pigeon-holed into a diagnostic categorisation by the psychiatric community. The problem with such psychiatric labels, however, is that they can only ever be that: arbitrary labels. The existence of mental disorders based on biological causes is highly disputable and psychological distress cannot be waved away under the guise of a single classification or explained by a list of behaviours and so-called symptoms.

Psychiatric medicine tends to put everything into discreet boxes, as far as is possible. The *Diagnostic and Statistical Manual of Mental Disorders (DSM)*, therefore, lists mental disorders or illnesses with specific symptoms/behaviours. In this way, people's difficulties can be neatly labelled and tackled from core, central tenets. Psychiatric medicine has also broken up appearance struggles in this way, with separate labels for seemingly different sets of presentations: body dysmorphic disorder, anorexia, bulimia, and so on. Yet, such clear lines simply do not exist. Twenty-five to thirty-nine per cent of those diagnosed with anorexia, for example, are diagnosed with co-morbid BDD (Grant et al., 2002) and such co-morbidities exist across the whole trajectory of appearance disturbances. These are not separate illnesses at all, but, rather, markers on a solo continuum, all jagged divergences on one single line.

Aside from any so-called co-morbidities, the concept of diagnosable mental illness is itself flawed. According to clinical psychologist Lucy Johnstone (2000), psychiatric diagnosis relies hugely on subjective judgements that depend on the context and culture in which one lives. This is not to say that mental anguish is not real; on the contrary, the psychological suffering experienced by many is tremendous and unfathomable. Yet, we have to ask ourselves if applying seemingly airtight delineations to this suffering is serving us. As far as diagnoses go, they might help people to gain access to services and social benefits and can also come as a relief to some sufferers and families, who might feel that they now, at least, have a name for their pain. There is a danger, however, of missing the story, the person, and the emotional suffering behind the diagnosis. When we talk about someone with anorexia, for example, we are talking about a person who meets the *DSM* criteria, which includes losing a dramatic amount of weight and exercising excessively. However, anyone who has ever been given this label will be quick to point out that such criteria are extremely limiting and reductionist. Speaking from my own personal experience, my psychological distress related to my disordered eating was at its height *after* my weight had increased and I had stopped exercising excessively, among other things. At this point, I would not have been classified as anorexic. Yet, it is exactly at this point when I needed the most help.

Psychiatric labels are created by committees using highly questionable methods. Shockingly, over two thirds of the members of the advisory task force responsible for the most recent edition of the *DSM* (*DSM-5*) have been shown to have links to pharmaceutical companies, instantly raising questions about the motivation behind the growing number of mental disorders and their lists of symptoms. Rather tellingly, some of the most emphatic concerns about the *DSM* have, in fact, come from committee members of the *DSM* itself. Professor Allen Frances, from the *DSM-IV* committee, has publicly criticised the way in which *DSM-IV* helped to create what he calls "epidemics" in the USA: a tripling of diagnoses of ADHD, a twentyfold increase in the diagnosis of autism spectrum disorder, and a fortyfold increase in paediatric bipolar illness (Johnstone, 2014). Frances fears that "DSM-5 will radically and recklessly expand the boundaries of psychiatry. Many millions will receive inaccurate diagnoses and inappropriate treatment" (Johnstone, 2014, p. 13).

In *A Straight Talking Introduction to Psychiatric Diagnosis*, Lucy Johnstone points to the fact that Dr David Kupfer, chair of the *DSM-5* committee, failed to come up with a convincing defence in the face of these justifiable criticisms:

> In the future we hope to be able to identify the disorders using biological and genetic markers that provide precise diagnoses that can be delivered with complete reliability and validity. Yet this promise, which we have anticipated since the 1970s, remains disappointingly distant. We've been telling patients for several decades that we are

waiting for biomarkers. We're still waiting. (Kupfer, cited by Johnstone, 2014, p. 14)

Sufferers of mental distress and their families are also frequently hoping for such biomarkers, desperate for a clear-cut equation to explain their suffering and point to distinct treatment options. I remember having a brain scan at Great Ormond Street Hospital during one of my admissions under the diagnosis of anorexia and it seeming to be the highlight of my nine-month stay for my parents. My mother and father were desperate for a certain, measurable reason for my behaviours; they wanted to see why their daughter had entered this upside-down world of self-starvation in a black and white brain scan. Perhaps unsurprisingly, the brain scan indicated some abnormalities. My family shared a collective sigh of relief. The problem was that this brain scan did not actually tell us anything at all. It was taken at a time when my body was in a desperate state of starvation. As soon as this body began to receive some nourishment, my brain scan began to return to "normal". Did the starvation cause the changes, as I now believe they did and as a growing body of research is increasingly pointing to? Or had the changes caused me to starve myself, as my parents so desperately hoped all those years ago?

In so many ways, it would have been wonderful to discover a biological reason for my distress that day in the fMRI scanner. Yet, any discovery would have almost certainly missed the point. Those of us engaged in battles with our bodies are people with stories. We are not a set of diagnostic criteria, a series of seemingly "abnormal" behaviours, a conglomeration of unfortunate genes and tripped switches in the brain.

Within the medical model, it is not uncommon for every event in the person's life is commonly seen as a trigger for the "illness". These triggers may be noted down but never questioned again, since the culprit is, henceforth, deemed to be the mythical underlying pathology. Those of us with a diagnosed mental disorder, therefore, are highly likely to be medicated with little further enquiry into the distressing events in our lives. From this moment onwards, patients in the mental health system are so often seen as the label they have been diagnosed with before they are seen as the persons they are intrinsically. All of this becomes even more ridiculous when we consider that two individuals who meet the criteria for the same mental disorder might share only one symptom (e.g., major depressive disorder requires only five out of the nine criteria). Assuming that all individuals with the same diagnosed mental disorder behave in the same way, therefore, is simply madness itself.

As soon as we put a label on an appearance battle, we take it out of the political and societal arena and place it firmly in the hands of the psychiatrists, who tell us that we are unwell and treat us accordingly. Over the years, I have had the words "anorexia", "clinical depression", and "BDD" on my medical files and not one of these labels has even come close to explaining my experiences or helping me to move forwards with my life. I wonder how different things might have been if I had been sat down and asked to tell my story, instead of being weighed and asked tick-box questions from a computer screen. I also ponder the suffering that could have been negated if, instead of being told that I was ill, the context of my suffering had been considered. Was I ill, or simply responding to an unbearable set of life circumstances in the only way my adolescent self could imagine?

When we consider the wider context of each and every person struggling with the appearance of their physical bodies, we might decide that they are not ill but, rather, responding to unthinkably painful experiences and emotions. The suffering itself has ignited the behaviours, not some underlying illness or pathology. Support from such a premise would move away from a focus on the behaviours and instead shine a spotlight on the underlying suffering. I am certain that had my own treatment included a greater focus on my inner anguish, it would not have taken me almost two decades to move beyond the seemingly inescapable pain. My treatment for anorexia largely focused on weight restoration and healthy eating habits, my treatment for clinical depression solely on medication, and my treatment for BDD on various exposure exercises. While I do not doubt for a moment that these things were both necessary and helpful (I might, indeed, have died without some of them), they failed to address, or help me to move beyond, the inner pain that seemed to eat away at me from the inside out.

In her germinal article on anorexia, Susan Bordo famously described psychopathology as "the crystallisation of culture" (Bordo, 2003, p. 138). In this phrase she hoped to capture the reality that so-called mental disorders, far from being anomalous features of pathological individuals, offer instead an insight into a culture's pressures, incitements, history, and structures of power. Weiss would agree, believing that our identity projects "derive their significance not merely from an individual's intentions but from the situation out of which they emerged and in which they are expressed" (Weiss, 1999, p. 1)

Disordered eating patterns offer a clear and powerful window into the make-up of our current culture. They are a crystallisation of this culture, a direct metaphor of our time. Susie Orbach eloquently agrees:

> Like the psychological symptom of hysteria that Freud described so well in late nineteenth-century Vienna, anorexia nervosa is a dramatic expression of the internal compromise wrought by Western women in the 1980s in an attempt to negotiate their passions and desires in a time of extraordinary confusion . . . such psychological symptoms are the understudies for the unspeakable. They express both the rebellion and the accommodation that women come to make in the context of a social role lived within circumscribed boundaries. The starvation amidst plenty, the denial set against desire, the striving for invisibility versus the wish to be seen—these key features of anorexia—are a metaphor for our age. (Orbach, 1985, p. 4)

The same could equally be said of any appearance battle. In mental health in general we have come to pathologise, and even demonise, the individual, neglecting to consider the systems around them, including their families and their culture as a whole. Richard Brothers, an eighteenth-century religious leader, when asked why he had been committed to Bedlam, replied, "I and the world happened to have a slight difference of opinion; the world said I was mad, and I said the world was mad; I was *outvoted*, and here I am" (Brothers, quoted in Colton, 1820, p. 75). It thus seems that society rarely attempts to truly understand the underlying metaphors beneath what they conveniently label as mental illness, attempting rather to manage and even eradicate the symptoms in order to manage and eradicate its own discomfort.

Such a mentality can be seen in the massive emphasis psychiatry places on medication for mental distress, with the efficacy and safety of most such drugs being highly questionable. The conventional view of antidepressants, for example, is that they correct a chemical imbalance supposed to be present in depression. Shockingly, the evidence underpinning the chemical imbalance hypothesis is pitifully scanty and entirely unsatisfactory (Healy, 2015). Professor David Healy, a UK-based leading psychiatrist and psycho-pharmacologist, explains that lowered serotonin levels in depression have been marketed as an established fact while, in truth, such a postulation is little more than a myth. Professor Healy points out that SSRIs began to be marketed for depression after concerns emerged about tranquilliser dependence in the early 1980s and were sold alongside the idea that depression was the deeper illness behind external manifestations of anxiety. The approach was an astounding success, central to which was the explanation that SSRIs restored serotonin levels to normal, an idea that later became the myth that they remedy a chemical imbalance. The small difference found in some studies between antidepressant drugs and placebo can be explained, for example, by their mood-suppressing properties, which can cause people to feel more indifferent to their environment than they normally would. As psychiatrist Joanna Moncrieff (2009) explains, antidepressants mostly cause a person to forget their feelings for a while and little more.

Specificity is one of the most elegant and ingenious characteristics of our biology's signalling system. If we come into contact with stinging nettles, for example, the signalling system that activates the inflammatory response will release histamine solely at the locality of the resultant rash, as opposed to releasing histamine throughout the body. In a similar way, when we are confronted with a stressful experience, the release of histamine in the brain increases blood flow to the nervous tissues, thus boosting the neurological processing required for survival: a process which does not initiate the inflammatory responses in other parts of the body. The majority of psychiatric drugs, however, affect multiple systems of the body, leading to a whole host of unwanted and frequently dangerous so-described "side-effects". Tragically, a study based on the results of a ten-year survey of government statistics by Null and Dean (2003) concluded that adverse reactions to prescription drugs, including psychiatric drugs, are responsible for over 300,000 deaths a year.

So-called mental illnesses are not simply candidates for drugs and the management of symptoms, but, rather, an invitation to inspect a shadow-side of our culture that we are, perhaps, too terrified to acknowledge.

Until the early twentieth century, Western painters depicted the ideal female body as having a body mass index (BMI) of between twenty-seven and thirty (Bonafini & Pozzilli, 2010). By the mid-twentieth century, however, the ideal female body had shrunk to a BMI of around nineteen, with the majority of idealised bodies having a weight 15% less than the healthy weight (Martin, 2010) It is generally agreed among researchers that the current idealised female body weight portrayed in the media is an unhealthy body weight for most women. Exposure to media images within which an unhealthy body weight is promoted as the ideal is correlated with a drop in female body satisfaction and an increase in body image related anxiety (Anschutz et al., 2008).

It is interesting, as Naomi Wolf, the author of *The Beauty Myth* notes, that thinness and dieting became female preoccupations around 1920, when Western women obtained the right to vote (Wolf, 1991). Whereas the average model now weighs 23% less than the average woman, this figure was only 8% less a generation ago. The average model, actress, or dancer is now thinner than 95% of the population. Is it any wonder that 90% of women now think that they weigh too much? Naomi Wolf writes,

> This great weight shift must be understood as one of the major historical developments of the century, a direct solution to the dangers posed by the women's movement and economic and reproductive freedom. Dieting is the most potent political sedative in women's history. (Wolf, 1991, p. 187)

At the point when women received the vote, with all of the knock-on events this heralded, the group identity has been argued by Wolf and others to have been greatly threatened. Men were no longer the powerful gender, the only gender to have earning power, no longer the breadwinners. Many men might have experienced their identities being threatened in a massive and unprecedented way. The outsiders in this case were women, greatly threatening social order as it had been known for centuries. Exclaiming that the female form should be thin in order to be desirable is to arguably wipe out any respect of femininity. The social message currently fed to so many unsuspecting young women is that the body can be altered at will to fit the ideal and that the shape of the body is completely within a woman's control. The shape that should be moulded is that which is most attractive and desirable, that which communicates a woman's power, her femininity (rather ironically), and her self-control. Failing to reshape the body into the form society deems acceptable is claimed to be weak, to be greedy, and to be undeserving of respect and affection. The diet industry is built upon these very premises, professing that you can change your body, become a better woman, and achieve ultimate bliss by following this meal plan, this diet, or this exercise regime. Weight loss is held up as the Holy Grail, as a central purpose of what it is to be a female. The women's intellect, personality, and deeper yearnings are thrown unceremoniously aside.

A woman who buys into these myths can be said to be a woman firmly under control. Wolf asks us to consider how every aspect of these myths strips a person of her identity as a woman. Losing enough weight to fit the ideal means a loss of breasts, loss of hips, loss of buttocks . . . and renders, in short, a woman androgynous. That for which she was celebrated in former times quite literally disappears. Perhaps the woman's starved ovaries will even stop menstruating. In addition to these physical changes, starvation takes up most of your mind and the majority of your energy. Starvation makes you quiet, submissive, and conformist. There is no energy available to be anything else.

Many theorists have attempted to explain anorexia, bulimia, and other manifestations of disordered eating as a private issue. Yet, as Wolf points out,

> if suddenly 60 to 80 percent of college women can't eat, it's hard to believe that suddenly 60 to 80 percent of their families are dysfunctional in this particular way . . . Just as the thin Iron Maiden is not actually beautiful, anorexia, bulimia, even compulsive eating, symbolically understood, are not actually diseases. They begin, as Susie Orbach notes, as sane and mentally healthy responses to an insane social reality; that most women can only feel good about themselves in a state of permanent semi-starvation. (Wolf, 1991, p. 198)

Wolf also usefully notes that eating disorders are often viewed as springing from a compulsive need for control, which rather nicely smoke-screens the place where the control is truly erupting from: society itself:

> . . . surely it is a sign of mental health to try to control something that is trying to control you, especially if you are a lone young woman and it is a massive industry fuelled by the needs of an entire determined world order. (Wolf, 1991, p. 198)

I cannot agree with Wolf more that disordered eating behaviours are a fight for survival, a combat against control, a battle against a system that denies who you are and who you authentically wish to be. Adam Phillips also agrees, arguing that self-starvation and other divergent eating behaviours are, in fact, an extreme experiment in living and of clinging desperately on to life (Phillips, 2001). Phillips views phenomena such as anorexia as an ambition of compensation. In other words, self-starvation is seen as an attempt to compensate for a loss or disappointment that has affected the person so very deeply as to leave them with a fear of dependency on others and a resistance to making connections for fear of a repeated loss. It makes tremendous sense that this shattering fear could manifest as a refusal of food or, more correctly, as a refusal of appetite. By refusing the appetite, we refuse the innate human characteristic to desire, with such desire reminding us of our neediness, our neediness reminding us of our dependency, and our dependency reminding us of relationship. By becoming a desireless, "pure self" through refusal of one's appetite, any recognition of neediness and of the other is buried and, perhaps most importantly, there is a repression of any recognition that our neediness was once traumatically let down or violated. The double bind, however, is that by denying any dependence on others by denying the need for food, an increased dependence results as the physical state weakens.

Denying oneself food could be viewed as a strategy for survival, as a symptom developed to negate something more threatening than the idea of death: the idea of living in recognition of vulnerability and traumatic loss and the seemingly impossible task of re-establishing trust and dependence. By directing their pain and anger on to their bodies, sufferers enter a pseudo-world in which they have no need to truly address their pain and anger in relation to the actions and treatment of others. In this way, they negate any requirement to face up to the pain of living in a society that vilifies the body and violates trust at every corner.

Survival, it could be argued, is also attempted by striving for the body to somehow magically disappear. Many people who intentionally starve themselves explain that they are never small enough, no matter how much weight they lose, and that they will not be truly satisfied until they disappear completely. Alongside this desire to disappear, there is often a seemingly dichotomous desire for love and attention. Quite often, as the person becomes more and more unwell, the drama around them gets bigger and bigger; they become the centre of attention and are given no option of being invisible, despite their shrinking bodies. The very things they have railed against became the very things taking centre stage. It could be argued that the desire to be seen, or, more accurately, for the true Self to be seen, had been at the heart of the self-starvation all along.

This desire to be seen for whom one truly is stands side by side with a desire to be heard. Repressed anger is also something found to be strongly present in populations exhibiting disordered eating (Curiel-Levy et al., 2012). People with an eating disorder diagnosis have been shown to display less aggressive behaviour, with a strong tendency not to assert themselves. The denial of the Self and the pushed-away anger is then seemingly turned inwards and directed against oneself. Instead of fighting and punishing those around him, the person fights and punishes himself. Instead of asserting her anger and giving voice to her pain, the person flings her anger and suppressed emotion on to her own appearance, believing if she can somehow look perfect that she will become perfect and finally secure the love of those around her.

What begins as a desperate bid for containing and yet displaying one's anger can very quickly become, for some, a raging battle between life and death. This was certainly my personal experience. As I systematically withheld adequate nourishment from my body, I found myself spiralling into a very deep depression and into behaviours that had not existed before I refused my body the fuel it needed. The physical and psychological ramifications of self-starvation can indeed, in and of themselves, trigger all manner of distress. Over sixty years ago, a now-famous experimental study was conducted by Ancel Keys and his colleagues at the University of Minnesota (Keys et al., 1950). Thirty-six physically and psychologically healthy young men were studied over the course of nine months. During the first stage of the experiment, which was three months in length, the men ate normally while their behaviour, personalities, and eating patterns were studied in detail. During the next six months, their calorie intake was cut to around half of their usual intake while the in-depth monitoring continued.

One of the first observations to be made during the six-month semi-starvation period was that the participants experienced a dramatic increase in food preoccupations. Concentration on usual, everyday activities became increasingly difficult on account of being plagued by continuous thoughts about food and eating. As the experiment progressed, the men were noted to play with their food. They also began to make "weird and distasteful concoctions" (Keys, 1950, p. 832), marrying foods they would never have considered eating together prior to the experiment. Those who ate in common dining rooms were observed to smuggle out bits of food and later consume them in the privacy of their own rooms in a "long, drawn out ritual" (Keys, 1950, p. 833). Towards the end of the starvation period, some men would take up to two hours over a meal they would have previously consumed in a matter of minutes. Pleasure taken in watching other people eat also increased.

The participants were often caught between conflicting desires to gulp their food down and consume it slowly. Long periods would be spent planning how to use their daily food allotments. The use of salt and spices increased greatly, as did the consumption of tea, coffee, and chewing gum. Many experienced periods of uncontrollable binge eating, rapidly followed by severe feelings of guilt and self-reproach. Some stole food from supermarkets, others found themselves eating unpalatable foods followed by feelings of nausea and self-disgust.

Thankfully, most of the men reported normalisation of their eating patterns after five months of re-feeding. It is of particular note that the men selected for this experiment were the most physically and psychologically robust the researchers could find: an intense selection process gave the researchers their final participants. Despite being extremely psychologically healthy prior to the experiment, most of the men experienced substantial emotional deterioration as a result of semi-starvation. Depression became more severe during the course of the experiment, with elation observed less and less frequently. Mood swings were extreme for some of the subjects. Frequent outbursts of anger became common, despite the men being of calm disposition prior to the experiment. Levels of anxiety increased, with habits such as the biting of nails and smoking developing suddenly. Apathy also became very common, with some men even neglecting some areas of their personal hygiene despite being highly fastidious before their participation in the study.

Standardised personality testing with the Minnesota multiphasic personality inventory (MMPI) revealed that semi-starvation resulted in significant increases on the depression, hysteria, and hypochondriasis scales. For one man, gross personality disturbances were evident on MMPI scales after ten weeks of semi-starvation. Extreme low mood and general disorganisation were particularly striking consequences for the men who had become the most emotionally disturbed. Social changes were also extreme. Previously extrovert and fun-loving personalities became isolated and withdrawn. Humour and sense of comradeship diminished alongside feelings of social adequacy.

The Minnesota experiment has a lot to teach us about the process of restrictive eating, which has become so commonplace and culturally acceptable in Westernised societies in recent years. These psychologically robust and physically fit men descended into many of the behaviours and deviant thought processes frequently labelled as anorexic or bulimic *purely as a response to physical semi-starvation.* They were not predisposed in the ways often cited: dysfunctional families, perfectionist attitude, rigid personalities, life traumas. Starvation itself was enough to make these men obsess over, and hoard, food, to experience altered sensations of reality and of themselves.

This is not to discount, however, the irrefutable role of difficult life experiences in disordered eating behaviours, which we shall return to in Chapter Seven. Psychological distress, usually rooted in childhood experiences, typically motivates the seeking of coping strategies such as food restriction and self-harm. Self-soothing and coping strategies can come in many forms, with self-starvation, bingeing, and purging being just some of them. As the brain is starved of adequate nutrition, however, grey matter reduces in several regions along the corticol midline of the brain, reaching from the occipital cortex to the medial frontal areas (reductions which are, thankfully, mostly reversible with adequate nutrition and weight restoration) (Mainz et al., 2012). These brain changes all too quickly pave the way for entrenchment in our disordered eating behaviours and black-and-white ways of seeing the world. In this way, what began as a societally acceptable coping strategy and survival bid rapidly becomes a diagnosable conglomeration of seemingly inescapable distress.

Kim Chernin, in her book *The Hungry Self,* agrees that the beauty myth creates a catalyst within which a host of factors can come neatly into play and provide the perfect conditions for disordered eating (Chernin, 1985). She also adds that we are a unique generation of women, in that we are the very first in history to have the opportunity to surpass the social achievements and social status of our mothers. This has never been the case for any other group of women in any other period of time; we are truly in wholly new and unchartered territory. What this means for so many of us is that we cannot look to the women who have gone before us to ascertain how our lives are likely to look.

In every other generation, women have grown up with the certainty that their lives would look similar to their mothers' lives and their grandmothers' lives before them. The current generation of women, however, are much more likely to live their lives completely differently to previous generations. People who experience low body image satisfaction and go on to starve themselves or engage in other perplexing eating behaviours are known to feel overwhelmed by the amount of choices available to them in regard to what they could and should do with their lives. We are in an age where the world, for the first time for women, is truly sold as our oyster; we can become doctors, enter politics, go travelling, have a family, and even, as some would have us believe, seemingly "have it all". The question, at its deepest level, is a question of identity. Since we are without historical female figures who have experienced the plethora of choices available to us, we are, perhaps, yet to discern useful ways of growing into our new roles and identities. Are we maternal or career women? Are we nurturing or power craving? Are we family orientated or goal driven? And can we, indeed, ever be everything?

Self-starvation stops all of this confusion conveniently in its tracks. When the most vital decisions in your life become about what is on the end of your fork, wider resolutions are put rather nicely on hold. Starvation keeps the individual on the bottom rung of Maslow's hierarchy of needs. Until the body is fed, higher issues such as career choices must be put off. In this way, we remain in limbo, in a helpless and almost child-like state, with life's choices and responsibilities held usefully at arm's length. As Grace Bowman puts it,

> the initial diet, I thought, was a means to lose a bit of weight but, in fact, it became more about evading the pressure and anxiety in my life . . . anorexics come to the (wrong and misplaced) conclusion that their shape is their identity, and it is their shape that controls their future. (Bowman, 2007, p. 32)

Chernin states that it has become clear to her, through her work counselling young women, that restricted eating always coincides with an underlying developmental crisis. It is not surprising, therefore, that the age of onset for many such difficulties is frequently during adolescence. A more recent trend is also seeing older women experiencing their first episode of eating-related distress after the birth of their first baby. Controlling what one puts into one's mouth could, in part, be understood as an attempt to make the whole world stand still. The most terrifying element of eating healthily again can, therefore, be the fact that life begins moving and there is a need to figure out a way of moving with it. This is especially difficult if you are without examples of people who have taken your particular path in your family or cultural history. This might also be part of the explanation as to why fewer men engage in extreme eating behaviours, although the incidence of disordered eating in the male population is also on the increase, as we shall explore in Chapter Five. Alongside a weaker version of the beauty myth, men can look to their forefathers to get an idea of how to live their lives and perhaps find some comfort in the knowledge of what this life might look like. Many women of this generation are simply not afforded such a luxury.

> Let me ask you something, in all the years that you have . . . undressed in front of a gentleman has he ever asked you to leave? Has he ever walked out and left? No? It's because he doesn't care! He's in a room with a naked girl, he just won the lottery. I am so tired of saying no, waking up in the morning and recalling every single thing I ate the day before, counting every calorie I consumed so I know just how much self-loathing to take into the shower. I'm going for it. I have no interest in being obese, I'm just through with the guilt. So this is what I'm going to do, I'm going to finish this pizza, and then we are going to go watch the soccer game, and tomorrow we are going to go on a little date and buy ourselves some bigger jeans. (Gilbert, 2009, from the film adaptation of the book).

CHAPTER FOUR

Altered appearances, questioned identities

"It was just a normal mirror, a round sheet of glass encased in a white plastic frame, but as I reached for it, my hand trembled.

"... how different could my face be? It might be red and scarred a bit, but it would still look like me, right? Taking a deep breath, I held it up to my face.

"All of a sudden, that normal little mirror became a window into hell"

(Piper, 2011, p. 1)

The epigraph was taken from the Introduction to *Beautiful*, by Katie Piper, a deeply inspiring book written shortly after the twenty-four-year-old model and television presenter was the victim of a vicious acid attack, leaving her face severely burnt. Katie now heads the Katie Piper Foundation, a London-based charity, which helps people to come to terms with many forms of visible difference. Katie writes incredibly movingly about the psychological hurdles she encountered and the existential crises she experienced as a result of the altered appearance of her face. Approximately 1% of the adult population have a scar, blemish, or physical irregularity that severely affects their ability to lead their lives as they would otherwise, according to the Office of Population Censuses and Surveys. Visible differences, therefore, are not uncommon and it is estimated that over one million individuals in the UK are currently living with a visible difference of some kind (Faces, 2010).

Visible differences are, of course, experienced and coped with in very different ways by different people. Whether congenital or acquired, they can understandably ignite appearance struggles or compound existing appearance-focused distress. Any alteration or perceived difference in our physical appearance has the potential to lead to a crisis over our identity, as we shall see as we move through this chapter. We shall also see that while some people do indeed become distressed by such differences, others cope exceptionally well and continue to have healthy self-concepts and high levels of confidence and self-esteem. We shall also look in this chapter at the phenomenon of people intentionally causing changes in their own physical appearance, creating disfiguring scars on their own flesh as a way of modulating and expressing their inner pain.

There are three broad causes of visible difference: congenital discrepancies (e.g., cleft palate and port-wine stains), traumatic events (e.g., fires, road-traffic accidents, and also self-harm practices), and disease processes. Many medical conditions (e.g., psoriasis and acne) can directly change a person's appearance while others may cause visible differences indirectly, such as in the treatment of cancer. The definition of the medical term "disfigurement", however, is not clear-cut and depends on an interaction between social norms and individual values and attitudes. Some cultural practices, such as facial branding for example, may alter appearance and compromise normal functioning, yet are not perceived as disfiguring. For the purposes of this book, we will be concerned with visible differences that potentially cause some level of distress to the individual and/or to the society in which they live.

Two overlapping perspectives have been adopted when looking at the experience of people with a visible difference (Cash, 1990). The first perspective is largely social and cultural in nature, and is often termed the "view from the outside". Studies taken from this perspective have been concerned with how appearance influences social perceptions and interactions. A large body of literature has found that many people with visible differences experience behavioural avoidance, with one early study, for example, sadly finding that people tend to stand further away from individuals with a facial difference (Rumsey et al., 1982).

The second perspective, the "view from the inside", is concerned with the impact of appearance on individual perceptions of self-concept, emotional well-being and quality of life. A large amount of evidence indicates that self-perceived appearance—the view from the inside—is only marginally related to the social reality of appearance and that this holds true across the whole appearance spectrum (e.g., Ben-Tovim & Walker, 1995). The severity of the visible difference, therefore, is not a good predictor of the severity of possible resultant emotional suffering. In a prospective study of burns patients by Isaacs (1996), even those with injuries of 1% burns or less experienced clinically significant levels of psychological distress. Perhaps surprisingly, much of the research seems to suggest that adapting to a major alteration in physical appearance can be more straightforward than adjusting to relatively minor blemishes, particularly when these blemishes are of an unpredictable nature, as is the case with many skin conditions. Body image is not a static phenomenon and can interact with the episodic nature of a range of factors, including skin disease. It has been found that, in people with skin disease, their conceptualisation of their body image can vary with the episodic nature and visibility of their condition (Thompson et al., 2002). Thompson and colleagues suggest that less extreme differences might result in greater variability in the reactions of others, with this unpredictability contributing to a sense of a lack of control and resulting in raised anxiety levels. More obvious differences, on the other hand, typically provoke more consistent reactions, thus facilitating the development of more stable, and perhaps, therefore, more effective, coping strategies.

There is a prevailing assumption, however, that people with more extreme visible differences need greater levels of psychological support, with those deemed to have less obvious differences being considered as not needing so much help and guidance. This simply is not the case. A person's subjective perception of the visibility of their difference is a far stronger predictor of the level of psychological distress than the severity of the condition itself (Robinson, 1997). All people experiencing appearance changes or differences, regardless of how seemingly minor, should have access to psychological support. It is also important to note that appearance changes require dedicated attention even when seemingly more "severe" impairments are present. In an early study by Coates and colleagues (1983), the appearance-related side-effects of chemotherapy, such as hair loss, were ranked by sufferers as being more distressing than resultant symptoms such as nausea, insomnia, breathlessness, and fatigue. Pitifully, however, the lack of sensitivity in body image measurement in cancer has been repeatedly noted (Mock, 1993).

People with visible differences frequently report experiencing difficulties in forming relationships, meeting negative reactions from others, and encountering discrimination (van der Donk et al., 1994). Social encounters may be made even more complex by the inability to use facial musculature, for example (perhaps on account of facial palsy or Moebius syndrome), which might lead to unconventional non-verbal and verbal communication and incorrect assumptions made about a person's level of intelligence and ability to interact. Given such potential reactions and perceptions, it is hardly surprising that many individuals with visible differences experience higher than average levels of psychological distress, including anxiety, low mood, and low self-esteem (Lansdown et al., 1997). A recent study found that 60% of a community- and clinic-based population with visible differences experienced a significant impact on everyday life, including negative thoughts about the self, avoidance, and reluctance to participate in social events (Rumsey et al., 2012). Feelings of anxiety and shame can also be particularly strong, with many people attempting to conceal their disfigurement from others. In another study, 9% of the women questioned concealed their port-wine stain even from their partners (Lanigan & Cotterill, 1989). One sufferer of acne explains,

> the cruellest legacy of my acne is the profound conviction that I'm different to others, that I am unworthy, that I can never hope for ordinary happiness . . . anyone meeting me for the first time must be filled with repugnance and pity. (Richardson, 1997, p. 61)

Much research strongly suggests that the personality characteristics of proneness to shame, low self-esteem, and appearance consciousness are first developed in childhood and later modified by wider social experiences (Leary & Kowalski, 1995). Shame involves a painful sense that aspects of the self are bad, inadequate, or worthless, with an underlying belief that, should these aspects be exposed, rejection could result. Shame would appear to underpin many of the emotional disturbances and maladaptive coping strategies engaged in by some people with visible differences, including excessive concealment, avoidance, and self-blaming. The origins of shame proneness have been attributed by Gilbert (1997) to a failure of recognition of being a good and able child, pressure to conform to society's expectations, and direct attacks on the self, a point we shall return to in more detail in Chapter Seven. Shame is now understood to be one of the most powerful, painful, and potentially destructive experiences known to humans. Shameful children, and, indeed, adults, are usually painfully focused on the negative aspects of the self and, thus, become highly attentive to that which is shameful, acutely self-conscious, and focused on perceived personal inadequacies and supposed deficits.

Shame can be a dangerous experience, since it can often lead to a wish to hide or to escape. One study, for example, reported a doubled suicide rate among Danish adults with clefts, a very disturbing statistic indeed (Herskind et al., 1993). Furthermore, Gupta and colleagues (1993) found that over 5% of their sample of psoriasis patients had active suicidal ideation and almost double this figure had expressed the wish to die. The tragic story of Melissa Martin-Hughes, an eighteen-year-old girl driven to suicide in 2012 by her acne, shocked many people, yet such occurrences are not uncommon. As we have already explored, a visible difference does not need to be life-threatening, or even severe, in order to cause extreme distress to the person concerned. Melissa, a grammar school student predicted to achieve three As at A-Level, hanged herself after reportedly spiralling into depression on account of her acne. She had also been taking the controversial anti-acne drug Roaccutane, which itself has been linked to incidences of depression and suicide.

Virtually all people experience acne at least once during their lifetime, with approximately 70% of the adolescent population having a recognisable degree of acne at any one time (Brown & Shalita, 1998). The occurrence is also increasing, especially among adult women, with 40–50% of all women over the age of twenty affected to varying degrees (Lowe & Forster, 1997). The appearance of the skin can profoundly affect overall body image, with improvement in acne severity having been shown to lead to greater satisfaction with unrelated body aspects such as weight and shape (Gupta et al., 1990). As with other visible differences, symptoms such as depression and low self-esteem are more common in acne sufferers than in the general population (Fried & Wechsler, 2006). Unfortunately, acne sufferers frequently become used to thinking about their looks in a critical, negative, and self-conscious way, with these thoughts tending to remain after their acne subsides (Kellett & Gawkrodger, 1999). Shame can be a particularly prevalent feature of acne, in part due to widely held societal misconceptions that the sufferer is in some way responsible for the condition of their skin. Pernicious myths, such as poor personal hygiene or excessive chocolate consumption causing acne, might lead a person to feel responsible for, and, therefore, ashamed of, their condition.

Skin condition and appearance are the most common concerns for people diagnosed with body dysmorphic disorder, with around 65% focusing on it and worrying about acne and scarring (Phillips, 2005). By definition, however, an individual cannot be given the diagnosis of BDD if he or she is deemed to possess a greater than slight visible defect. A diagnosis, therefore, is only rendered if a person meets both objective criteria (i.e., a clinician's assessment that the patient's defect is slight or imagined) and subjective criteria (i.e., reports of preoccupation, impairment, and skin concern related distress). Of importance to skin conditions such as acne is how a clinician defines a *slight physical abnormality*. In the majority of BDD prevalence studies to date, people deemed to have moderate or severe acne have been excluded from investigation (Uzun et al., 2003). In a fairly recent and thoroughly executed study, however, 14.1% of people with moderate to severe acne met formal criteria for the diagnosis of BDD, with the researchers concluding that "a significant proportion of patients, regardless of their acne severity at the time of examination, have substantial distress and preoccupation related to their facial appearance" (Sarwer & Margolis, 2007, p. 222). Again, the reductionist nature of psychiatric diagnosis becomes pitifully obvious.

Some acne sufferers have been found to limit exposure of their blemishes through social avoidance and the concealment of their skin (Kellett & Gilbert, 2001). Many might also struggle with the uncertainty and subsequent anxiety, as in the case of sufferers of other skin conditions, of not knowing exactly which behaviours are potentially contributing to their skin condition. This could lead some people to feel acutely trapped and fearful of their actions related to many areas of their lives. Acne has been correlated with an increased risk of restrictive eating, for example, as sufferers might attribute the acne to their food choices and eating habits (Lee et al., 1991). Acne has also been linked with compulsive behaviours such as excessive picking and/or scratching of real or imagined lesions. Other compulsions can include the excessive use of soaps and other products and the engagement in rigorous cleaning methods. I personally engaged in all of these behaviours while in the throes of acne, with food restriction being the most problematic for me, given my history of disordered eating behaviours. Where I once saw layers of fat embedded in every foodstuff, I later saw potential pimples as my acne episode ensued.

In a cruel Catch-22 situation, negative psychosocial experiences might also affect the progression, and even the onset, of appearance-changing conditions such as acne, eczema, and psoriasis. It has been found repeatedly that stress often precedes the onset or exacerbation of many dermatological conditions (e.g., Al-Abadie et al., 1994). Many sufferers, therefore, could find themselves in a vicious circle of stress leading to a worsening of their skin condition, which, subsequently, leads to more stress, and so on. Such stress can then lead to self-soothing behaviours such as skin picking and mirror checking. Interventions aimed at alleviating stress, therefore, are vital in improving the physical condition as well as the psychological struggles associated with dermatological conditions. A whole new discipline, known as psychodermatology, has recently been built up around this very premise.

The discipline of psychodermatology has its roots in research as far back as 1865, at which time Hillier, working with eczema patients, implicated mental excitement, nerves, and anxiety as a cause of skin disease (Hillier, 1865). Later, in 1982, Teshima and colleagues found that emotional stress had the capacity to influence the immune system, often manifesting in cutaneous illness (Teshima et al., 1982). More recently, extensive research by Linda Papadopoulos, an expert in the field of psychodermatology, has suggested an association between stressful life events and the onset of skin conditions (Papadopoulos et al., 1998). Again, returning to my own experience, my acne erupted after an unwelcome period of separation from my future-husband. It was then further compounded by my skin picking and excessive use of abrasive topical treatments, among other things.

Like acne and psoriasis, a serious burns injury can cause consider-able damage to skin integrity and often leads to scarring. Such an injury can also impair physical function, with scars across joints, for example, severely limiting the range of motion. In addition to these difficulties, burns injuries often necessitate surgery, with all the emotional trauma such surgery might bring: how will I look when I wake up? Do I risk my life for surgery with purely aesthetic goals?

James Partridge, OBE, was severely burned in a car fire when he was just eighteen years old, suffering 40% burns to his face and body. In his book, *The Challenge of Facial Disfigurement* (Partridge, 1990), thousands of people were prompted to change the way they thought about visible differences. The warm response to his book led him to found Changing Faces in 1992, with a view to championing the rights and inclusion of people with facial differences. In a 2007 interview, James explained,

> I knew it was bad from people's reactions. They would look into the hospital room and then turn away. When I finally saw myself, I was shocked to the core . . . The thought of taking this face into the street and meeting old friends . . . the self-consciousness level was of absolutely colossal proportions. The face is so much how we commu-nicate. It's our self-image. It's what other people remember. (Benjamin, 2007)

The question of self-identity becomes very pertinent with burns and, indeed, with any other facial injuries or visible differences. If the face is the medium through which people recognise us, who do we then become when our faces are no longer recognisable even to ourselves? It can often be difficult for people to access the adequate support needed to explore these questions, particularly once any medical dangers have been ameliorated. Many people, indeed, might feel ashamed to seek help if their visible difference is of a non-life-threatening nature, which they most typically are. Papadopoulos and Walker (2003) found that people with skin conditions and other visi-ble differences do indeed often face such trivialisation of their distress, which only promotes less openness and increased experiences of shame.

While people with visible differences are more at risk of appear-ance distress, low self-esteem, and social interaction difficulties, not all are affected in the same way. Many people find ways of coping effectively and come to see their difference as playing a minor role in their lives (Rumsey, 2002). A new wave of research is now emerging which focuses on the strengths and resilience of people with visible differences, as opposed to their difficulties and problems. One study by Meyerson (2001) identified family support, faith, humour, a sense of self, social skills, determination, and networking as influencing resilience. In one early study the low level of psychological distress experienced by a sample of people with port wine stains was related to "extraordinary support from family members" (Kalick et al., 1981, p. 205). I recently had the absolute pleasure of afternoon coffee with Stephen Bell, the founding managing director of a successful event management and planning business based in Chelsea, who was born with four of the fingers of his right hand fused together on account of a rare condition called syndactyly. His absolute joy for life is hugely palpable and deeply infectious. He explains,

> My personal experience of having Syndactyly has been generally really positive; from an early age, my family taught, encouraged, and helped me to be comfortable in my own skin. I guess nobody is 100 percent[sic] perfect. I have never ever tried to hide my fingers and hand, as this would only cause unnecessary attention. Some people never even notice but I am always more than happy to explain this unique condition and answer any questions. As with a lot of situations in life, it is often a case of assessing the situation and going with the flow. I let these conversations progress naturally, as I do not want to force anyone in to learning about my condition. If someone starts staring or glaring, then I will very politely just ask them, "Have we met before?" The majority of reactions I get when asked about my fingers is respectful, positive and encouraging. (Bell, 2015)

Self-esteem has also been shown to be an important factor in psychological adjustment to a visible difference, as individuals who possess high levels of self-esteem are less likely to perceive the possibility of rejection (Thompson, 2001). Encouragingly, seventy per cent of respondents to a survey of members of the Cleft Lip and Palate Association in the UK reported positive consequences of having a cleft lip and/or palate (Cochrane & Slade, 1991). Even those who grapple with challenging social interactions may come to understand that any negative experiences say nothing about themselves as a person, but, rather, point to a struggle in the other. As Melanie Gaydos, a model born with a cleft and a rare genetic condition which affects the skin and hair, explained in an interview for the "What's underneath" (Stylelikeu.com, 2015) project,

> My interaction with people is stressful. We are all mirrors to each other and I think a lot of people tend to project . . . so I have to remember that if there is ever anything, if anyone should say something to me or judge me in a certain way, it is really just a reflection of themselves and of their own issues that they're dealing with.

She goes on to explain,

> I'm always asked what I think of beauty standards of today and I'm kind of like ugh, and primarily because I've always thought of myself as beyond all that. I never thought I was beautiful but I also never thought I was ugly. For me, beauty was always more of a feeling and a state of being.

Melanie is also able to see the positive aspects of being born with visible differences:

> I have thought about what life would be like if I was born without a cleft palate and maybe with a full head of hair and I think I would be really boring. I think it wouldn't be very exciting, not to imply that I think your lives are unexciting but, I don't know, even though I have been through a lot, they're my experiences and I like where everything has brought me today. I like the way I am.

Melanie stopped wearing wigs four years ago and now feels comfortable enough to emerge in public without hair. Some visible differences are indeed amenable to camouflage techniques, for example using make-up, prosthetics, clothing, hair and so on. However, camouflage can certainly bring up its own issues, particularly in relation to identity, sometimes leading people to wonder if others are actually responding to the *real me*. Covering up and visibly altering one's true appearance can lead to the sense of a barrier being artificially present between the self and the other and may reinforce the belief that one must hide certain aspects of the self in order to negate rejection. The person may also come to believe that any positive attention cannot be assimilated since is it not perceived as being attributable to their true and authentic Self. In addition, concealment fails to address any underlying identity struggles. Such avoidance of displaying the appearance as it is can suffocate the development of new coping strategies and may prevent the questioning of unrealistic beliefs (Cahners, 1992). There is even some evidence to suggest that distress related to visible difference can be partially explained by the attempt to conceal, to avoid, and to hide (Kent, 2002). The promotion of camouflage services can potentially encourage the belief that a visible difference should be hidden, which is a far cry from promoting the personal and societal acceptance of every person just as they are and every body just as it is.

Personal accounts of living with visible differences testify to people feeling more at ease with familiar others who are perceived as seeing beyond superficial differences to the real person beneath. Socialisation with people beyond close friends and family can, therefore, become a central challenge for somebody learning to live with a visible difference. People with acquired differences have been found to shift between a pre-altered vision of the self and an identity as a person with a visible difference. James Partridge (2005) proposes that many people go through a third stage, within which they transform their sense of self through the adaptation of attitudes that are incompatible with society's idealisation of cosmetic purity in order to rebuild self-esteem.

Self-esteem is also mediated by the level of importance an individual places on physical appearance. According to research findings by Mendelson and colleagues (2000), those who believe that physical appearance goals are central to important life aspirations are, unsurprisingly, at greater risk of low self-esteem related to a visible difference. Unfortunately, Western societies frequently promote the belief that physical appearance *is* central to life goals, thus further advancing the notion of appearance being a strong predictor of achievement and fulfilment. Many researchers, such as Nichola Rumsey and Diana Harcourt, have pointed to the role played by the media in creating and compounding the pressures on those distressed by their appearance (Rumsey & Harcourt, 2014). As we explored in Chapter One, the bombardment with images of "beautiful" people can both encourage us to critically evaluate our looks and also to make inaccurate appraisals of our appearance based on unrealistic comparisons. Sadly, and perhaps rather ironically, a prime culprit is advertising by plastic surgery clinics specialising in visible differences, in which the desired end product is frequently portrayed using images of seemingly "perfect" models photographed using a soft-focus lens (Rumsey & Harcourt, 2004). Thankfully, people such as Katie Piper and James Partridge are intrepidly challenging these unrealistic appearance standards, boldly living lives which unwaveringly point to the characteristics of true beauty, such as selflessness, compassion, and love.

Kleve and colleagues (2002) note that a central task in the adjustment process to a visible difference is the ability to de-focus from the difference and develop a broader perspective of the self. Rosen (1997) agrees and believes that any therapy should refrain from directly challenging over-valued beliefs about the person's visible differences but instead aim to uncover and challenge the meanings hidden underneath the negative body talk. The focus, it would seem, should be on how one feels from the inside, which can transform without anything needing to change physically on the outside. When people are helped to realise that the inner Self remains untouched and unchanged by any physical changes, beautiful breakthroughs in self-acceptance can occur.

While visible differences can be caused by medical conditions or accidents, they can also be self-induced. Skin picking, for example, can occur in both the presence and absence of any dermatological condition and can lead to physical injury such as wounds, scars, and infections and result in high levels of psychological pain, including distress, embarrassment, and guilt (Deckersbach et al., 2002). In extreme cases, skin picking itself can cause extensive visible differences and necessitate medical intervention (Kondziolka & Hudak, 2008). Skin picking is more common in women than in men (Teng et al., 2002) and more prevalent in individuals with developmental disabilities such as Prader–Willi syndrome (Didden et al., 2007). It can be automatic, which is associated with a lack of awareness of the behaviour as it occurs (e.g., picking mindlessly while watching the television), or focused, which is characterised by preceding negative feelings or the urge to pick within the individual's awareness (Walther et al., 2009). Higher levels of focused skin picking have been correlated by Hayes and colleagues, among others, with skin-picking severity, anxiety, depression, and avoidance. Skin picking is also a known correlate of body dysmorphic disorder (Grant et al., 2006).

In a case study cited by Martinson and colleagues (2011), a fifty-five-year-old lady given the pseudonym of Evangeline was referred to psychological services with a primary presenting concern of skin picking. She had been picking incessantly at her skin for twenty-four years and reported commonly picking it until it bled, explaining that she had great difficulty in stopping once she started to pick. This caused her a great deal of distress and social impairment. In particular, she felt an acute lack of control alongside feelings of guilt, shame, and embarrassment as a result of her skin-picking behaviours. These negative emotions commonly ignited greater urges to pick and vicious circles of picking behaviour. Evangeline covered up large parts of her body with clothing due to extensive scabs and scarring and remarked that she would be "mortified" (Martinson et al., 2011, p. 413) if anyone saw what her skin looked like. She had started picking her skin after a series of stressful events involving a threat to her beloved family.

People engaging in high levels of focused skin picking often talk about getting "stuck in the mirror", with reduced awareness of the passage of time (Capriotti et al., 2014). Many hours can pass, after which the individual feels intense shame and guilt over the physical damage caused, wishing they could turn the clock back and resist the urge to pick. Similar desires have also been cited by people who intentionally pull out their hair, a phenomenon known in psychiatric circles as trichotillomania, which is also associated with low self-esteem and intense feelings of shame and guilt. Such behaviour is characterised by noticeable hair loss (alopecia), an increase in tension just prior to hair pulling, and pleasure associated with the act of hair pulling itself. It has been hypothesised by Azrin and Nunn (1973), to be an adaptive response to stress and is maintained by a variety of both internal (e.g., anxiety) and external (e.g., being in the house alone) cues.

Another way in which visible changes to the physical body can be self-generated is through what is commonly referred to as self-harm, or self-mutilation. Armando Favazza, an eminent psychiatrist specialising in this area, defines self-mutilation as "the deliberate, direct, non-suicidal destruction or alteration of one's body tissue" (Favazza, 2005, p. 10). Self-mutilation has been found to occur at a rate of 4% in the general population (Briere & Gil, 1998), although this is almost certainly a conservative estimate. Many of us were perhaps shocked to learn that Princess Diana had been engaging in both purging and self-mutilating behaviours, and possibly also humbled by her brave honesty on the subject. In an emotional BBC television interview for Panorama in 1995, Diana admitted to cutting her arms and legs, explaining that "you have so much pain inside yourself that you try and hurt yourself on the outside because you want help" (Bashir, 1995). Self-harm is particularly common among adolescents, with an average age of onset of twelve years (Fox & Hawton, 2004). In the UK, between 20,000 and 30,000 adolescents present to hospital annually due to self-inflicted harm. There is some evidence of increasing rates in recent years, especially in young women (Bhugra et al., 1999). There are also many people, of course, who do not present to medical services after a self-harm episode. Like Princess Diana, many keep their self-harm hidden for many years or perhaps even indefinitely, often as a result of shame and guilt, which is frequently underpinned by low self-esteem (Hodgson, 2004). People who hurt themselves might also be afraid that they will be stopped from cutting, burning, and so on if they seek help, a terrifying notion indeed, given that these behaviours are often experienced as aiding the ability to cope with life in some way.

Rather than being connected with suicide, self-harm is often viewed by experts in the field as a form of therapy that actually enables the mutilator to avoid taking their own life. As Favazza explains, "suicide is an exit to death, but self-mutilation is a re-entrance into a state of normality" (Favazza, 1996, p. 271). Favazza does recognise, however, that self-mutilators are also at an increased risk of suicide. Other psychologists, however, disagree with Favazza's claims, with one study finding that 85% of people questioned self-harmed with the expressed intent of killing themselves, with many of them explaining that their suicidal intent was rarely recognised (Liebling et al., 1997). Alternative functions of self-harm have been offered by Sharkey (2003), such as self-harm as a coping mechanism used to facilitate tension release, alleviate unpleasant emotions, and induce a shift in affective state. It has also been viewed as an attempt to assert self-control over threatening environments, the will of others, overwhelming thoughts and emotions, or a compromised body. It has been suggested that the origins of emotional pain are often covert, unclear, and challenging to confront, and the act of deliberately harming oneself can transmute this pain into a more tangible, physical pain "which at least can be attended to and controlled through physical interventions. An emotional wound cannot be sutured" (Clark, 2002, p. 788). In this way, self-harm can serve as a method for validating and attending to emotional suffering and a way of "speaking" a pain that perhaps feels impossible to express in any other way.

The increase in self-mutilation in recent decades has also been blamed, at least in part, on the beauty ideals embedded in Western culture. As one ex-self-mutilator explains,

> A woman who injures her body is condemned because her behaviour mutilates society's expectations of passivity and beauty. In hospital a charge nurse, male, told me I'd look prettier if I plucked my eyebrows and put on makeup. Is it any wonder that I went on to slice up my face? I was visibly saying "fuck off" to my abusive keepers. (Harrison, 1997)

Cutting of the skin can be seen as particularly metaphoric, since it is through the contact with the skin, as Marilee Strong reminds us, that a newborn baby begins to experience herself and the world around her (Strong, 2005). Warm and loving touch is one of the newborn's primary needs. As we grow, the skin becomes the organ through which we receive and express tenderness. Interestingly, the skin and the brain are intimately linked, since they both grow from the same embryonic cell layer, the ectoderm. The skin, therefore, is an exposed part of the nervous system. Self-mutilation of the skin can be an expression of traumatic touch. While there are a myriad of reasons cited for self-harm, a recent review of the literature most frequently found associations with childhood experiences of emotional neglect, psychological or physical abuse, especially sexual abuse, with twenty-one studies identified as reporting associations between deliberate self-harm behaviour and sexual abuse (Fliege et al., 2009). In an early study by de Young (1982), 58% of the forty-five sexually abused young girls and women she interviewed injured themselves by cutting, burning, attempting to break bones, or self-poisoning. In *Women Who Hurt Themselves*, psychologist Dusty Miller describes self-harm, including mutilation, self-starvation, substance abuse, and unnecessary cosmetic surgeries as a "trauma re-enactment syndrome" (Miller, 2005, p. 40).

Sexual abuse is particularly damaging to the psyche for a number of reasons, not least because a person's brain is rarely able to process such traumatic overstimulation. Since sexual abuse violates the boundaries of the body, it is perhaps not difficult to imagine how practices which highlight and reassert the boundaries of the body, such as cutting, can emerge in retaliation. Cutting can be seen as a way of demonstrably marking one's edges. Bovensiepen (1995) also suggests that cutting can serve as a reliving of the painful penetration of the penis into the containing object, with such acts enabling the person to take control of, and, therefore, manage, distressing thoughts and feelings related to the abuse. Studies have also indicated that self-harmers might be seeking self-identity through their mutilation and attempting to counteract any "loss of self" or dissociative experiences (Breen et al., 2013). Mutilating the body could, therefore, be viewed as an attempt to express emotional pain and to seek and reassemble a dismembered self. When one is not certain, quite literally, who one is, it can take something as stark as cutting or self-starvation to bring one dramatically and fully into one's body, serving as a reassurance that one does actually exist, that one is actually alive. As Lindsay explains in *A Bright Red Scream*,

> I stood in the bathroom, looking in the mirror, and I didn't recognise myself . . . It was my face looking back at me in the mirror, but my soul wasn't there. It was just a body to me, and I didn't feel part of it anymore. I felt I had lost control of my thoughts, my emotions, and my actions. And when you have lost control of everything, what do you have left? I saw the box of razors my parents kept in the medicine cabinet. It just seemed to make sense at the time, though I didn't know exactly why. I was only scared and searching. Later on, the more I cut, the more I understood why. (Strong, 2005, p. 36)

Psychologists call this sense of an internal split a *dissociation*. Rather terrifyingly, a mind that has employed dissociation as a survival method can come to feel as though it is disintegrating, as though it no longer has any connection to the person or to their sense of self. As psychologist Michael Wagner explains, "It's equivalent to feeling that you are no longer going to exist" (cited in Strong, 2005, p. 40). As we drive the razor blade through our skin, make ourselves vomit and pull out our hair, we perhaps feel intensely connected to our flesh and can experience being brought back to life and to existence in a raw and tangible way.

> One comes to see that it is not so much the nature of the act that counts but its meaning. (Chasseguet-Smirgel, 1990, p. 77)

CHAPTER FIVE

Gender, sexuality, and the pursuit of authenticity

"Not to be both masculine and feminine, simultaneously, is to have one's personhood deeply wounded, fragmented, resulting in partial selves"

(Abalos, 2002, p. 8)

"I think heterosexuality and homosexuality are a kind of psychosis, and the truth is somewhere in the middle"

(Jeanette Winterson, cited in Jaggi, 29 May, 2004)

I ndira Gandhi once famously stated that her "theory is that men are no more liberated than women" (Habyarimana, 2013, p. 49). On 25 June 2009, Michael Jackson died of acute propofol and benzodiazepine intoxication. He was fifty years old. His tragic death followed a tortured life, saturated in appearance distress and self-loathing. As early as 1970, Michael explained in a Jackson 5 interview for *Soul Magazine* that his brothers called him "big nose" and his father constantly teased him for its size (*Soul Magazine*, August 19, 1970). Later, in 1985, he spoke openly with Steven Davis, first editor for *Moonwalk*, about his battle with acne, explaining that my skin broke out real bad. It was tough—especially after everyone calling me cute for such a long time. And the more I worried about it the worse it got . . . I wore hats, I kept my head down all the time, I wouldn't look at people when I talked to them. I wouldn't say nothin' hardly. It was terrible. I felt I didn't have anything to be proud of. My success meant nothing. (Davis, 1985)

Between 1990 and 1992, Michael appeared to be starving himself and confided in a few close friends about his anomalous eating behaviours. Sadly, Michael appears to have suffered from both vitiligo and lupus, with skin lesions and changes to his skin pigmentation only adding to his distress.

We tend to think of appearance difficulties as being a primarily feminine issue but this, quite simply, is not the case. We usually associate dieting, for example, more readily with women and yet, in the nineteenth century, it was men, in fact, who were the archetypal dieters. The prominent supporters of dieting at this time, were generally male (such as William Banting and Bernarr MacFadden), as were most of their followers (Stearns, 1997). Stearns traces the transformations in weight perceptions to the late nineteenth century, when middle-class men and women were seen societally to be equally culpable for the amount of flesh on their bones. The focus for men, however, tended to be on muscle development, with advertisements increasingly depicting muscular men with large yet fat-free bodies. Stearns also points out that men left fewer diaries than women did, so we have less direct evidence of how widely they internalised these new injunctions.

Considerably more research to date, however, has focused on female appearance difficulties in comparison to male-focused research, with most research consistently finding that men report less body dissatisfaction and eating pathology than women. Despite this, recent analyses focusing on effect size rather than statistical significance suggest that many of these gender differences are actually quite small (Striegel-Moore et al., 2009). Furthermore, men might be less likely to talk about, or seek treatment for, any appearance distress, since it seems to be less socially acceptable for them to struggle with such issues in the first place. As Richard Klein puts it in *Eat Fat*,

[As] a man, I'm not supposed to be as preoccupied about fat as women. Women are obliged to consider thin as a precondition for success. A man of course doesn't feel the same pressure, but the pressure is there and it's internalised. Not only does the world mostly hate his fat, he hates it most himself. (Klein, 1997, p. 36)

Men, in fact, represent 10% of clinical eating disorder cases (Muise et al., 2003) and are increasingly presenting with the full range of clinical appearance difficulties. As we have seen, one is almost equally as likely to be labelled as suffering from body dysmorphic disorder whether male or female (Rief et al., 2006).

Susan Bordo argues that men and boys are increasingly being subjected to the same

complexly and densely institutionalised system of values and practices within which girls and women . . . come to believe that they are nothing (and are frequently treated as nothing) unless they are trim, tight, lineless, bulgeless, and sagless. (Bordo, 2003, p. 32)

Content analyses by the American Psychological Association (2007) have suggested that men in media content are primarily evaluated based on their sexual appeal or sexual behaviour and that television comedies regularly focus on the lack of sexual appeal of male characters by mocking overweight men (Fouts & Vaughan, 2000). For men, the current Western ideal is a mesomorphic (v-shaped) body with broad shoulders, a well-developed upper body with a flat stomach and narrow hips. An undifferentiated sexual gaze on the male body was found in television advertisements by Gill (2009), for example, showing young, white, attractive women gazing at young, toned, muscular, and bare-chested men.

One USA-based report by Garner (1997) found that 43% of 548 men surveyed by *Psychology Today* were dissatisfied with their bodies. Research suggests that men might experience and perceive body dissatisfaction differently to women, particularly in regard to a focus on the muscular exemplar over the thin ideal (Ridgeway & Tylka, 2005). While women are more likely to be categorised as suffering from anorexia, for example, men are more likely to be diagnosed with muscle dysmorphia, which has frequently been referred to as an unrecognised form of body dysmorphic disorder. Although females are up to three times more likely to be diagnosed with anorexia or bulimia, males are three times more likely to exhibit sub-threshold binge behaviours and are roughly equal to women in regard to the number of cases of binge eating (Hudson et al., 2007). There has also been a recent increase in the awareness of males who intentionally starve themselves, with the prevalence of men's dissatisfaction with their bodies having increased exponentially over the past few decades (Gray & Ginsberg, 2007).

The psychiatric diagnosis of muscle dysmorphia is characterised by the pathological pursuit of muscularity and includes disordered eating and exercise-related practices that are orientated towards the attainment of greater muscularity. Disturbingly, boys as young as six have reported a strong preference for a more muscular physique (Frederick et al., 2007). The obsessive compulsion to build muscle can result in significant disturbances to quality of life and psychological functioning (McCreary & Sasse, 2000), just as with other appearance struggles. The media, again, appears only to have compounded these issues. While there are, indeed, more diet-related articles in women's magazines, there are a considerably greater number of fitness-related articles in men's magazines and advertisements. Studies have reported associations between the internalisation of appearance ideals and reading fitness magazines among male college students (Morry & Statska, 2001) and the perceived media pressure among male adolescents (Knauss et al., 2008).

Men's magazines and adverts regularly implore men to engage in self-care regimes in order to negate so-depicted "undesirable" bodies. In this way, men are fed the message that self-care transmutes into beauty, with this beauty resulting in inevitable authority. According to Michel Foucault, the body is an object of power and, therefore, is socially objectified in order to be controlled, observed and reproduced (Foucault, 1979). In the Foucaldian view, the body is seen as *docile*, with the optimal process of normalisation being the fully individualised self-regulation of the body. The body as an object of power perhaps becomes all the more pertinent in current Western society, within which the traditional male role of breadwinner is being starkly threatened by a capricious economy in many geographical areas. It could be argued that whereas men once asserted their masculinity through their role as the sole material provider for their families, they now must establish their masculinity in other ways, with one socially acceptable method being the appearance of the physical body.

Attempts to assert one's masculinity through the body are no more evident than in the pursuit of unrealistic musculature, which is most likely to commence in adolescence. Murray and Griffiths (2015), for example, offer the woeful case report of a fifteen-year-old boy named Johnny. Johnny's mother brought her son to the attention of mental health services, reporting that she had become concerned about her son's eating habits, which included cutting all fat particles out of school meals, carefully selecting high-protein, low calorie foods, and attempting to increase the frequency of his meals with the goal of building muscle mass. In addition to his obsessive eating habits, Johnny followed an intensive exercise regimen, even continuing to train in periods when he was physically injured. Johnny reported intense muscular dissatisfaction and significant body shame and distress around potential exposure of his body, which prevented him from going to the beach with his friends. He even applied dark make-up to the ridges of his abdominal muscles in a bid to make them stand out more.

Johnny described experiences of bullying around the time of the onset of body-building behaviours. Many of his friends had reached puberty before he had and he appears to have felt threatened in his masculinity, which has been shown to be a frequent precursor to the development of unrealistic body-building goals (Murray & Touyz, 2013). Grieve (2007) identifies four general categories of variables which he believes influences the development of such an obsession: socio-environmental factors (e.g., media portrayals and influences), emotional factors, psychological factors, and physiological factors (e.g., body mass). Thankfully, Johnny's symptoms improved after a sequence of family therapy, an increasingly popular treatment for appearance distress. For others, however, the pursuit of the "perfect" male body can become chronic, haunting the individual for many years.

There is also growing evidence to support the link between men's pursuit of the muscular ideal and their use of appearance and performance-enhancing drugs (APEDs) (Bahrke, 2007). The most commonly used category of APEDs are anabolic–androgenic steroids (AASs), but these are rarely taken alone and often used in conjunction with a range of legal and illegal substances, such as fat-burning supplements, thyroid hormones, analgesics, pro-hormones, and nutritional supplements. The side effects of APEDs are numerous, including psychiatric and physical complications, with over 88% of APED users reporting such manifestations (Hildebrandt et al., 2007). These can include acne, testicular atrophy, depression, anxiety, and aggression. Life-threatening side effects, including cardiovascular effects, may also occur. Protein supplements, while less dangerous, also have known side effects and are becoming shockingly common. In a study conducted by the Central YMCA and Centre for Appearance Research, one in five British men admitted to using protein supplements in a quest to become more muscular (Diedrichs et al., 2011).

The devastating physical effects of APEDs arise within the context of a recent medicalisation of the male body, as pointed out by sociology professor Federico Boni. Writing about *Men's Health*, one of the most popular male fitness magazines, Boni argues that the male body is now depicted as uncertain and risky, "to be protected from illness, disease and, ultimately, death" (Boni, 2002, p. 470). Keeping death at bay, he argues, is a typical theme of the magazine, with article titles such as "Eight harmless things which make us panic/No it is not a heart attack" and "Prevention/Will your body crash?" Ironically, however, while men are currently paying more attention to their physical health than ever before, they continue to evidence high rates of stress-related disease and deaths. In their quest for so-deemed physical perfection, increasing numbers of men are taking dangerous steroids, cutting important food groups out of their diets, spending untold hours at the gym, and engaging in a plethora of other activities which serve only to place more strain on their bodies and emotional well-being.

Less dangerous practices are also frequently explored by men in the quest to obtain the "ideal" male body. An increase in body depilation, for example, is related to the male muscular ideal. This is defined as the shaving or trimming of body hair from the neck down, which is a relatively new practice among men in the Western world. In one study 63.6% of men reported having engaged in some level of depilatory behaviour (Boroughs et al., 2005). While women depilate their body hair to evade the stigma of appearing masculine, men were found in the Boroughs (2005) study to depilate their body hair in an attempt to look cleaner, more sexually attractive, more youthful, and more muscular. In the same study, 18% of men rated their anxiety in the moderate to extreme range when asked how they would feel if they were unable to shave their body hair for a few weeks, indicating that, for a subset of men at least, body depilation is critical to maintaining positive feelings and lower anxiety related to appearance and body image. Depilation carries its own risks, however, including staphylococcus infections as well as increasing the risk of contracting the herpes simplex virus.

Another way in which men attempt to assert their masculinity through their physical appearance is via the penis. A number of studies suggest that men generally underestimate the size of their penis and believe it to be smaller than average. Such a belief can cause significant amounts of stress, anxiety, and low self-esteem. In one sample of over 25,000 men, 45% were dissatisfied with their penis size and wished it to be larger (Lever et al., 2006). The media only plays on such insecurities, with all manner of products now being marketed (including cosmetic surgery) to enhance penis size. The notion of an inadequate penis is socially associated with inadequate masculinity, with some men attempting to compensate for this perceived inadequacy in other ways: for example, by increasing muscle mass or removing body hair. Sexuality also comes into play here and male sexuality could now be argued to have become, at least in part, a medicalised sexuality. Since sexual potency is depicted as one of the main requirements of the male role, impotence is societally sold as a matter of grave concern. Again, returning to *Men's Health* magazine, Boni (2002) argues that a biomedical approach is taken towards male sexuality and impotence, thus removing control and engendering a detachment from the body (and from the penis) in particular. The body, in this way, becomes a piece of sexual machinery, and the sexual organs the tools by which sex is accomplished.

It came as a surprise to me to learn that low sexual desire in men has been pathologised and deemed to be a separate mental disorder by the most recent edition of *Diagnostic and Statistical Manual of Mental Disorders* (*DSM-5*). This "disorder" is clinically referred to as male hypoactive sexual desire disorder (HSDD) and is characterised by deficient or absent sexual fantasies and desire for sexual activity, which is not causally related to any medical condition, with resultant distress to the individual concerned. Prior to this, HSDD was listed under the sexual and gender identity disorders of the *DSM-IV*, having been first included in the *DSM-III* under the name of sexual desire disorder. Indeed, it has become a measure of what it is to be a man to have an insatiable sexual appetite. If such inclinations are not strongly present, society may deem the person "less of a man" and somehow "unwell", compounded by this presence of HSDD in the *DSM*.

Furthermore, many of us are wrongly inclined to assume that sexual violence is principally a female experience. After analysing prevalence rates in twenty-one countries, Finkelhor (1994) concluded that between 3% and 29% of men have suffered sexual abuse during childhood, thereby suggesting a reasonable statistical average of between 5% and 10%. This wide range obviously makes it difficult to determine the true extent of the problem on an international scale, although we can be sure that the percentage is uncomfortably high and that study estimates are almost certainly conservative due to under-reporting. Furthermore, available studies suggest that between 0.6% and 7.2% of men experience adult sexual assault (Tjaden & Thoennes, 1998), with a study by Tewsbury and Mustaine (2001) indicating a higher rate for college men (8.3%). Holmes and Slap (1998) have found that men who have been sexually abused experience, among many other things, increased rates of post-traumatic stress disorder, depression, anxiety disorders, bulimia, and poor self-image.

Issues related to sexuality also feed into the growing phenomenon of disordered eating among males. Despite growing numbers of men with food and body-image-related distress, experiences of stigmatisation and isolation continue to be frequently reported by men diagnosed with eating disorders (Andersen & Holman, 1997). Males' unique needs, it would seem, often fail to be addressed, including a consideration of masculine identity, gender role conflict, and emasculation (Fernández-Aranda et al., 2009). Men who struggle with aberrant eating behaviours are often invisible, as self-starvation in particular is seen as a "woman's illness" by both professionals and by society at large. This can make it difficult for males to admit that they are struggling, instead hiding their controlled eating habits, associated distress, and body weight changes. Although risk factors for restrictive eating are varied, there do appear to be gender-specific risks for men, including premorbid obesity, parental obesity, parental divorce, involvement in sport, family enmeshment, gender-identity struggles, and homosexuality. As is the case with females, males who deny their bodies of food also report higher incidences of childhood abuse than men who do not restrict their diet (Olivardia et al., 1995).

Disordered eating in the male population can take on further complexities when the male is homosexual, with research indicating that men with differing sexual orientations can have differing relationships to their bodies and body image. In one 2010 study, gay men scored significantly higher on drive for thinness and appearance-related anxiety than their heterosexual counterparts (Marino Carper et al., 2010). The same study also concluded that gay men might be more susceptible to media pressure and to comparing themselves with idealised media images, despite being no more likely to consume these media images than heterosexual men. This could be, at least partially, explained by research by Wiseman and Moradi (2010) indicating that negative childhood experiences related to gender non-conformity can increase the internalisation of media images. The stigma experienced by this particular section of the population might do well, therefore, to be addressed within any model of treatment. Stigma attached to being homosexual has been strongly correlated by Blashill and Hughes (2009), to an increase in psychological distress.

We may profess as a society to have moved beyond discrimination and stigmatisation of people with differing sexual orientations and, as such, are greatly fooling ourselves. Tears fell copiously as I recently watched a modern film adaptation of the life of Alan Turing, the British wartime code breaker and computer pioneer, whose cracking of the Enigma code is estimated to have shortened the war by up to four years, saving an estimate of up to twenty-one million lives. Turing was prosecuted in 1952 for being gay and given an unscrupulous choice between two years in prison or chemical castration via a hormone therapy not dissimilar to the Nazi "cure" for homosexuality used in the Buchenwald concentration camp. Two years later, tormented by the side effects of the hormones, Turing committed suicide. He was just forty-one years old. Homosexuality is, of course, no longer a criminal offence and we now have, for the first time in over 500 years, through the Sexual Offences Act, a criminal code which does not discriminate on the grounds of sexual orientation. Our treatment of lesbian, gay, bisexual, transgender, and intersex (LGBTI) individuals, however, continues to be pitifully shameful in many quarters, with LGBTI adolescents being significantly more likely to be bullied or physically assaulted than their heterosexual peers (D'Augelli et al., 2002). Among LGBTI youths recruited from youth centres by Telljohann and Price (1993), 70% reported some kind of harassment, such as being subjected to rude comments, discrimination, profanities written on lockers, and threats from students' parents. The kicking to death of Ian Baynham, a sixty-two-year-old gay man, in Trafalgar Square in 2009, is an appalling reminder that, even in places as seemingly liberal as London, members of the LGBTI community are not always safe.

In the first research study to specifically mention gay culture, Silberstein and colleagues (1989) observed that the homosexual male subculture places an elevated importance on all aspects of a man's physical self, such as body-building, grooming, dress, and handsomeness. Dawn Atkins, co-author of *Looking Queer*, cites her brother, Michael, explaining, "We are told that we are unnatural . . . so proving our sexuality and attractiveness becomes an obsession—a way of proving our worth" (Dececco & Atkins, 1998, p. 53).

It is similarly worthy of note that women and girls are exposed to the same messages about female beauty standards regardless of their sexual orientation, yet also display differences in their respective relationships with their bodies. Lesbians are often excluded in body image research, with the rationale most commonly offered being that they are not attracted to men (Dececco & Atkins, 1998), a very narrow-minded line of reasoning indeed. This, alongside the suggestion that women are not as concerned about the attractiveness of their partners as men are, creates the assumption that lesbians are not as concerned about their body image as heterosexual women and, therefore, not so strongly affected by society's unrealistic body standards. In an early influential study, Smith (1989) found that a woman who is identified as less physically attractive is more often presumed to be a lesbian. Lesbians, therefore, appear to be trapped within a society that places tremendous value on physical appearance while concurrently holding the view that lesbians are less attractive and less concerned about appearances in general.

The first clinical study to examine body image in lesbians specifically did not take place until 1990. Striegel-Moore and colleagues (1990) studied body image among fifteen lesbian and fifteen heterosexual students, finding few differences in self-esteem, body esteem, and disordered eating between the two groups. The exercise patterns and body image concerns of lesbians were examined in another study, conducted by Cogan (1999). Interestingly, though perhaps unsurprisingly, many of the women in this study were conflicted about how they thought they should feel about their weight and overall body image and how they actually felt. Many of these women believed that lesbians were not, and should not be, concerned about the appearance of their bodies, causing intense dissonance in their thinking. These findings suggest that it might be more difficult for lesbians to admit to, and seek help for, appearance distress, given their possible sense that they should not be having these worries in the first place. Sadly, such women might go on to use food and fasting as coping mechanisms, not only for the reasons commonly cited but also, as Thompson (1995) found, to deal with their own or other people's homophobia. As Laura Brown explains in *Lesbian Psychologies*,

> The more a lesbian has examined and worked through her internalised homophobia, the less at risk she is to be affected by the rules that govern fat oppression. The more a lesbian shames and stigmatises herself for her lesbianism, the more it is that she will also actively fat-oppress herself. (Brown, 1987, p. 299)

It might also be more difficult for lesbians to talk about their appearance worries with their peers for fear of misinterpretation of intent. As one woman put it,

> If we were to talk about our bodies then someone might mistake it as trying to come onto them, or be sexual . . . Heterosexual women are obsessed with talking about their bodies with each other, and I think it must be good to be able to get feedback. However, there is no threat there. (Kelly, 2007, p. 880)

The picture we are beginning to build is thus of a more complex society to navigate for homosexual individuals where body image is concerned. It appears to be the case that societal homophobia can lie at the very heart of appearance struggles in this section of the population, with people who identify themselves as homosexual attempting to prove their self-worth, which might have been acutely questioned on account of their sexuality, via their appearance. While the female ideal focuses primarily on thinness, the gay male ideal focuses on being slender, muscular, or a combination of both. The pressures on gay males, therefore, could pose additional risks, resulting in both dieting and body-building behaviour.

Another important topic within this area is that of variations of sex development. Estimates by Chase (1998) suggest that one in every 100 births have some morphological anomaly, which is observable enough in one in every 1000 births to initiate questions about the infant's sex. Such anomalies have recently come to be known as disorders of sex development (DSD), a rather pathologising term. The concept of DSD is frequently rejected by gender identity charities and activists who prefer the term "intersex", or "variations of sex development". The frequency of individuals receiving "corrective" genital surgery, due to the diagnosis of DSD, is estimated to run between one and two per 1000 live births (Backless et al., 2000). Importantly, core gender identity has been suggested to result from a child's interactions with parents as well as the child's perceptions of their own genitals (Money, 1985). In children with *variable* genitalia, leading researchers in the area argue for surgical intervention as soon after birth as possible for the child's psycho-social well-being. Interestingly, penis size ultimately dictates whether a child is reconstructed as a male or a female in most cases (Griffin & Wilson, 1992). Consequently, it is common for infants with an XY chromosome to be raised as a female. On the website of the UK Intersex Association, we can obtain adults' perspectives of being born as a child with sexual variability. One young woman named Mairi MacDonald (2000) laments,

> I had been assigned as male—but I was not, I was intersex . . . I could not understand why I was the way I was and I had no language with which to express what was inside me . . . However, given the choice of "male", "female", "intersex", I would unhesitatingly select "inter-sex"—but society does not give me that option so I select "female". I do so with deep reservations, gritting my teeth at a society which will not accept my right to simply be who I am . . . there is a multi-faceted complexity to my sense of self which the two labels imposed by society cannot embrace. (www.ukia.co.uk).

Ruth Gibian notes that "our entire Western system of thought is based on binary opposition; we define by comparison, by what things are not" (Gibian, 1992, p. 5). Sex and gender are not clear-cut, easily definable entities, as our Western systems of thought would have us believe. While our sex is based in our biological characteristics, our gender is socially constructed and involves a complex interplay of hormones, genetics, culture, and socialisation. Western understandings of gender, in fact, have changed tremendously over time in ways that reflect social and political concerns. For thousands of years prior to the Enlightenment, a one-sex model of the genitals predominated in which the boundaries between male and female bodies were seen as being "of degree and not of kind" (Laqueur, 1990, p. 25). While gender was an important marker of cultural role and social status before the scientific, social, and political transformations of the late eighteenth century, it was regarded as being independent of biological sex (Shaw & Ardener, 2005), whereas we now tend to view biological sex and gender largely interchangeably. While for some people their gender-based struggles might be confined to the type of masculine or feminine clothes they wear or the career paths they follow, for others the struggle might lead one to question whether they are male or female on an intrinsic level.

The overwhelming feeling that one belongs to the opposite sex (often referred to as gender dysphoria) and ought, therefore, to have one's body changed to align with the intensity and conviction of one's feelings, is commonly referred to as transsexualism. The transsexual conviction has been found in children as young as three years of age (Green & Money, 1961). While transsexualism is an ancient phenomenon, it only really became widely known in the course of the twentieth century, when the possibility of sex-change surgery arose. Studies carried out in the USA, Australia, Sweden, the UK, and the Netherlands conclude that transsexualism is rare and that more men than women, in a ratio of approximately three to one, undergo a sex-change operation (Kuiper, 1991). People who identify themselves as transsexual often feel they were mistakenly born into the body of the "wrong" sex, thereby presenting a clear challenge to the assumption that biological factors determine gender and gender-based identity.

Transsexuals may opt to undergo sex reassignment surgery, with female to male sex changes being seemingly considered to be a more spectacular phenomenon culturally than male to female sex changes, perhaps simply since they are three times less common. As Orobio de Castro (1993) points out, the body of a man who becomes a woman appears, while the body of a woman who becomes a man seems to disappear. For some people, the need to completely change sex feels unnecessary. In the Netherlands, for example, there are a group of female-to-male transsexuals who halt mid-way into the medical process of surgery, hormones, voice training, and so on. They might have had their breasts removed, for example, but retain their vaginas and are at ease with their bodies. This group, by refusing to identify as male or female, radically deconstruct the two-sex system. Theirs, however, is an illegal existence (the law forbids an unclear sex) and, thus, they must keep their choice a secret.

I am reminded of the famous example of Joan of Arc (who wore male clothes and rallied French troops to victory against the English in the fifteenth century), with her refusal to wear women's clothes being one of the reasons given for her execution. The similarity between her story and that of modern-day transsexuals lies in the fact that Joan placed herself on the borders of sex and gender. She was viewed as an ambiguous female because she had not been converted into womanhood by marriage and remained a virgin. Transgenderism also straddles such borders. Transgenderism arose in the public consciousness in the 1980s and refers to people who wish to be both male and female, which usually concerns men who wish to acquire female characteristics without changing their sex completely. Often, there is not a strong desire for the removal of the penis and not the aversion to the original sex noted by most transsexuals.

Again, with such issues of sex and gender, we return once more to the core issue of identity and the affiliation of our identity with our physical body. Whether heterosexual, homosexual, male, female, transsexual, or transgender, we all seem to be striving for the same thing: integration of and acceptance of the self. Striving and falling short of our authentic self would appear to be at the root of all our bodily fixations. Interviewing men who choose to wear women's clothing, Schrock and colleagues received many comments related to the pursuit of authenticity:

> Shelly felt "freer to be me . . . more confident . . . more spontaneous . . . like my inner strength is coming out".

> Erin felt "comfort in terms of fulfilling my inner sense of identity, of expressing on some level who I really am".

> Jenny felt "much more aligned. Actually, I like myself; all of a sudden, I look in the mirror and go 'yeah!'" (Schrock et al., 2005, p. 326)

The medical model would seen primarily to pathologise and, therefore, demonise the pursuit of such authenticity, with the introduction of gender identity disorder (GID) appearing in the *DSM* around the time that homosexuality was scrapped as a psychiatric diagnosis. Moore is certainly not alone in the belief that "the GID diagnosis . . . is an attempt to prevent adult homosexuality via psychiatric intervention with children" (Moore, 2002, p. 1). Deplorably, transsexuals must persuade a psychiatrist to label them with GID before surgeons and endocrinologists will agree to aid them in the transformation of their bodies. It could be argued that GID legitimates the stigmatisation of transsexuals, which, in turn, fosters discrimination as well as distress and even suicidal ideation among this group. Those on the "for" side of the debate for classifying GID as a "mental illness" point to the suffering and distress experienced by these individuals, yet there is an acute lack of empirical evidence for such hypothesised anguish. Child distress, for example, is not a common reason for referral of children diagnosed with GID (Barlett et al., 2000). Rather, the basis for clinical referral is most frequently parents' or teachers' concerns regarding the child's involvement in cross-gender play, or the parents' desire to prevent homosexuality in their child (Doering et al., 1989).

Much controversy erupted during the preparation of the fifth edition of the *Diagnostic and Statistical Manual of Mental Disorders* (*DSM-5*) over the psychiatric categorisation of gender identity variants (GIVs), with some experts vehemently arguing for the removal of GIVs from the *DSM* altogether. There is a complete lack of any coherent theory, never mind a neurophysiological model, of so-called "normal" gender development that could give us any biological basis for pathology. Rather, we create such pathology where none exists, as is so recklessly the case in other "mental illnesses". As Meyer-Bahlburg explains,

> In the absence of an empirically grounded detailed theory of the mechanisms and processes of gender identity development, the available empirical evidence does not permit a categorical, universally valid statement that GIVs are . . . mental disorders" (Meyer-Bahlburg, 2010, p. 16).

A further form of gender transformation is that of "gender bending", which refers to self-identified women who are regarded by others as having some common masculine attributes, or self-identified men regarded to be uncommonly feminine. With women, such identification steps beyond "tomboyism" and enters the realm of being repeatedly mistaken for the opposite sex. Speaking to sixteen American "gender bending" women, Devor (1997) found that they encountered constant difficulty in obtaining social acceptance, while also being continually incorrectly assumed to be lesbians. Betsy Lucal writes stirringly about her experiences of being repeatedly assumed to

be a man on account of her mannerisms, style of dressing, and grooming practices:

> For me, the social processes and structures of gender mean that, in the
> context of our culture, my appearance will be read as masculine.
> Given the common conflation of sex and gender, I will be assumed to
> be a male. Because of the two-and-only-two genders rule, I will be
> classified, perhaps more often than not, as a man-not as an atypical
> woman, not as a genderless person. I must be one gender or the other;
> I cannot be neither, nor can I be both. This norm has a variety of
> mundane and serious consequences for my everyday existence.
> (Lucal, 1999, p. 785)

For Betsy, some of these consequences have included being thrown
out of female public toilets, being called "Sir" in shops and restau-
rants, and being challenged when paying for things by credit card on
account of the female name written on it. She also experiences many
positive consequences of being mistaken for a male, such as being able
to walk freely on the streets at night without fear of harassment and
being treated more respectfully in male-dominated situations. Despite
these seemingly desirable consequences, Butler is quick to point out
that, as a society, "we regularly punish those who fail to do their
gender right" (Butler, 1990, p. 140). Betsy Lucal is not alone in her
experiences of being ridiculed when people realise she is actually a
woman, with a group of harassing teenagers on one occasion calling
out mockingly, "Does she have a penis?" (Lucal, 1999, p. 792). Such
encounters have led Betsy to make attempts at increased femininity
without any personal conviction, in addition to hiding away and
avoiding public restrooms on occasion. As another "gender bending"
woman explains,

> The source of my problem is society's attitude. I mean lots of people's
> attitudes towards the way they think women should look. It's not my
> problem really, it's their problem, but I'm the one who gets the shitty
> end of the deal it seems . . . I used to think it was my fault . . . I always
> wanted to kill myself because I thought I was worthless because
> people knocked me down so much. (Devor, 1987, p. 31)

Men who display so-called feminine attributes, or identify as being
bisexual, are treated no more respectfully. According to Mandel and
Shakeshaft (2000), men who choose to express a different masculinity

continue to be pathologised, vilified, silenced, ignored, and ridiculed. Jackson, a bisexual university student, explains:

> Even as a kid, I discovered that most people don't have that openness, and I learned to behave like a real man . . . meaning that people would excuse my mixed race, but not my mixed sexuality. Teachers were always the first to diagnose a problem, and the playground was fertile for a lot of name-calling. (Davidson, 2009, p. 621)

Again, we find that societal expectations can lead to mental anguish and emotional wounding, as opposed to societal acceptance of all bodies in all forms. In much the same way in which societal non-acceptance of varying healthy weight levels and differing degrees of subjective beauty can cause identity crises and resultant misery, so, too, can the societal rejection of different gender-related appearance preferences stifle an individual's celebration of who he or she truly is, whether this be male, female, or both.

There often appears to be an unhelpful expression of narrow-mindedness in Western society. If we are not feminine or masculine enough, we do not fit the bill. If we are not thin enough, our skin clear enough, our muscles pronounced enough, our breasts buoyant enough, and our penises large enough, we are implored to improve, even perfect, ourselves in order to become acceptable and commendable human beings. This is madness, yet it is the reality of the society we currently find ourselves in. It would take just a little thinking outside of these boxes to help free so many of us from the unnecessary identity crises we are facing, a mere consideration that life is not so clear cut. Some of us carry extra weight, some of us are born with male and female body parts, some of us have skin conditions, some of us have small penises, and so on, *ad infinitum*. Perhaps one day we will come to understand that one size does not fit all. Perhaps one day we will learn to celebrate the beautiful uniqueness of who we each individually are.

> I highly recommend inviting the worse-case scenario into your life. I met Ellen when I was 168 pounds and she loved me. She didn't see that I was heavy; she only saw the person inside. My two greatest fears, being fat and being gay, when realised, led to my greatest joy. It's ironic really, when all I've ever wanted is to be loved for my true self, and yet I tried so hard to present myself as anything other than who I am. (De Rossi, 2011, p. 304)

CHAPTER SIX

Skin: a canvas for self-expression

"Wear your heart on your skin in this life"

(Sylvia Plath, 1982, p. 43)

"My body is my journal and my tattoos are my story"

(Johnny Depp, quoted by Wallis Simons, 2015)

T he body, as we have seen, can be a poignant site of self-expression. In current Western society, too many of us appear to be attempting to find and assert a self through the medium of the body, thus pinning our emotional pain on to our external flesh. This can take many forms. For some of us, this means obsessing over aspects of our physical appearance, for others, it means starving or stuffing ourselves, for others still, maiming or altering the body to either fit into socially acceptable standards or to rebel against them. Whatever the practice, the underlying metaphor is the same: a search for identity, a seeking after acceptance, a tremendous desire to return to the true Self.

Tattooing is one way of exploring self-expression through the body. Evidence of tattooing is present in even the very earliest human societies. Egyptian mummies from the period of the Middle Kingdom, for example, have revealed an extensive culture of body marking, with the motifs serving to ensure good health and to ward off evil spirits. Throughout the Mediterranean and the Middle East, tattoos were believed to protect people from the evil eye. They have also been used in Hawaii to remember dead relatives, and in Indonesia to mark and celebrate great accomplishments.

Tattooing was once also used as a state control mechanism by the Romans. By marking the unconsenting bodies of criminals and slaves, the Roman state could more easily restrain their movements, with their markings serving as a visible sign of their social role. Tattoos on the foreheads of criminals were commonplace until the fourth century, at which point Emperor Constantine forbade the inscription of faces. Perhaps the history of the tattoo can go some way to explain why tattooing as a social practice in Western civilisation has become entangled, in part, with deviance and criminality. Similar occurrences during the eighteenth century added further fuel to this fire, since the colonialist projects presented tattooing as a practice of the primitives who "needed" to be civilised.

Bringing us closer to the present day, the tattoo after the Second World War was associated with the working class, gangs, and drunks, while concurrently becoming one of the most common forms of teenage rebellion. Tattoos also began to be widely depicted in the mass media, with cartoons such as Popeye even sporting them. By the late 1960s, the tattoo as fashion re-emerged alongside the hippie and rock subcultures. While no longer being seen as a practice undertaken solely by criminals and deviants, tattoos, nevertheless, became symbolic of a deviant act and, therefore, served the desired rebellion of thousands of teenagers, hippies, and rock stars across Europe and North America. Punk culture epitomised this rebellion starkly. As Daniel Wocjik (1995) explains, the debut of punk culture in 1976 with the Sex Pistols included both body art and even self-mutilation from the beginning. Wocjik views these attacks on the body as a method of social rebellion:

> Having little access to dominant means of discourse, punks displayed their disaffiliation through such adornment, which was for them an accessible and direct channel of communication. By manipulating the standard codes of adornment in socially objectionable ways, punks challenged the accepted categories of everyday dress and disrupted the codes and conventions of daily life. (Wocjik, 1995, p. 11)

Where women were concerned, their punk code relied heavily on symbols of prostitution and harmful and constraining beauty practices, through the popular style of adornment that came to be known as the "bad girl look". The adoption of such clothing and make-up, according to Wocjik, was the way in which punk women "rejected established notions of feminine beauty, mocking sexist stereotypes through exaggeration, inversion, and parody" (Wocjik, 1995, p. 15). In this way, women adopting the bad girl look rejected the societal expectation to wear make-up, for example, by wearing excessive make-up, thus parodying the cultural ideal. In a similar way, tattoos and piercings were used by these women as a means of rejecting feminine beauty stereotypes. Interestingly, punks would often either do the tattoos and piercings themselves or get a friend to perform them, thus even more strongly asserting their independence from society and self-efficiency within their own subgroup or tribe.

Men have historically been more likely than women to get tattoos, but this trend has recently been reversed, with women now making up around 60% of the tattooed population (Mifflin, 1997). While women have traditionally tended to choose a site for the tattoo they are able to hide relatively easily (such as the shoulder, the hip, or the ankle), men often opt for a site they can most easily expose, such as the upper arm. Women frequently lean towards more feminine designs, such as flowers or winged creatures, but, again, this trend appears to be changing. Tattoos are increasingly being chosen by women as a means of rejecting expected ideals of femininity, with it now being more commonplace for women to choose tribal-type designs and more visible places for their tattoos, such as the wrists and neck.

Four primary overlapping functions of the tattoo have been identified (Blanchard, 1994). First, the tattoo functions as a ritual. In a culture bereft of rites and rituals outside of religion, with organised religion itself in rapid decline, the tattoo can serve as a physical mark commemorating an important life event. Such events can range from winning a sports event to the survival of a serious illness. In this way the tattoo is used, in a sense, as a rite of passage. Second, the tattoo can function as a means of identification. By inscribing chosen images onto the body, the tattooed individual might be identifying themselves as part of a given group. Third, tattoos can also have a protective function, serving to give their bearers a sense of protection from harm in the same way in which they were used to ward off evil spirits in ancient cultures.

Last, the tattoo can have a primarily decorative function, perhaps demonstrating stylishness or rebelliousness, or attempting to heighten sexual desirability.

Historically, people who were more likely to have tattoos were people whose bodies were regulated by the nation state, such as military personnel, prisoners, and the working class. This trend could be viewed as an attempt to reclaim the body, with individuals choosing to have tattoos in order to reassert ownership of their state-controlled flesh. Within this context, it is interesting to note that tattooing has now become popular in the middle and upper classes. We might ask, therefore, what this suggests about people's sense of body ownership in our current culture. It would appear, for some of us at least, that we are we using body art practices such as tattooing and piercing to find and avow a self that belongs to us and not to the whims of wider society. All of these practices could be viewed as ways of reasserting control over a body perceived as being constrained by external forces and stifled by ridiculously rigid and unrealistic beauty standards. As Fisher writes, "Tattooing appears then as a means to re-appropriate the physical body from the socially dis-eased body, as a means to resist the cultural forces that have commodified the body, and continue to do so" (Fisher, 2002, p. 104). These "physically edited bodies", as Alessandra Lemma refers to them (Lemma, 2015, p. 3), might thus attempt to integrate the appearance of the body into a sense of self that transcends the societal gaze.

If tattooing and other forms of ornament, such as piercing, can be a means of resisting cultural forces, then it is perhaps unsurprising to note the correlation between possessing such an ornament and risk factors such as alcohol abuse, drug or antidepressant use, smoking, purging, self-starvation, and self-injury (Pérez-Cotapos & Cossio, 2006). Fakir Musafar, the most well known US promoter and practitioner of body modification, is keen to promote piercing, in particular, as a spiritual experience, while concurrently giving examples of women using it as an attempt to recover from sexual abuse. He quotes the words of one piercee, whose comments he cites as being particularly common among women with piercings who have been raped: "I'm getting pierced to reclaim my body. I've been used and abused. My body was taken over by another without my consent. Now, by this ritual of piercing, I claim my body back as my own. I heal my wounds" (Musafar, 1996, p. 325).

While piercing and tattooing have become increasingly socially acceptable and seen to be largely safe methods of adornment an industry focused on self-mutilation has risen up, in which practitioners carry out cuttings and brandings alongside piercings and tattoos. These practices have long been intrinsic to the lives of hunting and gathering cultures, in which the shedding of blood is seen to be a way of summoning the gods and both good and evil spirits. In modern Western society, we have access to the *Body Modification Ezine*, which provides links to body modification artists, many of whom provide photographs of their work. An exploration of their website uncovers pages on piercing, tattooing, scarification (scratching, etching, burning/branding, cutting of words and images into the skin), and surgical modifications, including facial sculpting, implants (in every area of the body imaginable), genital surgery, and amputations. Videos of many of the procedures are available for viewing and are certainly not recommended for the faint-hearted. Stories of personal experiences also abound, with many, talking of do-it-yourself scarifications using sharp objects and alcohol rubs.

It is now possible for people with physical modifications, who might have historically performed their act in secret, to have access to public acceptance and even adulation for the extent to which they are willing to go in the "personalisation", as Winnicott (1945) would have put it, of their bodies. In May 1999 the first large-scale body modification festival was held in Toronto, with participants being required to have "heavy modifications" in order to be permitted to attend. Attending practitioners included those performing headsplitting of penises and urethral re-routing, sub-incisions with implants into genitalia, and finger amputation. Many of these practitioners offered tattooing and piercing side by side with these more extreme forms of bodily adornment, thus, perhaps, heightening their perceived acceptability.

Contemporary Western culture, argues Morgen Thomas (2012), often views the practice of non-mainstream body modification as an attention-seeking trend, the sign of a masochistic or sadistic personality, a symbol of affiliation with a deviant group, or a symptom of psychological instability. Dominant society often questions the motivations and mental capacity of individuals who engage in extreme modification and frequently ascribes labels of social deviance and psychopathology to them, without considering other reasons for the modifications, such as the assertion of personal identity and autonomy. *Mods*, as they have come to be referred to, are often, therefore, labelled as "sick" and in need of mental health intervention. One Mod, explains,

> To me the mods feel natural and normal so I'm not going to announce them, but on the other hand, I do take my time explaining them because I don't want [people] to think there's anything mentally wrong with me. (Thomas, 2012, p. 5)

Another explains, "The public believes I am over the edge, crazy, not in the right mind, and I enjoy every moment that I can prove their shallow outlooks false" (Thomas, 2012, p. 6).

It is, in my opinion, narrow-minded to label mods as "ill" or "crazy" on account of their body-alteration choices. It would appear to be more likely that they are responding to the communal body of society referred to by Favazza (1996), which is obsessed with binary categorisation and a view of health steeped in images of pristine, smooth, and youthful bodies. I am deeply grateful to have been in contact with the most tattooed man in Britain during the writing of this book. "The King of Ink Land, Body Art, The Extreme", as he likes to be known, offers the following perspective:

> Life is precious and wonderful. We are created beings and a fantastic species. Underneath we are all the same. However, not everything makes sense for a great number of reasons. From a naked baby to a clothed adult, we are born with plain skins. I knew my human plain skin format was an error at a young age and began to develop my human vessel. I saw this as a way of taking control over my life journey by shaping it and colouring it in a way that would make me happy.
>
> At the age of nine, which is half the legal age for tattooing, I knew that pictures would be my skin colour and destiny. Not happy with being a plain skin, I attempted to change my body at twelve before tasting the first experience of body art physically at the age of sixteen. That day changed my life forever. This was not an addiction; it was something I was correcting. I was evolving into who I felt I truly was.
>
> My identity is living, breathing, talking Art. My appearance makes me happy. I cannot see myself without my body modifications. I would not be me!

While people from all walks of life engage in body art practices, people with physical illnesses or disabilities might have particular reasons for adorning their bodies in these ways. In a culture that places such high importance on speed and productivity, people with disabilities are often grossly undervalued, with body art sometimes being one attempt to modulate this. As Adam Cline, a sufferer of muscular dystrophy, explains,

> I have reclaimed my body through physical adornment because, for me, this coincides with my mentality. I have pierced and tattooed myself, my body, to complement my disability. Body art gives me a new way of looking at myself. Anyway, I figure if people are gonna stare because of the chair—I might as well give them something interesting to look at. A chair by itself is pretty boring. (Cline, 2014, p. 1)

Cline also believes that his piercings and tattoos show people who assume that his intellect must also be compromised that he can think for himself. Perhaps this is the key to all forms of bodily ornamentation. It is possible that they are all an attempt to show the world that we can think for ourselves and do not need society telling us what we should do, how we should behave, what our bodies should look like, and, ultimately, who we are. The body may be seen as the one thing the self truly owns and the one medium, therefore, through which we can strongly assert this self. "Tattooing sits within the skin, as the skin sits within the frontier of culture and self" (MacCormack, 2006, p. 78).

While tattoos, piercings, and other bodily adornments have been correlated with psychiatric disturbances, researchers such as Preti and colleagues (2006) argue that they should be seen as a desire to assert an individual's identity rather than as a marker of psychopathology. In a society within which conformity is the order of the day (we should all be thin and beautiful or muscular and handsome), some of us are answering back using the very bodies with which our society wishes us to display our conformity. It could be said that instead of acquiring another muscle bulk at the gym or losing another pound on the scales, we transfigure our bodies as an act of defiance, as an alternative means of asserting our own control, agency, and autonomy. While the stories of scarification and self-mutilation might shock us, it is difficult to deny the lurch of fascination we may have with these individuals who are willing to go so very far to assert ownership over their bodies. We could call them "crazy" and "masochistic", or we could call to account the societal conditions which drive people to take such drastic measures in order to claim back their bodies and very selves as their own.

In the midst of mod-culture rebelling against Western ideals of the body, a French artist known as Orlan began a project in 1990 called "The Reincarnation of Saint Orlan". The venture comprised a series of nine operations/performances to redesign her face and body using cosmetic surgery. Using the facial features of women from Renaissance art, Orlan created a prototype with the use of computer technology. It might have seemed, superficially, that Orlan was attempting to become the epitome of beautiful women throughout art history and to publically display the process of plastic surgery in the construction of a woman. Interviews with Orlan, however, paint a very different picture and a completely alternative set of motivations, which challenge Western notions of homogeneity through an engagement with aberrant body forms (Clarke, 1999). Orlan presents photographic images preceding surgical treatment (with her face marked up with haunting black dots and lines), during surgical treatment (leaving nothing to the imagination), and post treatment as her skin begins to heal. This timeline of images contrasts the *natural* woman, untouched by cosmetic surgery, with the cultural impact of technology and plastic surgery. Orlan would appear to accept a Foucauldian notion of the body, in which the body is understood to be a surface for the inscriptions of culture rather than a biological entity alone. She explains,

> I have always questioned the status of the body in our society. I have always been working on social, political, cultural and religious pressures, which prints them in the flesh and in particular in women's flesh. The first part of my work before the surgery questioned my Occidental culture and my identity. My current work is about non-Occidental cultures. I use the new image of myself that I have coined in order to produce new images and new pieces of art.

> Surgery is not my job. I have been the first artist to use aesthetic surgery in another context—not to appear younger or better according to the designated pattern. I wanted to disrupt the standards of beauty. (Frank, 2013)

Much of Orlan's work has focused on adding to the skin and the body through plastic surgery, facial implants, and structural alterations, practices that are all on the increase in current Western culture. Rather worryingly, the industry for taking away from the skin, in the form of skin lightening, is also expanding rapidly. The preference for lighter skin and the discrimination of those with darker skin continues to heavily influence intergroup and intragroup relations. Sociologists and anthropologists continue to document discrimination against people with darker skin and also to draw correlations between skin tone and socioeconomic status (Hunter, 2005). Furthermore, researchers continue to find that darker-skinned people are sometimes viewed as less intelligent, less trustworthy, and less attractive than their lighter-skinned counterparts in some cultures (e.g, Herring et al., 2003). People with a lighter skin tone enjoy substantial privileges that continue to be unattainable to those with darker skin, including earning more money, completing more years of schooling, living in more affluent neighbourhoods, and marrying people of higher social status (Espino & Franz, 2002; Hughes & Hertel, 1990; Murguia & Telles, 1996; Verna & Herring, 1991). As Margaret Hunter (2002) explains, light skin colour, which is frequently used as an indicator of beauty, can operate as a form of social capital, for women in particular.

The practice of skin lightening is far from new and has been practised for many years all over the world. References to African-American women using powders and skin bleaches, for example, appeared in the press as early as the 1850s. Historically, women in particular would create their own treatments or purchase products such as creams and lotions, many of which contained highly toxic materials, including mercury or lead. At the turn of the twenty-first century, however, the quest for light, freckle- and age-spot-free skin dramatically accelerated, with the market for skin lightening products exploding in many parts of the world. The production and sale of merchandise offering lighter skin has now become a global industry generating multi-millions. In addition to official marketers, there has also been a boom of lightening products on the black market, with illegal sellers producing, transporting, and selling a wide range of unregulated lightening products.

Bans have been placed on the importation of skin lighteners in some countries, such as in South Africa, though there continues to be widespread use of these products nevertheless. In South Africa the use of such products now constitutes a serious health issue, since many of these products contain mercury, corticosteroids, or high doses of hydroquinone. Mercury is highly toxic to the body, with sustained exposure potentially leading to neurological damage and kidney disease. Hydroquinone, which was originally an industrial chemical, is effective in suppressing melanin production; hence, exposure to the sun damages skin that has been treated with it. Long-term hydroquinone use can lead to ochronosis, a disfiguring condition resulting in blue-black discolouration of the skin. In addition, the overuse of topical steroids can lead to eczema, bacterial and fungal infections, Cushing's syndrome, and even skin atrophy. These unwanted manifestations can lead to increased use of other skin products in an attempt to ameliorate the unwanted changes, leading to a vicious circle of skin disease and resultant psychological distress.

I was extremely disturbed to learn that the mercury soaps used by many Africans are most frequently manufactured in the European Union, with Italy and Ireland leading the production of this toxic, mercury-laced soap. One company located in Lancashire, England, was forced to close following out-of-court settlements related to two former employees who had given birth to stillborn or severely malformed infants due to their mercury exposure. Shockingly, the company, up until then known as W&E Products, subsequently secured a £750,000 grant from the Irish Industrial Development Authority to relocate to Ireland, where they changed their name to Killarney Enterprises Ltd and continued trading until 2007, at which time they were finally shut down permanently. Their soaps contained up to 3% mercuric iodide. While the distribution of mercury soap has been illegal in the EU since 1989, its manufacture has remained legal as long as the product is exported. While mercury-based soaps are often marketed as antiseptics and as body odour prevention, they are known to bleach the skin and are much more commonly used for this specific purpose. They continue to be frequently smuggled back into the EU for sale in shops catering for African immigrant communities.

Researchers estimate that 25% of women in Bamaki, Mali, 35% in Pretoria, South Africa, and 52% in Dakar use skin lighteners, as do a massive 77% of women traders in Lagos, Nigeria (Adebajo, 2002; del Guidice & Yves, 2002; Mahe et al., 2003; Malangu & Ogubanjo, 2006). While skin lighteners were primarily used by rural women with lower socio-economic status in the 1970s, they are now reportedly used by women with diplomas and university degrees who work within well-paid jobs, in much the same way in which tattoos have worked their way up the classes in recent decades. A recent study by Ntshingila (2005) found that one in thirteen "upwardly mobile" black African women aged between twenty-five and thirty-five use skin lighteners, though it is possible that this is an underestimation, given the frequent shame attached to using such products. Women in India, the Philippines, Japan, China, Korea, and Mexico, among others, have also been found to use skin-lightening products extensively. In Japan, for example, the following advertisements can be found for skin lightening products in women's magazines and on billboards:

The sensation of *whiteness* (*shiro*) on your skin (Helena Rubinstein)

The best shortcut to *whiteness* (Givenchy)

Let's cultivate *whiteness*, every day (Clinique)

What I have touched is a drop of *white* science (Yves Saint-Laurent)

Double action, for the skin of the future which goes beyond *whiteness* (Dior)

Clarins has discovered the *white* skin (Clarins)

A new experience of *whiteness* (Carita). (Ashikari, 2005, p. 74, original italics)

A great diversity of motives have been found for using skin lightening products, including enhancing life opportunities, increasing attractiveness of the skin, conforming to European and American beauty standards, reducing the effects of negative stereotypes, the desire for social dominance and power, enhanced ability to seduce others, and compliance with the wishes of close others. Again, one will note a number of parallels between these motivations and some of the driving forces behind other forms of permanent bodily alterations, such as tattooing and scarification. In short, the individual who uses methods of skin lightening is often an individual looking to assert a particular identity and a particular affiliation with a desired group. The pursuit of beauty and social belongingness, again, comes high up on the list. One letter entitled "The colour of me" in the *Jamaica Observer* in 2001 sums up many of these motivations rather succinctly:

I have been following the arguments about colour, and as a young Black woman (two years out of high school), I realise why my friends used to spend so much time bleaching. They were right. I was wrong. Fairer is better in our country. The guys say so, dancehall (music) says so, my friends say so, beauty contests say so, and learned adults say so! I have a good figure, and a cute face, but I am black. Therefore, I am saving up all my money to buy my pills and my Ambi, and I will even try blue soap. Hello! I need a life here in Jamaica. (Malangu & Ogubanjo, 2001)

Yet again, we find ourselves returning to Western ideals of beauty at the heart of body alteration practices. It appears that while many of us are engaging in all-consuming attempts to stamp out physical deviances from the beauty ideal by becoming thin, big-breasted, fair-skinned women with straight hair, and the socially promoted level of make-up, others are rebelling against this compartmentalisation through the exploration of other physical means of asserting our individual identity, such as tattoos, piercings, and socially deviant clothing. Either way, the Western beauty ideal is deeply affecting many of us, with such effects reaching out far beyond the Western world. Globalisation and the boom of the mass media mean that a teenager in the Philippines, for example, can be bombarded with Western images of thin, fair-skinned women and might come to assimilate this unrealistic ideal for themselves.

Beauty contests, or pageants, are one means by which women from all over the world are assailed with images of idealised Western beauty. The first beauty contest along the model of today's pageants was held in the USA in 1880, with the prototypical Miss America competition originating in 1921. These contests have proliferated and are, by now, extremely popular events all over the world. In the USA alone, around 7,500 contests are franchised each year by Miss America and Miss USA, with several thousand more taking place independently at local level. The official website for Miss World, a competition that originated in the UK in 1951, reports that the pageant is held annually in 104 countries and is the most watched annually televised event in the world. As beauty pageants along the lines of the USA and UK models have exported to other parts of the world, much controversy and resistance has ensued. The contest for a Pan-African beauty queen became a source of controversy, for example, when a white South African woman became one of the twelve finalists; many

Africans protested that the face of Africa should be black. Similarly, the Miss World contest in Bangalore, India, in 1996 resulted in riots, as did the Miss World competition in Nigeria in 2002, when the pageant was scheduled during the month of Ramadan.

One young Nepalese woman, when interviewed about the spread of beauty pageants to India and Nepal, explained,

"Some felt we were copying Western style, or Western culture, accepting Western norms and values and it [the introduction of beauty pageants] is against our tradition, culture and norms; there was great controversy." (Regmi et al., 2008, p. 70)

Many of the beauty pageants across the globe adopt Westernised beauty standards, since winners will often go on to compete in international competitions, including Miss World. Indeed, Miss Nigeria went on to win the Miss World title in 2001, a victory put down by the Miss Nigeria organisers to having successfully pushed their standards towards thinner and taller contestants in line with international criteria. Sadly, during the audition process for Miss Nigeria, a couple of the chaperones pointed out a woman who had auditioned for multiple years, stating that "each year she comes back cleaner and cleaner" (Balogun, 2012, p. 375). When asked what they meant, they explained that each year she returned to audition, her skin looked fairer, which, in this case, was linked to skin and make-up treatments.

Skin-lightening practices are not the only phenomena in terms of eastern societies emulating western appearance ideals. Disordered eating, which, until recently, was considered to be a "Western disease", is now also becoming increasingly common in eastern countries. Dr Anne Becker, a researcher at Harvard Medical School, famously studied the impact of television on the eating patterns of adolescents in Fiji, a non-industrialised country (Becker et al., 2002). In 1995, before television was introduced to the island, only 3% of Fijian teen girls interviewed reported that they had engaged in self-induced vomiting in order to lose weight. By 1998, after television was introduced to the island, 15% of interviewees admitted to self-induced vomiting in the pursuit of weight loss. Becker and colleagues do not attribute direct causation to the introduction of television, but do suggest some correlation between that event and the increase in these purging behaviours. As young people are exposed to Western concepts of beauty and thinness, they are arguably in danger of losing their own cultural identity and of an increased risk of developing maladaptive eating patterns and, ultimately, distressing appearance battles.

Thankfully, many women across the globe are questioning these beauty ideals and refusing to lose weight, to have cosmetic surgery, to lighten their skin, and to engage in any such body alteration practices in order to conform to Western beauty standards. Hair texture, for example, has long been regarded as a culturally meaningful symbol of femininity. Long, wavy hair or salon-straightened hair is often associated with a European appearance, while tightly curled or kinky hair is typically correlated with an African heritage. Mary O'Neal, a student at Howard University in the 1960s, was among the early group of black women who stopped straightening their hair. She entered university as a fashion-conscious young woman who followed the conventions for black female grooming, including hair straightening. As a student, she became involved in the civil rights movement and became friends with a fellow campus activist, who encouraged her to cut her hair and stop straightening it, since unstraightened hair, in his view, was not the mark of a poorly groomed woman but, instead, a symbol of racial pride. Mary soon stopped straightening her hair and became the target of much ridicule on campus, though she did manage to recruit a few other women, including Muriel Tillinghurst, who recalled the day she got her first natural hairstyle: ". . . so when I went to the hairdresser that day, after she washed my hair, I said 'Don't press my hair'. And that just sent a boomerang around the hairdressing parlour" (Craig, 2006, p. 172).

It might amaze us that something as simple as not getting one's hair straightened could cause such a strong societal reaction. Yet, this is how entrenched in the beauty myth we have become. Marcus Garvey, pioneer of a mass African-American civil rights movement in the early twentieth century, emphatically implored his followers to "take down the pictures of white women from your walls. Elevate your own women to that place of honour" (Hope-Franklin & Meier, 1982, p. 114). Perhaps we would all do well to elevate our own Selves to that place of honour. Perhaps it is time as a society to accept ourselves fully, to begin to love again our shape, our skin, our hair . . . and every aspect of our deeper, limitless being.

Trying to hold on to your identities, even if they are the most spiritual, most holy of identities, is like trying to shove a camel through the eye of a needle. They are too coarse, too big, too untrue, too fabricated to get to the truth. (Adyashanti, 2006, p. 7)

CHAPTER SEVEN

Shadows of childhood

"The development of the child's personality could not go on at all without the constant modification of his sense of himself by suggestions from others. So he himself, at every stage, is really in part someone else, even in his own thought"

(Baldwin, 1902, p. 23)

A s we have moved through the early part of this book, it might have become increasingly clear that difficulties and self-destructive behaviours related to appearance struggles cannot simply be explained as disease processes or brushed aside as private affairs. Distress related to the perceived physical appearance of the body is firmly situated in a cultural and societal context and, as such, is far from being attributable to individual pathologies or "deviances".

The pervasive medical-model view of appearance struggles as "mental illnesses" roots its postulations firmly in the position that psychological distress owes significant accountability to our biology. Such attribution frequently points the finger firmly at our unsuspecting genes, which are held up as the "baddies" in our appearance-focused identity struggles. Yet, genes cannot even precisely determine the development of specific neural pathways; there are about 30,000 genes in the human genome, but over 100 trillion synapses in the brain. More accurately, a signal from the gene's environment, as opposed to an emergent property of the gene itself, activates the expression of that gene. According to the discipline of epigenetics, which literally means "control above genetics", it is our experiences that shape the actions of our genes. Simple biology cannot, therefore, be held solely accountable for any of our physical or psychological struggles.

In a landmark study in 2009, which used rodent models of maternal care, scientists showed how the frequency of licking and grooming in the early life of the rodents governed the development of brain and behaviour in the offspring, with effects that lasted into adult life (Champagne & Curley, 2009). Absent and poor maternal care was found to directly affect and shape the activity of the hypothalamus–pituitary–adrenal (HPA) axis (the main stress system of the brain), in addition to the forebrain regulation systems. Those pups exposed to poor maternal care developed a modified, frequently increased, HPA axis reactivity and a breakdown in the normal down-regulation of this system, in addition to increased anxiety, fear, passivity, and startle responses. It was found that rodent maternal care affects the transcription of genes that support glucocorticoid receptors, which are essential to the regulation of the HPA axis. Importantly, difficulties in childhood attachment, which we shall return to later in this chapter, have also been found to alter the structures, neuro-chemicals, and connectivity of the human brain, with severe childhood neglect typically affecting the ability of the HPA axis to regulate the brain and body's stress response (Corbin, 2007). One of the many tragic consequences of the simplistic bio-genetic approach is the failure of the mental health community to petition for primary prevention programmes aimed at keeping children safe and securely attached in the first five years of life. Such programmes are slowly springing up, however, including the Parent and Infant Partnership services (PIPs) increasingly springing up in the UK.

When we attempt to explore the aetiology of our appearance struggles, therefore, I believe it is more useful to focus on life experiences and sociocultural factors while maintaining an awareness that, while biological elements have almost certainly played a part in the drama, they hold no accountability *per se* if divorced from the life and even foetal experiences that would have given them their substance. This understanding takes a step beyond the current understanding of the stress-vulnerability model of mental illness, which claims that "weak" genes make us susceptible to certain pathologies and stress later triggers these vulnerabilities. The argument made by true epigenetics, rather, is that our bodies are made up of a vast network of parts continuously engaged in methods of intercommunication; we are far from explaining these mechanisms with the scientific knowledge we currently have.

This chapter explores the role of difficult life experiences in appearance struggles that, as we shall see from the literature, comes up time and again. Prevalence rates of childhood trauma in Western countries have been shown to be high, with the collective rates of neglect, physical abuse, sexual abuse and emotional abuse having been estimated to be up to 59% (Creighton, 2004). Trauma can be experienced by any person at any time when his emotional resources are overwhelmed. As such, we would be hard pushed to find a person on this planet who has not experienced some level of trauma at some point in his life. It might be useful, perhaps, to think about trauma within the core concepts of helplessness and terror. Trauma, by its very nature, renders the victim defenceless, with commonly cited resultant experiences being feelings of intense fear, loss of control, and threat of annihilation (Sadock et al., 2009). All too often, these traumatic symptoms become disconnected from the original event and take on a life of their own.

Sexual abuse is a particularly complex form of trauma, often leading to post-trauma stress. Feelings of helplessness can be absolute for people who endure such trauma, with up to 88% (of 89 women) reporting high to moderate levels of paralysis during a childhood sexual assault reporting high to moderate levels of paralysis during assault (Finn, 2003; Marx et al., 2008). Pereda and colleagues (2009) examined prevalence rates of childhood sexual abuse (CSA) in nineteen countries and found that all studies looking at long-term implications of CSA reported a relationship between histories of CSA and mental health issues later in life, including anxiety, depression, withdrawal, fear, suicide, low self-esteem, somatic complaints, aggression, self-destructive behaviour (including disordered eating), and acute stress. People with a history of sexual abuse have also been found by Hunter (1991) to exhibit a more negative body image and attach less importance to their physical appearance and by Wenninger and

Heiman (1998) to typically appraise their health more negatively than controls. It is also pertinent to note that children and young adolescents reside in the age of "magical thinking", whereby they typically possess a propensity for marrying up two separate, distinct occurrences as being directly correlational, or attribute everything that happens in their lives to some perceived flaw or "badness" within themselves. A child might correlate an abusive act with a personal misdemeanour, for example, and come to believe not only that they caused the abuse, but also that they acutely deserve it. Appearance-related distress in children and adolescents might also be rooted in such magical thinking. Sadness on account of trauma could be interpreted as originating in the size and appearance of the body, particularly in the modern, Western world within which we are constantly exposed to the myth that happy people are beautiful people and ugly people are sad.

Given the importance of relationships to a healthy self-concept, attachment theory might also provide some useful insights into the association of appearance disturbances and childhood experiences. A growing body of research, for example, indicates a strong relationship between attachment and disordered eating (Ward et al., 2000). The broken trust experienced by children who have been abused, neglected, or have had their self-worth strongly questioned by their carers would appear to negatively influence their ability to form secure attachments. These children suffer what van der Kolk (1987) has termed a "disorder of hope" (p. 154). Instead of perceiving themselves as a whole person, the child experiences herself as highly fragmented, only allowing selected aspects of herself to interact with, and be visible to, others. Children affected in this way might also attempt to dominate their own bodies in a desperate effort to understand and cope with the ways in which their bodies were dominated by others. As Stephen Cope (2001) explains, we learn at a very young age how to control and override the cues and needs of our bodies as opposed to responding to them. We end up doing to ourselves what was done to us.

In the early 1950s, John Bowlby, a British psychoanalyst and child psychiatrist, published his now famous report commissioned by the World Health Organisation (WHO), entitled *Maternal Care and Mental Health* (Bowlby, 1951). Within this report, he coined the term "maternal deprivation" to describe a range of conditions in which he found maternal care to be lacking. Bowlby viewed attachment behaviour as an evolutionary survival strategy for protecting the infant from predators. The goals of attachment include and subsume the instinctual behaviours of suckling, clinging, following, crying, and smiling, with the aim of all of these behaviours being to bring the infant closer to the mother. Bowlby postulated that unless there were powerful, in-built behaviours that activated this maternal care, the baby would be unable to survive and would, therefore, die. Bowlby noted an increase in attachment behaviours during times of fatigue, sickness, pain, or when additional care was required.

Researchers have now repeatedly confirmed the importance of attachment to healthy psychological development. Another psychologist we owe a particular debt to is Harry Harlow, who is best known for his social isolation experiments on rhesus monkeys (Harlow et al., 1963). Working in the late 1950s and early 1960s, Harlow bemoaned the fact that very little experimental research had been devoted to the subject of love. In his most famous experiment, Harlow gave young rhesus monkeys a choice between two different "mothers". One was made of soft terrycloth but provided no food. The other was made of wire but provided food from an attached baby bottle.

Harlow removed the young monkeys from their natural mothers just a few hours after birth and left them to be raised by these cloth and wire surrogates. Overwhelmingly, the infant monkeys preferred spending time clinging to their cloth mother, visiting the wire mother only to feed. Harlow concluded that contact comfort was essential to the psychological development and health of the young monkeys, even more so than the provision of food. His findings echo the work of John Bowlby, who believed that bonding occurs not only as a result of the reduction of primary drives (such as food) but also due to primary object clinging, which is a need for intimate contact, most commonly initially associated with the mother.

Unsurprisingly, even those monkeys reared on the cloth mother suffered abnormal development and were neurotic as adults. In subsequent studies, when provided with a rocking surrogate, the young monkeys suffered fewer abnormal developmental indicators. Relatively normal development and optimal adult functioning, however, only occurred in those given contact with a live monkey for at least thirty minutes a day. Harlow thus hypothesised that human infants also need interactive, nurturing touch to support normal development and to become psychologically healthy adults.

When we are touched, there is a pressure pushing on the skin at the point of contact. Just under the skin are pressure receptors called Pacinian corpuscles, which receive pressure stimulation and send a message to the brain. Signals from the Pacinian corpuscles go directly to the vagus nerve, an important nerve bundle deep in the brain. The vagus, sometimes called the "wanderer", has branches that wander throughout the body to several internal organs, including the heart. It is the vagus nerve that slows the heart down and decreases blood pressure. Importantly, the vagus serves the gastrointestinal system and strongly influences digestion, assimilation, and elimination. It is also the "switch" between our sympathetic ("fight or flight") and parasympathetic ("rest and digest") autonomic nervous systems. Furthermore, touch results in a decrease in cortisol, a stress hormone, and simultaneously increases the release of oxytocin, which promotes feelings of trust and bonding. Touch also makes the orbital frontal cortex light up, just like other rewarding stimuli, such as sweet tastes and pleasant smells. Babies who are touched and held frequently each day have an abundance of cortisol receptors in the hippocampus as adults, unlike babies who fail to receive positive touch and are exposed to stressful events: these babies typically grow into adults with a reduced number of hippocampal cortisol receptors (McEwen et al., 2012). When a stressful event then triggers a rise in cortisol levels, there are fewer receptors to receive it and the cortisol floods the hippocampus, affecting its growth. A smaller, or damaged, hippocampus is then less able to inhibit the further release of cortisol and the person can find himself continually suspended in high states of emotional arousal and stress.

Bowlby believed that in order to stay connected to the mother, or primary caregiver, the child develops organised patterns of coping with her personality. He believed that children go to great lengths, including making extensive cognitive distortions and emotional sacrifices if necessary, to remain connected to their mothers. A child's self-model, therefore, is profoundly influenced by how his mother sees and treats him: whatever she fails to recognise in him he is likely to fail to recognise in himself. The ongoing interactions between the mother and child lead to particular regulating styles, as well as to specific defensive strategies for excluding negatively perceived emotions, notably anxiety and anger (which, as we have seen, are central components of appearance struggles). These ongoing interactions would seem to create an attachment style within the child which determines how they organise their connections to important others.

The case of Nina, offered by Sue Gerhardt (2004), highlights the development of such emotional sacrifices rather patently. Nina grew up as an only child with a mother who was a fitness enthusiast and ate sparingly. Nina was the adoring focus of her parents, who had high expectations of her but did not have a good relationship with one another. She subsequently felt under constant pressure to meet her parents' needs, in particular the psychological needs of her mother. Nina could not even bear to stay away from home overnight on account of her mother potentially feeling left out and abandoned; she felt she could not have anything good if her mother was unable to have it also. Nina appears to have spent a large proportion of her childhood trying to make her parents happy and hiding any so-perceived negative emotions. In the process, she lost touch with her feelings and desires and began to starve herself as a teenager as a way of preventing her emotions from coming to the surface. Nina had tremendous difficulty separating from her parents as she grew up, due to the high levels of enmeshment. From Nina's perspective, ". . . they [her parents] needed her so much. How would they survive without her?" (Gerhardt, 2004, p. 129).

Attachment difficulties can have a whole host of agonising implications and can feed strongly into appearance struggles. If the primary carer's awareness of her own emotions is lacking or if she is overly preoccupied with her feelings, it might be more difficult to notice and respond to her child's feelings. If the carer has not yet learnt how to tolerate his own emotions, he is less likely to find his child's feelings tolerable and might subsequently ignore or rebuff them. The child might come to understand that there is no regulatory assistance available for her feelings, leading to the potential denial and suppression of these feelings. These children often typically develop an avoidant attachment. Other children live with parents who are highly inconsistent in their response to emotions, sometimes supporting their child in their sense-making of feelings and sometimes pushing these feelings away. Such children also discover that help with regulating their emotions is not easily available to them and thus learn to exaggerate their emotions, while concurrently being strongly aware of their needs and fears. These children may come to develop an ambivalent attachment.

The most problematic of the attachment styles is frequently claimed to be the disorganised attachment type, in which children engage in erratic and contradictory attachment strategies. In these families, one or both parents have often been affected by traumatic events that have not been processed effectively, making it difficult for them to respond to their child's needs. Parents 'with these kinds of emotional difficulties often struggle to provide the most basic necessities for their child, such as emotional warmth and security. Disorganised attachment is displayed by approximately 15% of infants in non-clinical samples, though in maltreated samples the incidence rate can be as high as 80% (van IJzendoorn et al., 1999). Disorganised attachment has the strongest link with later psychological struggles, including appearance-related battles.

Attachment style is an important consideration when attempting to understand relationships and their association with appearance distress. Fraley and Shaver (2000) argue that attachment can be accurately conceptualised as two continuous dimensions: anxiety (monitoring the relationship and being sensitive to rejection or threats to security) and avoidance (avoiding closeness with the attachment figure). Secure attachment corresponds to low levels of both dimensions. Attachment security has been estimated to occur in around 58% of the population, with attachment anxiety occurring in 19%, and attachment avoidance in 23% (Bakermans-Kranenburg & van Ijzendoorn, 2009). Secure attachment is also related to body satisfaction (Cash et al., 2003). This is consistent with the findings of Brennan and Shaver (1995), who found their healthy eating and body satisfaction measures to be related to a preoccupied attachment style, implying a relationship with anxiety but not avoidance. It could be that those with high attachment anxiety are more sensitive to socially relevant cues such as appearance. Furthermore, people without secure early attachments are more likely to be victimised and traumatised and are also, therefore, more likely to develop pervasive symptoms of shame and dissociation (Kessler et al., 1995), which are two known correlates of appearance-focused distress.

An additional important finding is that anxiously attached adults have been found to be highly sensitive to relationship loss and to frequently have an incoherent sense of self, characterised by preoccupying anger or passivity (Tasca et al., 2009). It is not difficult to imagine how each of these facets can filter surreptitiously into appearance struggles. Being highly sensitive to relationship loss, the individual could become a people-pleaser in every sense of the phrase, using societal ideals as pegs upon which to hang their people-pleasing tendencies. Appearance ideals might then be embraced and lived out, encapsulated within the belief, perhaps, that being thin and beautiful, or muscular and handsome, are ways of hanging on to the relationships they are so very terrified of losing. This striving is overlaid by an incoherent sense of self, which renders the individual unsure of who they are in the first place.

It is perhaps unsurprising that attachment difficulties may find a voice through the medium of the body, since the body is potentially the most obvious reminder of our interrelatedness with others. As Lemma (2015) reminds us, we cannot give birth to ourselves. Our bodies bear testimony to the fact that we have life only through the existence, either past or present, of our parents. This truth is visually heightened by the fact that many of us bear some physical resemblance to our parents or possess some of their physiological attributes. It is also through the body that we experience most intensely a sense of closeness and intimacy with others and, therefore, the conflict between wishing to be connected to the other and the fear of being engulfed by them.

Appearance battles can be an attempt to find and cling to a separate sense of self. When one is not sure of whom one is, any focus on or attempt to manipulate the physical appearance can viscerally aid the sense of one's existence. Preoccupying anger might then be turned inwards and used to punish the self through the medium of the body, while passivity might hold the individual back from expressing their anger towards any external agent. A pervasive sense of identity confusion and fragmentation can result.

In a study by O'Kearney (1996), of women engaged in disordered eating behaviours, higher levels of anxious and avoidant attachment patterns were reported compared to controls. Similarly, another study compared 18–24-year-old patients being treated for eating disorders with controls and found that the severity of the eating problems was related to the security of attachment (Broberg et al., 2001). Furthermore, in a recent study of 224 college women, Cheng and Malinkcrodt (2009) found that attachment anxiety was associated with body dissatisfaction, but that this effect was mediated by media internalisation: women with higher attachment anxiety internalised the media thin ideal more than those with lower attachment anxiety. In addition, they found that more positive memories of parental care were associated with lower attachment anxiety and, in turn, lower body dissatisfaction. In a review of twenty-nine studies conducted by Zachrisson and Skarderud (2010), between 96–100% of people with clinical levels of an eating disorder reported attachment insecurity.

From these findings, it could be assumed that higher attachment anxiety causes a person to be more other-orientated and, therefore, more susceptible to negative social and societal influences. This is consistent with the finding that people diagnosed with anorexia in particular tend to be more interested in the needs of others than in their own needs (Curiel-Levy et al., 2012). The tripartite influence model proposed by Thompson and colleagues (1999) upholds such a postulation, incorporating three significant socio-cultural variables as predictors of body image and eating disturbances: cultural influences, parental influences, and peer influences. A wide body of research supports this model with associations having been found between the awareness and internalisation of socio-cultural standards of beauty and disordered eating, between parental influences and body-image difficulties, and between peer influences and appearance distress (Griffiths et al., 1999; McCabe & Ricciardelli, 2001; Shoemaker & Furman, 2009).

In recent research by Hardit and Hannum, young women who reported more anxiety in their relationships with others were also more concerned about their body size and shape. This might be because body size and shape can be "visible, concrete ways that young women come to evaluate and devalue themselves" (Hardit & Hannum, 2012, p. 473). Understandably anxiety within relationships can be a result of poor attachment, often with the mother or primary caregiver. A central tenet of attachment theory is the notion that infants develop beliefs about their lovability based on the quality of interactions with their primary caregiver. These beliefs and patterns of attachment have the potential to persist across the lifespan and influence personality, psychological functioning, and behaviour unless they are addressed and attended to.

Donald Winnicott, an English paediatrician and psychoanalyst, wrote extensively about the development of a false self within the mother–infant relationship. Such a self is given the opportunity to develop at the stage of first object-relationships, at which time the child is mostly unintegrated, since the "cohesion of the various sensori-motor elements belongs to the fact that the mother holds the infant, sometimes physically, and all the time figuratively" (Winnicott, 1965, p. 145). The infant, within this unintegrated phase, periodically acts on spontaneous impulses with the source of such spontaneity being the true Self. The mother then meets this gesture in either a good-enough or not-good-enough way (Winnicott's terms). The good-enough response meets the spontaneity of the child repeatedly, thus allowing the true Self to have life. The not-good-enough response is unable to accommodate the child's spontaneity. Instead, the mother substitutes the child's gestures with her own, thus promoting compliance of the child and the emergence of a false self.

If a child is repeatedly unable to act spontaneously from her true Self, she quickly learns that this true Self is not acceptable and is, therefore, to be hidden. The true desires, needs, and personality of the child are, henceforth, squashed and packed away, with a false self which more readily meets the needs, expectations, and demands of the mother, or primary caregiver, coming to centre stage. If this dizzy dance of suppression continues for long enough, the child might even begin to lose a sense of her true Self, growing up into an adult who simply has no idea of what her own needs and desires are, let alone having any notion of how to go about fulfilling them.

There is an acute danger of the child assimilating the view that his true Self is inherently flawed. This can all too easily lead to the desolating belief that he is unacceptable as a person and, therefore, unlovable at his very core. Such a belief is complicated by the fact that it typically develops in the pre-verbal stage and is, therefore, in part unconscious and can be devoid of relation to graspable memories.

Children who believe that they are unlovable typically grow into adults with low self-esteem; such low self-esteem has been strongly linked with transactions within the family system (Harter et al., 1996). Several studies have indicated that strong family relationships have a positive effect on self-esteem (e.g. Yabiku et al., 1999) while children and adolescents with inadequate family support demonstrate poorer mental health, delayed social development, and lower levels of well-being (Sameroff et al., 1998). Children's fears and social anxieties are typically related to levels of family cohesion, which has been defined as "the emotional bonding that family members have toward one another" (Olson et al., 1992, p. 1). Levels of cohesion can range from disengaged (little closeness and high independence) to enmeshed (very high closeness and dependency). Mid-range (separated and connected) levels of cohesiveness have been suggested to reflect positive family functioning. Research conducted by Gorbett and Kruczek (2008) found that the strongest predictor of social self-esteem in adults was the perceived level of family cohesion in their family of origin during childhood. Interestingly, the second strongest predictor was the number of siblings, with more siblings being related to stronger social self-esteem. Birth order or biological sex were not found to have any significant impact.

Importantly, any factor which has an impact on self-esteem can be experienced as a trauma by the child. Such trauma can be particularly acute if the child has been singled out by the parents and treated poorly in comparison to the treatment of their siblings. Many possible hypotheses have been offered for such singling out, including:

- The *scapegoating* hypothesis: singling out and blaming one child serves a function for the family system. Marital tensions, for example, might be misplaced on to a single child.
- The *projection* hypothesis: unacceptable and uncomfortable feelings within the parent are attributed, without justification, to an individual child. Depression within the parent, for example, could contribute to this kind of distorted view.
- The *symbolisation* hypothesis: the child is a representation of another figure to the current parent and the negative feelings carried from this relationship are misattributed to one child.
- The *lack of bonding* hypothesis: the mother's difficulty in bonding to one child might be the result of an unwanted or difficult pregnancy or postnatal depression.
- The *transgenerational* hypothesis: parents, who themselves were rejected as children, feel compelled to repeat this behaviour with their own child.
- The *goodness/badness of fit* hypothesis: the temperamental style of the individual child and parent are very different and the parent has difficulty relating to this child.
- The *family secret* hypothesis: one child is singled out as a punishment for holding a family secret, such as that of hidden parentage. (Rushton & Dance, 2005, p. 421).

When a child is singled out by their parents and treated poorly, in whichever way and for whatever reason, their self-worth can be thrown strongly into question. In one study of individuals diagnosed with body dysmorphic disorder, more than three quarters reported a perception of childhood maltreatment, with emotional neglect being the most common form of such perceived maltreatment (Didie et al., 2006). When a child is neglected emotionally, the propensity might be to turn any resultant anger in on themselves, reliving the trauma of being mistreated by mistreating themselves. In this way, the psyche is given an opportunity to resolve the trauma, although the person could become so deeply entrenched in the cycle of self-destruction that years, if not decades, might be spent attempting to reach a resolution. It is also possible that, in an effort to cope with painful emotional states that overwhelm them, maltreated children develop external behaviours that help them to avoid painful emotions (Briere & Scott, 2006). Such tension-reducing behaviours can include self-harm, mirror-checking, and disordered eating. Recent research findings suggest, for example, that emotional dysregulation mediates the relationship between childhood emotional abuse and eating disorder symptoms (Burns et al., 2012). People who have had traumatic experiences are more likely to report disordered eating than those without experiences of trauma, particularly binging and purging behaviours (Ackard et al., 2001). In addition, between 30% and 50% of people with eating disorder histories report experiences of childhood sexual or physical abuse (Smolak & Murnen, 2002).

Attachment trauma can arise solely from a child's needs failing to be adequately met. The attachment system is activated when a child is afraid and needs comfort, reassurance, and safety and is traumatic when he or she fails to get it. A sense, then, of not being good enough, of not being lovable and worthy of any attention, can travel with the child into adulthood, setting the stage for a series of relationships within which the person desperately seeks to be loved while simultaneously feeling as though they lack the resources with which to make this a reality.

Traumatic early experiences can both stem from and result in unhelpful interactions within the family unit. Transactional analysts would say that repeated transactions between the child and his caregiver are aggregated and internalised to form the basis of developing child, parent, and adult ego states. Eric Berne, one of the early transactional analysts, observed that people live out their lives based on early decisions, something he called a script, which he described as a complex set of recurrent transactions based on early life experiences. He believed these scripts to be the result of the repetition compulsion, which describes the way in which people have a tendency to repeat unhappy childhood events in a bid to resolve them. We all have unique scripts, which we are very likely to have written early in our childhood years. Since our scripts have an onset, a course, and an outcome, they are often likened to, or even mistaken for, disease. Berne would argue that tragic life scripts, such as suicide, addiction or diagnosed mental illnesses are not in fact disease processes but simply the result of scripting. Thankfully, given that scripts are based on early life experiences and subsequent decisions, they can be altered and even revoked completely by similarly strong decisions.

Transactional analysis is built on three forms of ego function, namely the parent, the adult, and the child. The child ego state is preserved in its entirety from childhood. In this child state, the person might speak, act, and even think as they did when they were four years old. Such a state often emerges in times of mental distress or when great pain or elation is experienced. The adult, on the other hand, is essentially a computer, a state within which data is processed and gathered and predictions are made. In this state, the person may be mostly detached from their feelings and internal processes. The parent is made up of behaviour copied from parents or authority figures. Such a state can be nurturing, oppressive, or both.

A child brought up in a stable, loving household would seem to be most commonly raised by the nurturing parent ego-state of his parents, with their child and adult playing only supporting roles. Tragic life scripts, on the other hand, are more likely to emerge out of childhood households full of attributions and injunctions, within which the parents might predominantly reside in their child or adult ego states. Attributions tell a child what she must not do and injunctions tell her what she must do in order to remain in the parents' favour. Many of us, therefore, could have learnt from a very early age that we win favour by exhibiting certain behaviours and refraining from others. According to Berne, we then use these acceptable and non-acceptable behaviours to write our life scripts, continuing to believe that we must live within certain parameters in order to be worthy of love and acceptance. If we come to believe that we are unworthy of love and affection, we might also fail to provide these things for ourselves, which can lead to the acute lack of self-care we so often see in people engaged in appearance struggles. We gradually learn to take care of ourselves as we grow up and receive our first lessons in self-care from the way our primary caregivers look after us. Children whose parents provide a reliable source of comfort also develop the strength and resilience to better cope with difficult life experiences (van der Kolk, 2014). Children without such early sources of comfort might, conversely, find challenging experiences emotionally unmanageable.

Different parenting styles can also spring from these core ego states. Three such parenting styles were first proposed by Baumrind (1971): these are authoritarian, permissive, and authoritative. Authoritarian parents are characterised by controlling means of asserting absolute standards. Permissive parents, on the other hand, are typically non-punitive and make very few demands. Finally, authoritative parents attempt to offer rational directions while encouraging verbal give-and-take and explaining their reasoning to their child.

Numerous research studies suggest that authoritative parenting is most beneficial to self-esteem (Buri et al., 1988) and is related to lower utilisation of maladaptive strategies including passivity (Kaisa et al., 2000). Findings on permissive parenting styles appear to be somewhat inconsistent, although parental distress (including low mood) has been correlated with permissive styles, as characterised by a parent's ineffectiveness to monitor their children's misbehaviour and administer discipline (Zahn-Waxler et al., 1990). The authoritarian style would appear to be the most damaging to children's psychological health with researchers such as Shek (1999) finding that demanding parenting styles can lead to hopelessness, low self-esteem, and psychiatric morbidity in children.

The people we grow into, therefore, are patchworked from a complex matrix of relationships. If any of our core relationships are fractured, we might experience a resultant fractured self. As we have already seen, any crisis or uncertainty over our sense of self and identity can also lead to appearance distress. Psychoanalyst Hilda Bruch, who challenged traditional psychoanalytic approaches to treating disordered eating in the 1960s, examined the thinking patterns of people diagnosed with anorexia and described them as feeling incomplete in their sense of separateness and explained that an attitude of basic mistrust permeates their self-concept and all relationships, suggesting an early family life that had discouraged independence and the expression of feelings (Bruch, 1985). This sense of feeling incomplete is, I believe, at the very heart of all appearance battles, with the person seeking to become complete by attempting to perfect his physical body while concurrently struggling to find ways of coping with truly overwhelming emotions.

Appearance difficulties are most likely to emerge in adolescence. During adolescence, the parent–child relationship changes significantly as the adolescent begins to seek more independence, autonomy, and physical distance from their parents. Despite this, adolescents still retain a desire for high levels of support from their parents (Shoemaker & Furman, 2009) with a secure attachment at this stage of development seeming to depend upon three factors: first, the adolescent must have open communication with their primary carers; second, these carers have to be accessible; and third, they need to provide protection and help if necessary. When these conditions are met, adolescents are likely to maintain a sense of security and report higher levels of self-esteem (Diamond et al., 2003). It is also more probable that they will express negative emotions freely, without fear of criticism or abandonment. Adolescents who are insecurely attached, on the other hand, are more likely to perceive the expression of negative feelings as unwelcome and unsafe, thus making them more vulnerable to emotional problems, which could be played out through appearance battles. It has been found, for example, that for adolescents who carry insecure childhood attachments, the inability to reach out for emotional regulation is likely to make them vulnerable to self-harm as a way of self-soothing (Cooper et al., 1998).

Importantly, the majority of children and adolescents entering the mental health system on account of appearance distress do so via their parents and usually via their mother. Parents and primary caregivers seeking help for their children are more likely to blame any depression/anxiety and so on within themselves on the presentation of their child, believing that when their child gets better they, too, will then be all right (Anderson et al., 2006). Parenting in the modern world can be extremely stressful and many parents lack the support they themselves need in order to manage the unparalleled responsibility of bringing up a child. Parents who bring their children into the mental health system are less likely to seek or accept referrals to address their own needs. Evidence suggests that children have a 40–60% higher risk of developing their own mental health problems if a parent is mentally unwell (Beardslee et al., 1998), with the Social Care Institute for Excellence estimating that a about a third of children known to Child and Adolescent Mental Health Services (CAMHS) have parents with a psychiatric disorder (Kearney et al., 2003). It must be emphasised, however, that parenting exists on a continuum and that many parents with mental health problems provide warm, loving, and stable environments (Parrott et al., 2008).

While it might, indeed, be the case that a mother is anxious because her daughter is refusing to eat, for example, it could equally be the case that the mother's anxiety preceded any food avoidance on the daughter's part. Children might experience a range of worries if a parent is prone to difficult emotional states, perhaps feeling that they are to blame, feeling scared of their parent's symptoms, or fearing that they may develop the same presentations. Family Therapy can be one of the ways of beginning to unpick these interwoven threads and aid an understanding of the reasons, motives, and metaphors behind each member's behaviour and emotional state.

Family systems theory conceptualises the family as an organised whole in which all of the members are interdependent. Each individual's behaviour is viewed as being strongly influenced and determined by the structure, organisation, and transactional patterns of the family system. Similarly, the characteristics and behaviour of the members, as well as the functioning of the whole family system and its subsystems, are influenced by the characteristics and behaviour of each individual. Family system theory clearly states that the patterns within the system are circular, as opposed to linear. The family system, therefore, could be said to be a continuous creation loop, within which the reality of each of its members is created in tandem with the reality of each other member and with the reality of the family system as a whole. In the case of appearance battles, there could be a raised concern in family members for the struggling individual, who then consequently receives more attention. The individual might then, in turn, report more symptoms, gain more attention, and stronger diversions from other painful aspects of family life can be subsequently created. Such a cycle can become embedded and have negative consequences for each of its members. It is at this point that the cycle needs to be interrupted in some way.

Family therapy is one way of interrupting these negative cycles. The family could have become so entrenched in the drama that they are unable to see that the cycles exist or have the awareness and resources necessary to deviate from the recurrent interactions. Pleasingly, such family therapy is not in the business of laying the blame on individual members. Mothers, in particular, have received much attention for the negative effects of their behaviours and dispositions on their children, but Minuchin, the father of family systems theory, is quick to point out the misleading nature of such unidirectional interpretations, rather stating,

> It is an epistemological error to state that an overprotective mother is creating anxiety in her child. Rather, mother and child have created a pattern . . . which . . . triggers concerned behaviour in the mother, which exacerbates the child's fears, which escalates the mother's concern, and so forth. (Minuchin, 1985, p. 290)

It would be reductionist to suggest that the fault lies with any single person. The aetiology of appearance struggles is far more complex than this, as we have seen and shall continue to explore. Moreover, each parent within the appearance struggle vortex may have come with a history of battles of his or her own. A mother's attachment to her own mother, for example, is a good predictor of her infant's attachment, particularly for secure and disorganised patterns of attachment (Benoit & Parker, 1994). Family therapy aims to soothe the system and each individual, while calling each to take responsibility for his or her own part. To see the person who is distressed by her appearance solely as the victim is also inaccurate. She, too, must accept some responsibility in the systemic drama if she is to have any hope of understanding her difficulties and moving on.

Reassuringly, an individual's attachment style is not carved in stone. There are many beautiful biographies, for example, given in *The Transcendent Child* by Lillian Rubin (1996), of adults who live deeply fulfilled lives despite challenging childhood experiences and difficult attachments. While research findings suggest a significant level of attachment stability across the lifespan, attachment styles and states of mind are open to revision. Mary Main, co-author of the adult attachment interview, has spoken to many individuals with "earned security" who report high levels of relational adversity in childhood but, nevertheless, demonstrate secure attachments as adults (Main, 1995). Perhaps through good relationships in adulthood, positive interventions, and so on, these adults have managed to develop useful and healthy ways of relating to others, thus moving beyond their early attachment difficulties. While it is certainly the case that early attachment influences the establishment of neurological pathways in the brain, recent developments in neuroscience indicate that the plasticity of the brain (neuroplasticity) allows neuro-generative growth in adulthood when optimal relational conditions such as empathy, emotional attunement, and validation are experienced. It certainly does not necessary follow, therefore, that insecure attachment in childhood will continue to haunt us throughout our lives.

"You are the bows from which your children as living arrows are sent forth" (Gibran, 1991, p. 17).

CHAPTER EIGHT

Embraced emotions

"If you bring forth what is within you, what you have will save you"

(Valantasis, 1997, p. 149)

W
e have moved beyond a paradigm of appearance struggles as mental disorders, towards a view that they are understandable responses to difficult life experiences within the setting of one's social, cultural and societal context, resulting in a suppression of the true Self. For appearance struggles to be moved beyond, therefore, rejected aspects of our life journey would appear to need assimilation and the metaphor behind the appearance battle understood. A core element of this process is the experience, acknowledgment and acceptance of our emotions.

Immanuel Kant believed that "there can be no doubt that all our knowledge begins with experience" (Kant, 2007[1781], p. 15). Emotion is often typically described as involving changes in experience (feeling, affect), autonomic nervous system activation, expressive behaviour, and instrumental behaviour (Weins, 2005). Language provides us with discrete labels for our emotions, yet such airtight delineations do not exist and fail to communicate the complexity and richness of our emotional lives. According to Daniel Goleman, author of *Emotional Intelligence* (2009), our emotions act as powerful guides in facing circumstances too important to leave to cognition alone, such as bonding, danger, and loss. Our emotions, in short, are present in order to keep us safe. Each emotion brings with it a call to action, pointing us in a direction that has previously served us in handling challenges in some way. Biologically, what we have been born with in terms of emotional circulatory is what has worked best for the last 50,000 human generations, with the deliberate forces of evolution having shaped our emotions over the past million years.

According to some theorists, our appraisals of every encounter are shaped not only by our own judgements and personal history but also by our evolutionary past. Our emotions are impulses to act. The root of the word emotion, in fact, comes from the Latin *motere*, meaning "to move". The prefix "e-" suggests a moving away, a tendency towards action embedded in every emotion. If our emotions exist, therefore, as impulses towards action then any inaction could be argued to be synonymous with suppression of the emotion. When we feel a particular emotion and refrain from acting on it, the emotion (quite literally, the energy in motion) is forced underground and must be expended in another way. For some of us, the suppressed action can take the form of anger towards and punishment of the self.

Suppressed anger can take the form of self-harm behaviours, for example, which often involve the expenditure of energy from the hands (such as in cutting and skin picking). Theoretical, clinical, and empirical works alike, in fact, indicate that self-mutilation primarily constitutes an emotional regulation strategy (Chapman et al., 2006). Repressed emotions can also be used to fuel other destructive behaviours, such as self-starvation, which requires an immense amount of physical and psychological energy to sustain. Numerous research studies indicate either an increase in outwardly directed anger or a greater degree of suppressed anger in people with clinically diagnosed depression (e.g. Luutonen, 2007). Other studies support the notion that anger directed towards the self is linked with chronically low mood, with researchers such as Goldman and Haaga (1995) finding that participants diagnosed with depression had increased levels of inhibited aggression and covert hostility, but did little to express their aggression. Depressive symptoms are known to be common correlates of all appearance-focused struggles.

Repressed fear can also feed into our difficulties. The hyper-alert resulting from repressed fear can lead to self-soothing and danger-avoidance behaviours such as mirror-checking, hair-pulling, and excessive exercise. Given the nature of difficult childhood experiences, within which many of us would have been unable to display our anger, flee the situation, or allow our fear to have adequate expression, we might have had no choice but to bury our emotions. These emotions, and their physiological and psychological implications, sadly, might continue to haunt us until they have been attended to.

As we have seen in the previous chapter, difficult early life experiences and traumas often underpin appearance distress. Most of the early neuroimaging studies of people with traumatic life experiences focused on how subjects reacted to reminders of their trauma, but recent studies are beginning to unpick how these people's brains respond when they are not thinking about the pain of their past. In a recent study, Bluhm (2009) disturbingly found almost no activation of any of the self-sensing areas of the brain while subjects diagnosed with post-traumatic stress disorder (brought on by early life traumas) lay in the brain scanner thinking about nothing in particular. The only area that showed slight activation was the posterior cingulate, which is responsible for proprioceptive awareness. According to the researchers, there can only be one feasible explanation for their results: piteously, these people had learnt to shut down the brain areas that transmit feelings and emotions which accompany terror in response to their early life experiences. Unfortunately, these same brain areas are responsible for the registration of the full range of our emotions, which provide the basis for a sense of who we are.

In the constellation of experiences commonly referred to as post-traumatic stress disorder (PTSD) in the psychiatric community, there is a persistent, involuntary re-experiencing of a previously experienced traumatic event in addition to avoidance of stimuli associated with the trauma, emotional numbing, and increased arousal and reactivity. All of this results in an exaggerated fear response. While not everyone engaged in appearance battles will be diagnosed with PTSD, of course, I would argue that the vast majority of people entrenched in such battles will have experienced early life traumas and, therefore, some level of emotional numbing if these traumas have not been processed. The essential aspect of these experiences is that they generate doubts about survival, either as a body or as a psychological self. When our self-worth is questioned in childhood, the only way some of us are able make sense of it is to decide that we must be bad people in order to deserve being treated in this bad way. Such a belief can easily lead to self-hatred and subsequent self-harm in a plethora of forms. We might also cut ourselves off from our emotions, since the story these emotions tell (a story of our "badness") is just too difficult to bear. It has been suggested by Fox (2009) that self-starvation, for example, serves as a function to suppress and avoid feeling and that self-conscious emotions that arise as a result of perceived personal transgressions or failures are a core feature of body dysmorphic disorder (Fuchs, 2003).

A necessary element of moving beyond appearance distress, therefore, would appear to be the release of repressed and denounced emotions. Karla McLaren likens this process of emotional release to the three stages of tribal initiation, which have been described as:

1.   Being isolated or separated from the known world.
2.   Having an ordeal or brush with death.
3.   Being recognised and welcomed back as an initiated person (McLaren, 2010, p. 100).

Tribal knowledge explains that if stage three is not completed, for whatever reason, the initiate must cycle through the first two stages again and again, until the cycle reaches resolution. The initiation does not conclude until all three stages have been fully worked through. As McLaren explains, the psyche seems to concur with tribal wisdom on this point. Some of us who have experienced distressing early life experiences become trapped in isolation (stage one) and repeated ordeals of a tragic nature (stage two). We find ourselves suspended in no-man's land between feeling too much and feeling too little, oscillating between a sense of numbness and the seeking of experiences that will make us feel alive in some way, which might take the form of self-mutilation, self-starvation, and all manner of other things. Those of us engaged in appearance battles might continue to be entrenched in our difficult experiences, engaging in ordeal after ordeal, until we recognise and welcome back our emotions, which, in turn, will enable us to return to the world as an emotionally integrated, initiated person. The act, in this case the painful life event or events, must be brought through to completion if it is to be integrated into our psyche, thus enabling us to move on.

In order to engage with our emotions, we first need to recognise them. Alexithymia, defined as an inability to identify and describe emotions within the self, is found in varying degrees across all sections of the population, though it has been found in higher levels in people diagnosed with anorexia (Gilboa-Schechtman et al., 2006). Furthermore, self-starvation has been linked to difficulties with recognising emotions in others, as assessed using tasks which require participants to identify emotional expressions from faces and from the eyes only (Harrison et al., 2009). Other studies suggest that people diagnosed with anorexia pay less attention to, and are, therefore, less aware of, their emotions (e.g. Harrison et al., 2010). Similarly, individuals diagnosed with BDD who were asked to match identities of faces with emotional expressions, neutral expressions, and a control task of ovals and circles had significantly more difficulty matching the identity of faces with emotional expressions relative to the control group (Feusner et al., 2010a). Individuals diagnosed with BDD have also been found to have substantial trouble with correctly interpreting neutral expressions, especially in the realm of neutral–disgust confusion (Buhlmann et al., 2011). Moreover, individuals diagnosed with bulimia have been found by Sim and Zeman (2004) to exhibit poorer emotional awareness and identification skills. It would appear that for these three presentations of appearance difficulties, recognising and understanding emotions can be a veritable labyrinth, a muddled tangle likely to be experienced across the full trajectory of appearance struggles.

People engaged in appearance battles are known to wrestle with a lived sense of their own bodies, often feeling somewhat fragmented and painfully disembodied. One could argue that it would be impossible to starve, cut, or purge the body if one was truly *in* the body: such acts necessitate some level of dissociation and some semblance of divorce from the body and its intrinsic needs and whims. The Western focus on the mind epitomised by Descartes's pronouncement, "I think therefore I am", has arguably led to a massive neglect of the lived experience of the body which is the place, of course, where our emotions express themselves. Emotions, it would seem are not a mental phenomenon, but a visceral one. Many researchers agree that the body initiates our emotions, with our minds then following suit by trying to make sense of our physical sensations. In 1884 William James and Carl Lange proposed a theory linking the mental and physical aspects of emotion, which came to be known as the James–Lange theory of emotion. James (1890) unequivocally proposed that our physiological sensations precede any mental thoughts and attached emotion-based labels and actions. In this way, emotional responses are first experienced as physical sensations in the body, which are outside of our conscious control and choosing, and are then experienced as anger, happiness, dread, and so on in accordance with the ways in which we make sense of these physiological ambiences. As Antonio Damasio puts it, "all emotions use the body as their theatre" (Damasio, 2000, p. 51). A considerable body of recent research upholds such a view, including early research conducted by Laird (1974) which found that subjects described themselves as happier when in a smile expression and angrier when in a frown expression, regardless of their previous emotional state. Furthermore, research by Weins and colleagues (2000), indicates that heartbeat detection is associated with emotional experience. When students were shown film clips targeting different emotions, individuals who could detect their heartbeats (which was a measure taken separately) reported experiencing more intense emotions than poor heartbeat detectors.

The topic we are coming to here, which we shall return to in Chapter Ten, is that of interoception, which can be described as the sense of the inner physiological condition of the body. Given that emotions emerge within the body, people with more refined interoception may be more easily able to notice and sense their emotions and, therefore, less likely to become confused or overwhelmed by them. Sadly, people diagnosed with BDD have been found to typically have weakened interoception (Kunstman et al., 2015), as have people diagnosed with anorexia (Pollatos et al., 2008) and bulimia (Fassino et al., 2004). Many of the behaviours related to appearance battles can also create a chasm between oneself and one's interoceptive awareness, with practices such as food restriction, self-mutilation, bingeing, purging, exercising to excess, and so on all necessitating ignorance of the body's felt signals and sensations. This is one of the many reasons why mindfulness practices, which promote a lived sense and present moment awareness of the body, can be so very healing for those of us with appearance-focused distress.

People engaged in appearance battles are typically so utterly confused by our emotions because they have not yet learnt how to feel or contain them. Some of us are so "out of" our bodies that we have no idea how to interpret our increased heart rate, our sweaty palms, our tingling extremities, and so on. Subsequently, we can find ourselves overwhelmed by the intensity of our emotions to such an extent that we continually shut down completely, perhaps dissociating into our appearance battle-related behaviours. We have not regularly enough had the experience of feeling and moving through our emotions without falling apart. When we recognise our innate ability to tolerate extremes of emotions and sensations while maintaining equilibrium and awareness, we no longer have any reason to fear our emotions and they lose their power over us. Anger is the emotion many of us seem to have the hardest time with, yet this is also a necessary and completely containable constellation of sensations with an important story of their own.

As we have seen, research has supported an association between anger and disordered eating, with researchers such as Zaitsoff and colleagues (2002) finding that adolescents who restrict their eating are more likely to suppress angry feelings. Much of this anger is repressed because it is felt not to be allowed; some of us learn from a very early age that displays of anger are undesirable and synonymous with a lack of control. Despite its bad reputation, anger is a healthy emotion and simply a reaction to a perceived threat to ourselves, our loved ones, our property, our self-image, or some part of our identity. While anger in its aggressive state can certainly lead to actions that cause more harm than good, such aggression does not need to follow anger, which can be expressed (and, indeed, is naturally to be expressed) in a multitude of non-aggressive ways.

Anger is a core emotion resulting from difficult life experiences, and is, regrettably, the emotion that receives most bad press in modern society. We often make the assumption that anger goes hand-in-hand with aggression, yet early research findings by Averill (1982) indicate that most anger episodes do not lead to aggressive behaviours. Thankfully, recent research studies are beginning to treat anger and aggression as two separate entities. Our propensity to equate anger with aggression is grossly misplaced. Anger, fully felt and permitted its voice, simply states and heals our personal boundaries. These boundaries can be firmly and calmly stated in the presence of anger. It is only when we deny or refuse our anger that red displays of rage seem to have the power to erupt and consume us.

At the beginning of our lives, the fortunate ones among us would have been able to express our anger freely. This is not necessarily to say that we threw ourselves on the floor kicking and screaming as toddlers, though for many of us this indeed would have been the case. Anger is a strong emotion needing release and, as very young children, we would have intuitively felt that the way to do this was by moving the body. Such movement of the body can take aggressive and passive manifestations. Much of the way we deal with our anger as young children depends on the style with which we are parented. A sensitive maternal style characterised by positive affect and responsiveness to the child's signals, for example, has been shown to increase self-regulation in toddlers, resulting in free yet non-aggressive displays of anger (Feldman et al., 1999). Conversely, interactions coloured by maternal intrusiveness have been associated with childhood aggression and unregulated anger.

Both unregulated and suppressed anger can be counterproductive and both psychologically and physically unhealthy. When anger is misdirected and overly aggressive, it can certainly lead to a whole host of unwanted consequences, although appearance battles are more likely to occur if anger is denied and refused expression. Modern society arguably does little to promote the expression of emotions, however, with its emphasis on social conformism, and commendation of control and self-censorship. The suppression of emotions such as anger, however, can also have huge implications for our physical health. Emotional expression is always tied to a specific flow of peptides (which are compounds consisting of two or more amino acids: they perform a wide range of functions in the body including regulating hormones and resisting disease), hence any suppression of emotion can result in a disturbance in the psychosomatic network. Emotional repression causes blockages and an insufficient flow of peptide signals to maintain function at the cellular level, which sets up the conditions that can lead to disease.

How, then, can we move through our anger consciously? Of prime importance to those of us experiencing difficulties in our relationship to our bodies is, I would argue, the re-visitation of the anger attached to the difficult events of our past. Something, somewhere along the line, has caused us to repress our true Self and there will be some anger related to this event, events, person, or people, however much we might deny this to be the case. Earlier psychoanalytically trained therapists supported the use of catharsis in anger work, which translates from the original Greek as cleansing, or purification. Most definitions of catharsis emphasise two essential components: the emotional aspect (strong emotional expression and processing) and the cognitive aspect (insight, new realisation, and the unconscious becoming conscious). The result is positive change. Aristotle defined catharsis as the "purging of the spirit of morbid and base ideas or emotions by witnessing the playing out of such emotions or ideas on stage" (Aristotle, 2001, p. 1458). Some researchers perceive catharsis as emotional discharge (e.g., through crying), equating it with the expression of strong emotions. Others emphasise the cognitive aspect more fully and point particularly to the new awareness that emerges after assimilating traumatic events from the past.

The hydraulic model of emotions emerged from the psycho-analytic theory of catharsis. The analogy is that of fluid flowing through a system. When emotional distress remains unexpressed, it is stored and can create pressure in the system. Thus, venting emotions decreases tension and, thereby, reduces any negative psychological experiences. The greater the expression of negatively perceived emotions, therefore, the bigger the relief from psychological distress should be. Scheff (2001) argues, in a similar vein, that emotional expression is a human necessity and our primal way of dealing with hurtful experiences. He reminds us that the baby comes out of the womb crying: the ability to cry is not learnt, but, rather, the ability to suppress crying is learnt. When we subdue these innate biological necessities, our emotions are denied a voice and psychological suffering is provided with an accommodating forum. For some of us, this suffering is directed towards the physical body and played out there.

Kottler defines crying as "a language that transcends words, a way of communicating with its own special rules of grammar and its own unique vocabulary" (Kottler, 1996, p. 49). Crying is, thus, an authentication of feelings and of meaning, since speech is often inadequate to describe what and how we feel. The cathartic result of crying continues to be debated. While most people report feeling better after they have cried, it is not clear whether increased physiological and/or psychological well-being is caused by the act of crying itself, or by the empathy and solace a crying person usually receives from others. Either way, Janov, the father of primal therapy, believed that people cannot emerge from psychological distress without crying, while Gestalt theorists argue that crying is a necessary expression of loss connected to unresolved issues in the past.

One way in which crying promotes the re-emergence of the true Self might be through its expression of self-sympathy. For some of us who have had difficult childhood experiences, of whatever form and level of intensity, feelings of guilt and shame might have overtaken any ability to self-sympathise. I can honestly say that I was unable to feel any self-sympathy in the many years I spent ensconced in self-starvation behaviours, rather engaging in a constant blaming of myself for everything that had happened and berating myself for being the terrible person I believed myself to be. It was not until I met my husband in my mid-twenties and shared some of my difficult childhood memories with him that I began to question this world-view: he was angry on my behalf for some of my experiences and this began to awaken some dormant anger and self-sympathy in myself. I began to wonder, for the very first time, if everything really had been entirely my fault. I began to question whether some of my behaviours might have sprung from the context in which I had found myself as a child and adolescent and not, therefore, solely from some intrinsic badness within me, as had been my constant belief up until this pivotal point.

Somatic expressions of anger are necessary, as advocates of catharsis suggest, because language alone can be an inadequate means of expressing our feelings. While talking therapies have been popular since the time of Freud, recent research is indicating that talking alone might be inadequate when attempting to work through emotions related to the difficult events of our past. Many of us have struggled, at one point or another, to put a particularly emotive experience into words. Try as we may, no amount of effort would seem to convey the truth of the experience or the intensity of the emotions. One neuro-imaging study conducted by Rauch and colleagues reported that when traumatic memories are provoked in research participants, there is a decrease in activity in Broca's area, an area of the brain that plays a central role in the processing of language. Increased activity, however, is reported in areas that govern intense emotions (e.g., the amygdala) and visual images (e.g., the right secondary visual cortex) (Rauch et al., 1996). Therapeutic approaches that neglect the body will always be limited in that they miss the vital "talk" of the silent body, which clearly displays the deeper wisdom of the person and of their experiences. Talking therapies alone, therefore, while indeed they have their place, might not always be able solely to facilitate the emotional release necessary for a movement beyond our distress.

It is important to consider how we will move our bodies to release or work through anger, since even early research into catharsis suggested that not all movement was created equal. In one of the first experiments on the topic by Hornberger (1959), participants initially received an insulting remark from a confederate. Next, half of the participants hammered nails for ten minutes, an activity which resembles many of the venting techniques recommended by catharsis advocates, while the others did not get a chance to vent their anger. After this, all participants were given the chance to criticise the person who had insulted them. According to catharsis theory, the act of hammering the nails should have reduced participants' subsequent aggression. In fact, the opposite was true. The people who had hammered the nails were more hostile towards the confederate afterwards than those who were not afforded the opportunity of hammering the nails.

When we engage in aggressive acts such as punching pillows, screaming, and hammering nails, we seem to give rise to thoughts and feelings associated with aggression, which become linked together in our memory, thereby forming an associative network. Add to this the fact that anger is not correlated with aggression in its natural state, and we can perhaps begin to see why cathartic acts of an aggressive nature might not be the best way forward. Such aggressive acts could strengthen the association of anger with aggression in our minds, which, in turn, might lead to greater fear. Anger is not an emotion to be feared and can be expressed in a myriad of non-aggressive ways. When we allow our anger, it tends to flow through us effortlessly, enabling us to speak clearly (and calmly) about our needs and boundaries, as we have already discussed. With buried anger, however, the moment might have passed for this calm expression to the person or people concerned, necessitating the need to move our anger in other ways. Bodywork practices such as yoga and Qigong can be extremely helpful to this end, as we shall explore in Chapter Ten, as can be other non-aggressive forms of body movement.

With appearance struggles, we seem to have displaced our anger on to our bodies and are now called to return the anger to the place it belongs. We do this by moving towards the anger and allowing ourselves to truly feel it. If we manage to feel this anger while maintaining a position of non-judgemental awareness, a beautiful break-through can be given the opportunity to occur: we are able to experience, perhaps for the very first time, our capacity to feel our anger without being consumed by it. As we remain in contact with our feelings of anger while concurrently experiencing the positive visceral feelings associated with mindful awareness, we are able to step back and observe our unsettling physical sensations without becoming swept away by them. We learn that we are the observer of our emotions rather than identifying our emotions synonymously with who we are.

For many years, I believed "recovery" would mean that I would not feel sad and angry so often. I was wrong. Sadness, anger, and every other emotion will, of course, live on, as they are there to tell an important story and deliver a vital message. I continue to experience deep feelings of anger and sadness on a regular basis as various difficult occurrences emerge in my life, but the difference is that I now no longer feel overwhelmed by them and am increasingly learning not to identify with them. Anthony De Mello, a Jesuit priest and psychotherapist, tells the parable of a Zen master: before enlightenment he was depressed and after enlightenment he continued to be depressed. The big difference was that, after enlightenment, he no longer identified with his depression (De Mello, 1990, p. 59).

The ability to feel my emotions and emerge beyond them unscathed has been one of the most important elements, personally, in my re-emergence from my appearance-focused struggles. Not uncommonly, I had understood the importance of allowing my emotions their full expression many years before I actively entered into them, so unsure was I of my ability to deal with these incredibly uncomfortable feelings. Massive leaps towards my wholeness, however, were only really enabled to occur when I ceased my endless avoidance and escape tactics and allowed myself to bloody *feel*. This meant coming out of my head and fully into my body, however terrified I felt and whatever my suspicious mind told me: *it's a waste of time, it's silly, it's self-indulgent, it isn't going to help.* When I took this leap of faith, I was massively astonished at just how effective and life-changing the visceral feeling of one's emotions can really be. An example of such a personal catharsis could be described as follows:

Initial thought: "I have a sense that I hate my body. It is too big. It is too much. It gives me away and is the reason people reject me. If my body were different then people would love me. If I saw a different reflection in the mirror I would be able to love myself".

Accompanying emotions: *shame, guilt, anger, fear.*

Aware allowing: "I come into my body and place my awareness there. I notice a warm 'squeeze' in my stomach that seems to gather heat as I immerse myself in these sensations of shame and fear. There is also a slight heat in the back of my arms, accompanied by a prickly feeling. My chest feels somewhat constricted and my breathing is quite shallow. It actually seems to hurt a bit to breathe, as though my chest would rather collapse in on itself than expend any effort in expanding and contracting. There is a tightness in my throat similar to the feeling that usually comes just before I cry. My legs want to run; I can feel them buzzing and itching to move. My whole body feels restless. I notice a huge aversion to feeling this way and have a sense of being unsafe, as though I am being attacked in some way.

"I stay with these feelings. I bring my attention to my stomach, to my legs, to my arms, and, finally, to my entire body. I sense my body 'from the inside'. I do not attach any labels. I simply observe and feel, notice, and remain present.

"The heat in my stomach seems to be diminishing. I stay with this decrease and feel a gradual coolness there. I cry and sense a release in my shoulders as I let the tears fall. I observe my desire to push away certain thoughts and memories without doing so. Rather, I allow these thoughts and memories to play out as I keep my attention on the sensations in my body, all of which are slowly subsiding."

When I allow myself to enter into my emotions within this state of non-judgemental awareness, I find that a shift occurs organically in my sensing and thinking. In the above example, I sense respect for my body in place of hatred of it, a quiet understanding that I am safe and acceptable within my flesh. I gently slip into an experience of being vaster than my body and my feelings about my body. The notion of being attacked and derided evaporates and, in its place, emerges an impression of security, safety, and peace.

Once we have remembered how to move through our anger and other difficult emotions without becoming overwhelmed by them, some of us may find ourselves at the threshold of another stage. For want of a better word, we will call this stage forgiveness.

There is not, currently, a universal definition of forgiveness, no consensus on its most important dimensions, and no general under-standing of the steps and processes involved. When we ask a person "Have you forgiven?" we cannot really be sure of the question they are answering, and neither can they be certain of what we mean by what we ask. It is generally agreed, however, that forgiveness is one of many possible responses to interpersonal harm and is a positive and healthy reaction that involves a decision to relinquish anger that does not involve revenge (Pingleton, 1989). Recent findings by Coyle and Enright (1997) have established that forgiveness is related to positive mental health and decreased grief. It has also been correlated with more positive mood states and reduced anxiety (Freedman & Enright, 1996; Mauger et al., 1992). In addition, forgiveness is related to higher indices of better physical health and a lower cardiovascular stress response (Thoresen et al., 2000).

One influential theoretical model of forgiveness is Enright and Fitzgibbon's process model, which describes what needs to occur in order for forgiveness to take place. This four-phase model includes: an uncovering phase, which involves confronting the emotional pain resulting from an offence; a decision phase, in which the person realises that the decision to forgive might be personally beneficial; a work phase, where reframing facilitates perspective taking, empathy, and compassion; and an outcome phase, in which the person gains some emotional relief, which might also promote increased compassion towards others (Enright & Fitzgibbons, 2000). Emmons (2000) agrees, proposing that forgiving individuals have well-developed emotion management skills that allow them to work constructively through their emotional responses to transgressions.

In addition to forgiving others who have hurt us, self-forgiveness also needs to take place. The inability to forgive the self, in fact, seems to be more overtly common in people who punish their bodies. Often a surface level of forgiveness or denial of blame will be attributed to others, while a continued self-blame and self-hatred will be directed towards the self. Returning to my own personal experience, self-forgiveness was almost certainly the most difficult element of my re-emergence from my appearance struggles. I harboured extreme hatred towards myself on so many levels and for so many reasons. I blamed myself for not being a "perfect" daughter and constantly disappointing everyone. I berated myself for the personality charac-teristics that I believed invited my childhood bullying experiences. I tore myself apart for the pain and destruction I caused in my family on account of years of self-starvation. And later I would come to beat myself up for the physical ramifications of my disordered eating, which included crumbling bones induced by years of self-neglect. I truly did not know where to begin with all of this self-blame and self-hatred. In truth, it took me many years to make the decision that I deserved to be forgiven at all.

The main emotions that most frequently emerge after a battle with one's physical appearance are guilt and shame. There is often a quietness, a vast void, when the drama of an appearance battle is over. There are suddenly unfamiliar vacant hours that would have been spent in front of the mirror, cutting our arms, counting calories, and so on, and untold additional amounts of headspace. With this new and seemingly cavernous time and ability to think more linearly, we might find ourselves coming face to face with ourselves and how we have been living our lives for the past how-ever-many months and years. Up until this point, we might have been so wrapped up in our personal drama that we were unable to fully imagine or comprehend the impact our actions were having on those around us. In recovery, this realisation can hit us full force and threaten to pull us back into the vicious circle of guilt, self-hatred, and self-destruction.

Regret is wholly different from guilt, in that guilt contains the sense of having abandoned or betrayed the Self. With appearance battles, we might look back and feel as though we acted, somehow, without purposeful, conscious choosing; we were not present. Instead, it might feel as though our experiences were characterised by a divided consciousness and that we acted outside of our usual morals, values, and beliefs. We might even look back and be unable to connect with this appearance-disturbed person from the past, so detached do we feel from the behaviours we engaged in and the mental stance we were operating from. We might even ask "What was I thinking?" and, with this, experience an acute fear that if we cannot grasp the thoughts that led us to those painful behaviours in the past, then we cannot hope to negate such thoughts and behaviours in the future.

Anger at the self typically accompanies guilt, since we feel as though we have let ourselves down, as though our deeper Selves have somehow failed us. We might want to go back and shake our younger selves, to tell them in no uncertain terms to take a different path, but now it might feel as though it is too late. Our guilt might also be accompanied by the sense that we are powerless to change anything. We might feel unsure of how to make amends and how to integrate our past self with our current self and how to live as a person from our authentic centre once more.

This anger and these regrets are normal and healthy. As Henry David Thoreau advised, "make the most of your regrets, never smother your sorrow . . . to regret deeply is to live afresh" (cited by Baard, 2003, p. 2). It does not serve us, in fact, to push our anger and regrets away, to distract ourselves from them or to fool ourselves into thinking that we do not have them at all. To move past them, as in all things, we are called to enter fully into them and allow ourselves to hear the message they are attempting to deliver. We might fear that if we fully allow ourselves to feel our guilt and our shame we will become stuck in them. This is not the case. In my experience, we can only ever become trapped within emotions we refuse to see and accept.

My family forgave me instantly. When I asked for their forgiveness, in fact, they said that there was nothing to excuse. They had frequently shared their frustration and their anger with me over the years and were then, later, able to release the pain we had been through together, eager only to move on after so many years of darkness. It took a lot longer, however, for me to accept their forgiveness, which was a necessary step towards forgiving myself. The guilt I felt was so indescribably huge and all-encompassing that I felt utterly choked by it each time I so much as contemplated the agony I had put my family through. This festering guilt gave rise to new heights of self-hatred, which served only to keep me stuck in self-destructive cycles. It was only when I saw that my lack of self-forgiveness was keeping me hemmed in, restricting my freedom, and continuing to ignite pain in myself and in those who loved me that I began to question my position. I realised that I did not really have a present or a future if I was unable to heal and release the past.

The biggest obstacle I faced was my belief that I was unlovable. This sense pervaded my self-concept and made it impossible to forgive myself. While people told me they loved me and inundated me with very deep and profound acts of love, I could not assimilate these offerings since I did not believe I deserved them. I thought that if people saw the real me, the true me, they would be as disgusted with myself as I was and would ultimately reject me. I attributed any love I was shown to the false self, while continuing to believe that nobody could ever possibly love the true me, my true Self. This true Self I had long since decided was abhorrent and to be hidden from the world at all costs.

When I allowed my true Self to re-emerge, I could finally assimilate the love I was shown by others and move towards a place of forgiveness of others and of myself. This forgiveness enabled me to learn to love who I was, to let go of past hurts, and to finally move on, to echo the words of poet Mary Oliver, with my wild and precious life.

> This being human is a guest house.
> Every morning a new arrival.
>
> A joy, a depression, a meanness,
> some momentary awareness comes
> as an unexpected visitor.
>
> Welcome and entertain them all!
> Even if they are a crowd of sorrows,
> who violently sweep your house
> empty of its furniture,
> still, treat each guest honorably.
> He may be clearing you out
> for some new delight.
>
> The dark thought, the shame, the malice,
> meet them at the door laughing and invite them in.
>
> Be grateful for whatever comes,
> because each has been sent
> as a guide from beyond.
>
> (Rumi, 1995, p. 109)

CHAPTER NINE

Interlude: processes of sight and perception

"We must not, therefore, wonder whether we really perceive a world, we must instead say: the world is what we perceive"

(Merleau-Ponty, 1962, p. 18)

S ome of us may have had the following experience: we look into the mirror at a given time of the day and feel dissatisfied with what we see. Our thighs look too big perhaps, our arms are not muscular enough, or maybe the skin looks more blemished than we hoped it would be. Then, at a later point in the same day, we look into the same mirror and see a very different image. Our thighs look smaller, our arms more defined, our skin clearer. How is it that we are seeing one image at one moment and a different image the next? Seeing and perception are not passive processes but active ones in which we participate in the result. The human eye takes in ten million bits of information per second but only deals consciously with forty. The human visual system then divides the continuous pattern of light projected onto the retina into a discrete set of separate objects. We never experience reality as it actually is, since our brains would simply be overwhelmed by the vastness of the data. If we were to process every intricate piece of information in our environment, we would not have time to forage for food or escape danger. In short, we would not survive. Our ability to filter information is proposed to be an evolutionary mechanism: we would appear to rely on models rather than reality itself. Our emotions, according to neuroscientist Candace Pert (1997), decide what is worth paying attention to.

When we see something, the eyes send nerve impulses to a part of the brain called the lateral geniculate nucleus (LGN). For each nerve coming from the eyes, the LGN receives inputs from over eighty fibres coming from other parts of the brain. This visual information is then analysed in yet other areas of the brain, which themselves are linked to many parts of the body. When forming visual images, therefore, our brains must integrate information from the eyes with vast amounts of information from other sources, many of which are internal (Laszlo, 1993). The brain has about 100,000 times more internal connections than external sensors, and so is naturally more concerned with internal processes. As so many sages have aptly put it, we never see the world as it is, but as we are.

Gestalt theorists, in fact, are responsible for raising many of the research questions studied by vision scientists. Gestalt is a German word meaning configuration or pattern. According to this theory, there are six main factors that determine how we group things according to visual perception:

Proximity:	objects closest together are more likely to form a group.
Similarity:	objects similar in size or shape are more likely to form a group.
Closure:	our brains add missing components to complete a larger pattern.
Symmetry:	symmetrical items are more likely to group together.
Common fate:	items moving in the same direction are more likely to group together.
Continuity:	once a pattern is formed, it is more likely to continue even if the elements are re-distributed.

These processes of perceptual organisation are responsible for structuring the retinal mosaic into the global stimuli of perceived objects. It is not the eye, in fact, doing the seeing at all, but the brain attempting to make sense of the light projected onto the retina. Aldous

Huxley appeared to understand this before the related science had been developed to back him up, referring to the brain as a reducing valve in *The Doors of Perception* (Huxley, 1954). The processes of closure and continuity in Gestalt theory are perhaps the most relevant and interesting to our current discussion. If our brains do indeed add missing components to complete a larger pattern, how, then, do they decide which components to add?

Ambiguous figures provide a useful illustration of the influence of our concepts, beliefs, and expectations on perception. Such figures are static pictures that strikingly change their appearance upon prolonged viewing: a sudden mental switch occurs whenever two or more interpretations of a given picture are equally likely. In the classic ambiguous figure of the young woman/old lady and that of Rubin's vase (Figure 1), the input to the visual system (the light striking the rods

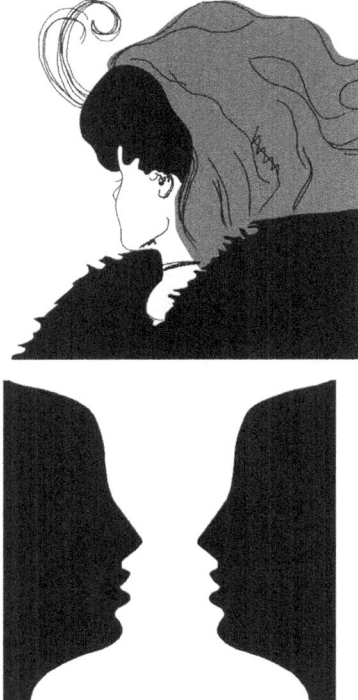

Figure 1.   Young woman, old lady, or both? (Hill, 1915).
An ornate candlestick or two faces? (Rubin, 1915).

and cones at the back of our retina) is the same, yet, when the figures reverse, we see things differently. Given that this difference cannot be attributed to the visual input, there must be some other reason for the alteration in what is seen.

In a beautiful twist of serendipity, I met a young and fascinating physicist named Chien-Yuan Chang on a bus from Luxembourg to Metz while in the final stages of editing this book. His specialism? Vision! After a wonderfully meaty discussion about the human eye, followed by French bread and vanilla tea, Chien-Yuan showed me a picture on his iPhone of a self-made ambiguous figure of his own image, which is reproduced with his kind permission below, along with the permission of the visual designer who helped him to create it, Yann Tong (Figure 2).

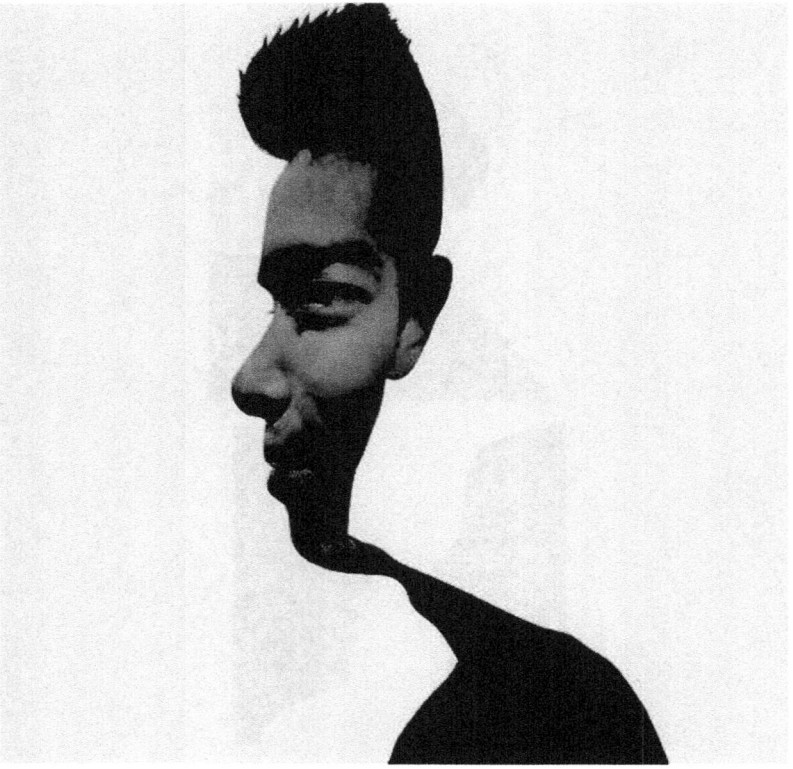

Figure 2. Side or front profile?

Hypothetical explanations about the neural processes underlying perceptual reversals of ambiguous figures fall mostly into two classes that emphasise either bottom-up or top-down factors. Bottom-up approaches assume that the perceptual reversal results from passive adaptation early in the visual stream (Toppino & Long, 1987). Top-down approaches emphasise attentional or expectational factors acting in a centrally governed active decision process near awareness and consequently later in the visual hierarchy (Vickers, 1972). Research conducted by Kornmeier and Bach (2005) concluded that perceptual reversals can be initiated during the first visual processing steps, a bottom-up approach, as early as 120 milliseconds. They found that disambiguation of ambiguous figures seems to occur 200–300ms before perceptual awareness is established. This is in line with the findings of others who have shown that Gestalt grouping occurs outside the focus of attention (Moore & Egeth, 1997).

Norwood Hanson (1958) summed up these ideas by saying that perception is theory laden. Our background theory, that is to say our concepts, beliefs, and expectations, influence what we see, or, more accurately, how we see them.

William James, author of *Principles of Psychology*, writes, "My experience is what I agree to attend to. Only those items which I notice shape my mind—without selective interest, experience is an utter chaos" (James, 1890, p. 255). Without some focus of our attention, we would become lost, as James explains, in endless reams of sensory information. We must, therefore, become attentional experts if we are to make sense of, and survive, the sensory-laden world. Julian Jaynes puts the following, eye-opening exercises to us in his perception-shifting book *The Origin of Consciousness in the Breakdown of the Bicameral Mind*:

> . . . consider the following problems; Does the door of your room open from the right or the left? Which is your second longest finger? At a stoplight, is it the red or the green that is on top? How many teeth do you see when you brush your teeth? What letters are associated with what numbers on a telephone dial? If you are in a familiar room, without turning around, write down all the items on the wall just behind you, and then look. (Jaynes, 1982, p. 27)

He then goes on to say,

I think you will be surprised how little you can retrospect in consciousness on the supposed images you have stored from so much previous attentive experience. If the familiar door suddenly opened the other way, if another finger suddenly grew longer, if the red light were differently placed, or you had an extra tooth, or the telephone were made differently, or a new window latch had been put on the window behind you, you would know it immediately, showing that you all along "knew", but not consciously so. (Jaynes, 1982, p. 28)

As Jaynes explains, most of the visual information to which we are constantly exposed on a daily basis is not consciously processed. Largely, we are conscious only of that to which we pay attention. There exist, within some occupations, so-termed attentional experts, such as fighter pilots, surgeons, taxi drivers, chess masters, and mail sorters. Polk and Farah (1995), for example, found that Canadian mail sorters' attentional skills were easily transferrable to sorting US mail due to US zip codes containing familiar elements, such as numbers, while US mail sorters were unable to effectively sort Canadian mail due to the existence of novel elements, such as letters. Task repetition, therefore, can automate specific behaviours that can then be generalised, in so far as the subsequent tasks contain similarities to the original one.

How easily a behaviour becomes automatic, would appear to be highly dependent on whether the external event is synchronised with specific internal feelings (Shiffrin & Dumais, 1981). As we repeat attentional patterns and preferences over time, orientation towards or away from certain stimuli becomes habitual. If we continuously focus our attention on a body part in the mirror, for example, with such attention being accompanied by a feeling of disgust, we are likely to continue to orientate towards this specific body part when we look into the mirror and to experience the same sense of disgust each time. In this way, an attentional pattern becomes automatic: *look into the mirror, focus on said body part, experience a sense of disgust, correlate this sense of disgust with one's own reflection, identify oneself as "disgusting"*.

Sadly, we can all too quickly find ourselves in a vicious circle, particularly if we are adolescents or young adults. One study found that while older adults selectively activate positive gaze preferences when they are in a "bad mood", younger adults tend to make mood-congruent gaze preferences. When in a negative mood, for example, older adults are more likely to seek out positive faces, while younger adults more commonly seek out negative ones (Isaacowitz et al., 2008). It would, therefore, follow suit that adolescents and younger adults are more likely to seek out negative aspects of their body in the mirror when in a negative frame of mind.

Goodale and Milner (2005) argue that we rely on two distinct kinds of representation when making sense of visual stimuli, since we have two very different decisions to make. One representation is based on the enduring properties of the scene and is used for recognising objects, people, and places. The second representation is centred on the instantaneous relationship between the object and ourselves and is used to guide our actions. Such a relationship is largely driven by our particular schemas. If we view our reflection in the mirror as having a direct relationship to our sense of self, we might continue to derive and interpret a sense of self from the reflection we are met with.

Marcel Proust once famously wrote, "the only true voyage . . . would be not to visit strange lands but to possess other eyes" (Proust, 1922, p. 291). The way we see the world and ourselves is largely dependent on our internal world, on our ideas, perceptions, and beliefs about the way things are and the way they should be. According to Wegner (2002), most of us understand our minds around the concept of an agent, which involves both intention and conscious will. He argues that we have a brain that interprets actions in terms of a "we think we did it" experience by way of keeping track of our actions and decisions. The influences and processes beyond these concrete actions and decisions are perhaps too complicated or covert to monitor. We tend to think, therefore, that we are in control of physiological processes such as vision whereas, in fact, they are determined largely by processes beyond our conscious awareness.

Early research by Libet and colleagues (1983) highlighted the phenomenon of physiological processes being beyond our conscious awareness poignantly. This research required participants to bend their wrists and fingers at a time of their choosing. The time at which the participants were consciously aware of the intention to perform the movement and the moment at which the hand muscles were activated were both recorded. Event-related potentials were also recorded in the brain to assess the readiness potential, which reflects the pre-planning of a bodily movement. A core finding was that the readiness potential occurred an average of 350ms *before* participants reported having a conscious awareness of the intention to move their fingers and wrist. Conscious awareness itself only preceded the movement by about 200ms. The conclusion drawn was that initiation of the voluntary process to move is developed well before there is any awareness of the intention to act. These findings have been replicated by more recent researchers, such as Trevena and Miller (2002), who also found that readiness potential occurs well before participants are consciously aware of the decision to mobilise.

Returning now to vision, only the representations computed can be conscious (Brogaard, 2011). Much of the research on conscious experience, in fact, has focused on visual consciousness, on our awareness of visual objects. This preference in terms of research is due to the possibility of controlling what is presented to participants and, thus, determining whether stimuli are or are not consciously perceived. The phenomenon known as "blindsight" has been thought to be an exemplar of perceptual processes. Blindsight occurs due to damage of the primary visual cortex, resulting in a scotoma, or region of blindness. People with a scotoma report no visual awareness of visual stimuli presented to them in their blind field. Rather fascinatingly, however, they have a preserved ability to predict attributes of visual stimuli, making above-chance predictions about the motion, location, and even colour of the objects they report not being able to see. Persaud and colleagues (2007) tested a patient with blindsight who was correct 70% of the time when asked to decide whether a stimulus had been presented to his affected visual field. Such blindsight is an example of "implicit processing" (residual functioning in the absence of explicit knowledge) (Weiskrantz, 1991). This mechanism might partially explain what is occurring when an underweight boy who starves himself looks into the mirror and sees an overweight body. The fat does not exist to the naked eye but is, nevertheless, processed and perceived implicitly as a result of underlying, residual schemas and self-beliefs embedded in the past.

Given that we are conscious only of the perceptual processes we pay attention to, I would argue that it is incredibly challenging to alter our perception of our appearance without addressing deeper levels of awareness, as we shall explore in more detail from the next chapter onwards. For now, suffice to say that it might be unwise to unquestioningly identify with our thoughts when we look into the mirror. Are we really "ugly" because our minds tell us so as we behold our reflection? Or does this perceived ugliness come from another place, a place that tells a story perhaps of wrong treatment by others, of early life experiences of a painful nature, of non-acceptance and of denial of the true Self?

Viewing ourselves in the mirror can be a highly emotional experience for some of us, as we have explored in previous chapters. Numerous studies have shown that emotional information subliminally presented to a subject may be perceived and processed on a high level, even without consciousness (e.g., Balconi & Mazza, 2009). Different kinds of analyses of sensory data, such as visual stimuli, are performed by the emotional and the cognitive system: a rapid computation of poorly processed sensory data is enough to decide if an external situation has an emotional meaning for an individual. Thus, when our emotions are triggered by looking into the mirror, the sensory data on which we have based our reaction might have been rapidly and poorly processed. When we feel abhorred by our mirror reflection, therefore, it might be useful to remember that our negative emotions are not being triggered by reality *per se*, but by poorly processed sensory data that have been interpreted based on our internal schemas and beliefs.

If it is difficult for you to believe that the image you are seeing with your eyes in the mirror might not reflect true reality, I would ask you to try out the following exercises.

Blind spot

All humans have blind spots, though in everyday life these often go unnoticed. To detect your blind spot, close your right eye, hold this book at arm's length, and look at the right hand dot with your left eye (Figure 3). Slowly move your head towards the picture. At a certain

Figure 3. Two dots.

point, the left dot will disappear. The missing spot will be filled in white by your brain, so that it appears as if nothing is missing.

Moving images

Sometimes stationary images can appear to be moving. If you stare at the circular design in Figure 4, you should see movement of some sort, such as pulsating or rotating. This is due to how the brain interprets the information it receives.

Figure 4.   Swirling/pulsing or stationary?

In the above examples, did you see what was really there or something else? Would you say that the visual reality and your perception of the visual reality were the same or different somehow?

Binocular rivalry

Binocular rivalry occurs when two images are presented simultaneously, one to each eye. These two images appear to alternate unpredictably as opposed to forming a third, stable image. You can experience this yourself by taking a cardboard tube or rolled-up piece of paper. Look through the tube with one eye while placing your hand about ten inches in front of the other eye. Next, angle the tube so that it points just behind the hand your other eye is focusing on. Your hand will now seem to have a hole through it, through which you can see what is at the other end of the tube. This hole appears because each eye has a different view and these two views compete for perceptual dominance (Thompson, 2015).

Seeing the world

The following exercise, for me, is the most powerful demonstration of the fact that we do not see reality as it is (cited by Hood, 2013, p. 217). Look at yourself closely in the mirror. Focus your gaze on your left eye and remain here for a moment or two. Now switch and focus your gaze on your right eye. Do you notice anything? If you alternate your gaze from the left to the right eye and back again, you cannot see your own eye movements from the left to the right and back. Your eyes are indeed moving, as you will be able to feel, yet you cannot see this movement. This is because our brains deliberately wipe out the visual experience of seeing the world every time we move our eyes (Hood, 2013). We are actually blind for an average of two hours every waking day, yet we would never know this. In this way, the world is constructed afresh each and every time we move our eyes.

Not a single one of us sees the world as it actually is. Those of us experiencing appearance-focused distress are no different. The problem is not that we fail to see a true representation of reality, but that we *think we see a true representation* and ascribe our identity to what is perceived. As Gareth Evans (1982) explains, the essence of self-consciousness is self-reference. When we look into the mirror, we have perhaps decided that what we see there is who we are because our bodies are our major external point of self-reference. Our body is the main way other people recognise us and, therefore, the main way we might have come to recognise ourselves. For many years, when I looked into the mirror, all I could see was a pale, ugly, blemished, too-big reflection. I could not even call this reflection a person, since I felt somehow subhuman. I decided that I must be subhuman due to the way I looked, yet had this completely the wrong way around. I saw a monster because I had already come to believe that this is what I was.

The picture book *The Goblin and the Girl* resonated with me very strongly at this time, which beautifully illustrates a little girl who sees a goblin when she looks into the mirror instead of a human being (Irani, 2012, reprint). Later on in the story, a little boy shows her unexpected kindness and acceptance and she is then able to look into the mirror and see herself as a little girl again. Within a deeper part of myself, I knew I was a person, yet my experience of myself was of something somehow less, which is what I saw when I gazed into the looking glass. The image I saw was informed by my childhood experiences of insecure attachment, demanded perfectionism, and of a myriad of experiences that slowly annihilated my self-worth. When my true Self began to re-emerge and as I learnt to love and respect myself again, the image in the mirror seemed to morph before my eyes; I saw a person instead of a goblin for the first time in many years. My external appearance had not changed, yet what I saw was a completely different image in front of me, an image seen through the lens of self-acceptance, of self-love.

> Gazing is such a wonderful thing, and one we know so little about. In gazing we are completely turned outwards, but at the very moment when we are most outward-turned things appear to happen within us that have waited longingly until they are unobserved, and whilst these things happen within us, without us, perfectly and strangely anonymously—their significance grows in the object outside, a convincing, strong name, their only possible name, in which we blissfully and

reverently recognise what is happening within us without ourselves reaching out for it, comprehending it only very gently, from some distance, under the sign of a thing that just now was alien to us and in the next moment will be alienated again. (Rilke, 2011, p. 11)

PART II

SPIRITUAL ASPECTS OF PSYCHOLOGICAL DISTRESS

"This too shall pass"

(Sufi saying in Fadiman & Frager, 1997, p. 48)

CHAPTER TEN

A mindful return to the body

"Space flights are merely an escape, a fleeing away from oneself, because it is easier to go to Mars or to the moon than it is to penetrate one's own being"

(Jung, in Serrano, 1966, p. 102)

"The true self comes from the aliveness of the body tissues and the workings of the body functions, including the heart's actions and breathing . . . the experience of aliveness"

(Winnicott, 1965, p. 148)

All of us, whether engaged in appearance battles or otherwise, surely yearn for a deep and pervasive knowledge of our own intrinsic beauty, which we would have naturally possessed as young children. Yet, perhaps we have little idea of how to go about remembering this. I have personally stared into the mirror thousands of times knowing that I was somehow good, that there was a deep and genuine loveliness beyond my perceived ugliness, but I could not feel it, could not grasp it. I wanted to move beyond the appearance-driven hell I had found myself in. I just did not know how.

Appearance battles isolate us, involve large amounts of preoccupation and take us away from our ultimate values—as an expression of our mourning, perhaps, over a loss or violation of these very things. Jung believed that psychological distress is an externalisation of our deepest hurts and fears which, thus externalised, give us something tangible to face and overcome. We seem to keep externalising and repeating our pain in order to provide ourselves with opportunities for integration and wholeness, with the manifestations of such pain perhaps directly symbolising the root of the pain itself.

Emotional pain resides within the body. Or, as an advertisement for a yoga-based programme for mental health poetically put it, "your issues are in your tissues". It would seem that modern society, with its emphasis on speed and productivity, is increasingly taking us "out of" our bodies and engendering greater and greater disconnection from the internal, lived experience of our emotional lives. When we are aware and tuned into our inner states, we are better able to notice and attend to our emotions before they overwhelm us. In this way, we are also afforded the opportunity to heed the interoceptive messages of our organism, which exist to keep us safe and contented. Our bodies speak to us continuously about what we need both physically and emotionally. When we return to the present-moment experience of the body, we naturally experience a deeper sense of self-trust and authenticity and an intuitive sense of how best to live our lives. William Blake frequently empathised with the belief that an authentic life—springing forth from open experience—is available to everyone and that "love ... breaks all chains from every mind" (Blake, 1788a, p. 472). Blake was genuinely troubled by the way in which people lose trust in their spontaneous experience, desires, and creativity and instead substitute a defensive or compliant false self. Blake advocated, rather, continuous open awareness as a way of breaking free of the "mind-forg'd manacles" (Blake, 1788b, p. 27) of our fears and defences. It is this idea of open awareness that shall be the focus of our musings in this chapter.

I would argue that an appearance struggle only becomes possible if we view the body as an external object and ignore its role as the enabler of lived experience. An understanding of the body as such a facilitator is intrinsically intertwined with self-awareness. We have already explored the phenomenon of dissociation, which describes a process by which we experience a lack of connection between our thoughts, memory, and sense of identity. This experience occurs on a broad continuum, with mild daydreaming on one end and the complete loss of a sense of self on the other. It would seem to me that those of us entrenched in appearance battles spend a significant proportion of our time in a semi-dissociative state, cut off from a sense of our self and the sensations and ambiences of our physical body. This cut-off state enables us to hurt and starve our bodies without the instinctive drive for self-preservation taking over and keeping us safe. If my awareness had remained truly in my body, I doubt that I would have been able to self-harm so virulently nor starve myself into such near obliteration. Returning to self-awareness, embedded within the body, might be the most efficacious tool, therefore, for those of us immersed in appearance battles. It is, after all, our very bodies we have chosen as a means to explore and express our inner pain while simultaneously cutting our awareness off from them.

Few have championed the importance of body awareness as emphatically as Maurice Merleau-Ponty, a French phenomenological philosopher with a passion for the centrality of human perception. Merleau-Ponty argued that the body is not only the source of all perception and action, but also the core of our expressive capacity and, therefore, the basis of all meaning. Our bodies and minds are the tools through which we experience the world and the means by which we become aware of our Self and our connection to all of life. The mind, more accurately however, is not separate from the body, but inextricably intertwined with it. Rather, we possess a body-mind, as John Dewey (1928) referred to it. Quantum physics has taught us that the mind is present in every cell of our bodies. Our body-mind (henceforth referred to as the body for ease of reading) would appear to be the means by which we unlock the knowledge of who we are: it duly guides us, but only if we stop judging and analysing it. A vital element of this lack of analysis is the understanding that the body is strong and vibrant (whatever physical state it is in), as opposed to the weak and value-laden body proposed to be in need of fixing and enhancing in the west.

Merleau-Ponty believed deeply that the key to overcoming our sense of disconnection from our selves and others is through the body. He also held the firm conviction that the truth of human experience is to be found in renewing our connection to perceptions and experience that precede knowledge and reflection. In this way, the movement beyond our appearance struggles necessitates engagement in the world of noticing and feeling, as opposed solely to the realm of thinking and analysing. Merleau-Ponty wrote repeatedly about the absolute importance of spontaneity and immediacy, thus advocating a bringing of our full attention and awareness into the present moment experience of the body, as opposed to analysis and rumination on the past and projection into the future. The call is not to "rise above" the body, as many religious traditions would suggest, but, rather, to enter fully *into* the flesh and find within it our wholeness, our transpersonal nature, and our innate sense of contentment and peace.

There are many practices in which we can engage to promote a return to present moment awareness, rooted in our physiological self. None of these needs to be complicated in any way. Meditation is one such tool, with Zen meditation, or Zazen, being one simple meditation technique. Zen meditation is a practice rooted in Buddhist spirituality, during which the person sits silently and focuses their attention on their breathing, often counting (usually from one to ten) every time they exhale. In the *Satipatthana Sutra*, the Buddha presents this straightforward technique as being at the very heart of liberation from suffering, teaching the mind to stay in the present moment.

The interest in the effects of Buddhist meditation practice has been growing rapidly in recent years, particularly in the area of utilising meditation as a therapeutic tool in healthcare. The mindfulness-based stress reduction programme (MBSR), developed by Jon Kabat-Zinn in the early 1980s, for example, has been rapidly gaining in popularity and is now used in many NHS settings across England (Kabat-Zinn, 1990). MBSR consists of multiple forms of mindfulness practice, including formal and informal meditation practice, as well as hatha yoga. The formal practice consists of breath-focused attention; body-scan-based attention to the transient nature of sensory experience; shifting attention across sensory modalities; open monitoring of moment-to-moment experience; walking meditation; and eating meditation. Together, these practices aim to enhance the ability to observe the immediate content of experience, particularly the transient nature of thoughts, emotions, memories, mental images and physical sensations.

MBSR has been found to reduce the habitual tendency to emotionally react to, and ruminate on, transitory thoughts and physical sensations (Ramel et al., 2004). It has also been found to reduce stress, depression, and anxiety and to modify distorted patterns of self-view (Chiesa & Serretti, 2009; Goldin et al., 2009). MBSR encompasses attitudes of non-judgement, a beginner's mind, trust, non-striving, acceptance, letting go, and patience. Qualities fostered by mindfulness are considered necessary for self-compassion to take root (Beddoe & Murphy, 2004), which is often achingly lacking in people with appearance-related distress. According to Neff (2003a), self-compassion involves three fundamental components:

1. Extending kindness and understanding to oneself rather than harsh self-criticism and judgement.
2. Seeing one's experiences as part of the larger humanity rather than as separating and isolating.
3. Holding one's painful thoughts and feelings in balanced awareness rather than over-identifying with them.

Neff has also found positive correlations between self-compassion and life satisfaction, social connectedness, emotional intelligence, happiness, and optimism. Self-compassion would also appear to act as a buffer against derogatory self-feelings and has been negatively correlated with depression, anxiety, neuroticism, rumination, self-criticism and thought suppression. A recent study expanded beautifully on previous MBSR research by demonstrating a strong relationship between increases in self-compassion and spirituality (Birnie et al., 2010). Participants in MBSR programmes have reported significant increases in both spirituality and state and trait mindfulness after programme participation, which has been found to then translate into greater self-compassion.

The Dalai Lama has frequently stressed that if contentment for oneself and others is desired, the focus should be on compassion (Dalai Lama & Vreeland, 2001), which he defines as a sensitivity to the suffering of self and others with a deep wish and commitment to relieve the suffering (Dalai Lama, 1995). Compassion-focused therapy refers to the theory and process underpinning the application of a compassion model to psychotherapy, which arose out of observations that people with high levels of shame and self-criticism often have tremendous difficulty in being kind to themselves, feeling self-warmth, and being self-compassionate (Gilbert, P., 2009a). As we have learned, shame and self-criticism are often rooted in experiences of abuse, bullying, emotional disturbances within the family, neglect, and a lack of affection (Andrews, 1998). Early experiences such as these can make us highly sensitive to threats of criticism and rejection; we might use self-denial and self-criticism as a defence mechanism, hurting and rejecting ourselves before others are given the chance to do so. We could find ourselves sabotaging relationships again and again because it is just too painful to carry the relationship through to a potential point of rejection.

Contentment is associated with peacefulness and a sense of well-being, which is devoid of any seeking behaviours. Animals only enter states of contentment when they have sufficient resources and do not have to be attentive to, or cope with, threats and dangers. Human beings are no different. The contentment system evolves in tandem with the evolution of attachment behaviour (Depue & Morrone-Strupinsky, 2005) and can only be ignited when we feel safe and secure. Caring and connecting behaviours of the primary caregiver have a soothing effect on the infant, with self-compassion often failing to develop if the child grows up without secure attachment. Insecurely attached children often become ruinously focused on others as constant sources of threat. To negate these pervasive feelings of lack of safety and discontentment, compassion-focused therapy aims to foster the following attributes of self-compassion:

Care for well-being: involves harnessing the motivation to be caring with the purpose of alleviating distress.

Sensitivity: involves becoming sensitive to distress and needs, thus being able to recognise and distinguish the feelings of the target of our caring.

Sympathy: involves being emotionally moved by the feelings and distress of the target of our caring. This includes the ability to experience others as being emotionally engaged with our lives as opposed to being passive or distant.

Distress tolerance: involves being able to contain, stay with and tolerate high and complex levels of emotion, as opposed to avoiding, diverting, invalidating or denying them.

Empathy: involves understanding the meanings, functions, and origins of another person's inner world. This also includes self-empathy, which is the ability to stand back from, and understand, our own thoughts and feelings.

Non-judgement: involves refraining from condemning, criticising, shaming or rejecting the self or others (Gilbert, P., 2009b, p. 203).

In research conducted by Ferreira and colleagues (2013), it was found that higher levels of self-compassion were linked to lower levels of body dissatisfaction and lower engagement in disordered eating patterns. Conversely, a critical attitude towards the self was found to be positively associated with dysfunctional behaviours related to eating and body image. Wester and Trepal (2005) have particularly advocated the use of compassion-focused therapy with people who self-harm, advising that sensory alternatives should not be threat-based but, rather, gentle and soothing. Rather than snapping an elastic band on the wrist or holding an ice-cube against the skin (as is the common recommendation) when cutting is motivated by the desire for a feeling of aliveness, Wester and Trepal suggest using a menthol rub to generate a pleasant, tingling sensation. Expressing gratitude to another person, taking care of a pet, or tending to a garden have also been offered by others as compassionate alternatives to self-harm behaviours (Gilbert, P., 2009b).

The development of self-compassion springs from the use of awareness to free the mind from ignorance, negativity and delusion (Das, 1997). Mindfulness in the context of self-compassion involves being aware of our painful experiences in a way that neither ignores nor ruminates on disliked aspects of ourselves or our lives (Neff & Germer, 2012). Included within this is the extension of compassion to the self without getting swept away by the storyline driving the suffering, a process defined by Neff as "over-identification" (Neff, 2003b). Anthony De Mello offers the following exercise against such over-identification, which he recommends engaging in no less than a thousand times a day!

- Identify the negative feelings in you.
- Understand that they are in you, not in the world, not in external reality.
- Do not see them as an essential part of "I"; these things come and go.
- Understand that when you change, everything changes (De Mello, 1990, p. 89).

Mindfulness includes an openness to new information, a height-ened awareness of multiple perspectives in problem solving and the creation of new categories for structuring information (Langer &

Moldoveanu, 2000). Such engagement provides the opportunity for the navigation of reality without biased information, enabling us perhaps to look into the mirror and see a truer reflection of ourselves, as opposed to a self overlaid with biased information such as "I am ugly" or "I am a bad person". A personal experience of such a state of unmarred awareness was the multiple occasions during the years I spent entrenched in disordered eating within which I would wake in the night, walk to the bathroom, and catch sight of myself in the full length mirror in the hallway. In my half-asleep state, my mind and cognitive biases were not fully engaged and I was often shocked and moved to compassion by what I saw. At those times, in a half-asleep state of increased cognitive openness, I would see the thin and sickly looking figure I truly was, as opposed to the too-big-bad-girl I would see reflected in my full waking state. I have also experienced such alterations in perception after periods of mediation and yoga and vividly remember one particular yoga class in which, while in sarvangasana (shoulder stand), I "saw" my legs for the first time in decades; I witnessed, appreciated, and marvelled at the form of my legs and felt intense gratitude to them for holding me up and enabling me to go on so many adventures over the years.

Mindfulness, as Hanh (1975) insists, is a way of arriving at liberation from narrow views and obtaining fearlessness and compassion. In terms of appearance struggles, the end product of mindfulness would ideally be the compassionate observation of the body without judgement, even amid a society that seems to dissect and judge the body at every turn. This is wildly different from the common perspective of those with appearance distortions, whose negative body schemas, automatic thoughts, core beliefs, and obsessional thinking serve as cognitive filters, resulting in a distorted view of their own person. As Stewart (2004) explains, limited information enters an individual's awareness at any given moment on account of normal attentional processes. This awareness is then narrowed even further by attentional biases. When a state of mindfulness is cultivated, however, it is as though the individual's surroundings have been illuminated by a vast light, much wider than the narrow, focused beam of their previous attention, which might have been restricted to a single theme (e.g., body dissatisfaction). This "light" allows the person to see details that had previously been filtered out by their limiting views of perception. This can facilitate the genesis of alternative views of the physical self.

Mindfulness-focused therapy for appearance struggles, therefore, aims to broaden a person's narrow perspective of herself and her body. Unwanted behaviours related to appearance distress can also be diminished through mindfulness practices. Rather than acting on an impulse, a state of mindfulness can promote reflection before acting, perhaps preventing a person from compulsively picking his skin or checking his body in the mirror. When such behaviours are considered mindfully, the intentions of the behaviour can be elucidated. The act of deliberate hair-pulling, for example, might come to be understood as an expression of anxiety, with the noticing of this anxiety having been made possible through the mindful awareness of the body and its sensations. By cultivating such awareness, we nurture the ability to recognise and change impulsive or destructive desires before they occur.

Mindful, or intuitive, eating can be a particularly useful practice for people engaged in food-related appearance struggles. Advocates of the intuitive eating approach draw our attention to the natural eating habits of young children, who take in just the right amount of energy and nutrients their bodies need without fear, worry, or the application of any self-imposed rules. They also point out how value-laden food becomes for us as adults and the ways in which it is used to comfort, to distract, and to anaesthetise us. As adults, there are too few among us without any self-imposed rules and regulations around food, with many of us relying on these rules as opposed to the inner wisdom of our bodies, which know exactly which nutrients they need and in what quantities. The dieting industry perpetuates this move away from our intuition to immeasurable degrees. Mindful and intuitive eating implores our return to the wisdom of our intelligent organism, prompting us to listen to what we need to eat and when, and to stop when we are satiated. In short, it is the practice of coming into the present moment and placing our full attention/awareness on both the signals of our bodies and on the experience of eating itself. An example exercise for mindful eating can be found in Appendix III of this book. Mindful eating has been shown to have positive effects on people who binge eat, for example, who have reported both feeling less depressed and bingeing less following an eight-week mindfulness programme (Kristeller & Hallett, 1999).

Mindfulness practices promote the observation and description of situations, thus enabling an experience of these situations through a non-judgemental, neutral stance. In many ways, we begin to see our lives from the perspective of the observer, as opposed to the perspective of the participant; we watch the story unfold as opposed to becoming wrapped up in, and identified with, the story. When we look into the mirror in this mindful state, therefore, we begin to leave the narrative behind. Thoughts such as "I have too many blemishes"; "I don't deserve to wear nice clothes"; "I look larger than I did yesterday"; "nobody is ever going to love me while I look like this", and so on are replaced with an aware observation in which judgements are heard, felt, and moved through without overwhelming us. With practice, it is possible to arrive at the joyful place of being able to look at our reflection without attaching any story to it at all.

I remember watching a video clip of a rather young and hippyish-looking Louise Hay at one of her early classes. This motivational author could fill a hall with hundreds of people as she spoke about people's intrinsic goodness and self-worth. One element of these classes was to provide participants with a small, hand-held mirror. Louise would then implore each person to look into the mirror and tell the reflection "I love you". People often seem to find this activity extremely difficult to do . . . and extremely moving when they manage to carry it out. I implore you to try this for yourself. Put down this book, find yourself a mirror, look yourself straight in the eye, and say "I love you . . .", followed by your name. Then notice what stirs within you. In many ways, Louise was recommending the self-compassion promoted so unabashedly by mindfulness practices. She was asking people, for just a few brief seconds, to lay their self-judgements aside, to look into the mirror and see themselves for the beautiful and worthy people they are.

T. S. Eliot, in his provocative poem "Ash Wednesday", asks God to "teach us to care and not to care. Teach us to sit still" (Eliot, 1950, p. 60). There might be a sense of mystique for some of us around mindfulness practices when, in fact, they are little more complicated than such still sitting (or still being), such letting go. Mindfulness is not concerned with getting rid of thoughts, as seems to be a common assumption. The function of mind is to think thoughts and our function, as awareness, is to rest non-judgementally with these thoughts without pinning our identity to them. Conscious breathing is a vital element in this non-judgemental resting with oneself. The word spirituality, in fact, comes from the Latin root *spiritus*, meaning breath, or breath of life. Breathing is the simplest and seemingly most effective way of cultivating awareness in everyday life. William James (1890) himself exclaimed that the stream of consciousness was nothing more than what, when scrutinised, revealed itself to consist essentially in the stream of his breathing.

Every human life begins with an inhalation and ends with an exhalation, and in between we take an average of one hundred million breaths (Loehr & Migden, 1999). Every inspiration is stimulating and energising to the sympathetic ("fight or flight") autonomic nervous system, while every exhalation is relaxing and stimulates the parasympathetic ("rest and digest") nervous system. Put simply, if increased vitality is required, the inhalation should be longer than the exhalation, while the exhalation should be longer if rest and relaxation are required (Edwards, 2005). The effects of our breathing on our physiologies cannot be over-emphasised. Breathing balances and brings equilibrium to all internal and external systems including digestion, circulation, neurochemical, and endocrine systems and all divisions of the nervous system (Reid, 1998).

The fundamental principle of breathing (sometimes called re-breathing) and relaxation therapy is that the speed of the mind and the quality by which one perceives his or her reality follows the speed of the breath. When we decelerate the breath, therefore, we slow down and, thus, increase the quality of our perception. Within mindfulness practices, and yoga in particular, a rich array of breathing techniques are taught, some of the most common of which can be found in Appendix III. Breathing is often seen as the one system under both our voluntary and involuntary control although, with practice, involuntary systems such as heart rate, brainwave activity, and the production of neurochemicals, such as endorphins, can also be brought under our voluntary control through conscious breathing (Reid, 1998). Possibilities like these have massive implications for those of us experiencing stress and anxiety in our lives, which are themselves expressed in our physiologies in the same way in which our emotions are, as we explored in Chapter Eight. Emotional arousal also goes hand-in-hand with altered breathing rate, a scientific understanding used in lie detector tests, which use ventilation rates as a measure of stress and correlate them with untruth telling.

A discussion on breath and anxiety would hardly be complete without a look at heart rate variability (HRV). The normal variability in heart rate is due to the autonomic neural regulation of the heart and the circulatory system, with the balancing action of the sympathetic and parasympathetic branches of the autonomic nervous system controlling the heart rate. HRV refers to the natural fluctuation in heart rate occurring with each breath, which is faster on the inhalation and slower on the exhalation. Teaching people to maximise this fluctuation has developed into a clinical procedure on account of its apparent links to autonomic balance: the sympathetic and parasympathetic branches alternate their control of the heart rate in line with the phases of the breath cycle (Rajendra Acharya et al., 2006). A strong alternation is thought to indicate a strong vagal tone (i.e., improved parasympathetic influence on the heart), with a diminished fluctuation indicating a relative dominance of the sympathetic nervous system.

Long, deep breathing can, therefore, interrupt cycles of stress and anxiety through the regulation of heart function via the vagus nerve (which itself acts as the "switch" between the sympathetic and parasympathetic nervous systems). Yeragani and colleagues (2002) obtained results of diminished HRV in participants diagnosed with depression compared to controls, while Borkovec and Costello (1993) found that slow-paced meditation with diaphragm breathing had a major impact on depression scores and anxiety scores. Yogic breathing has also been shown repeatedly to be a valuable resource for people suffering from stress, which is in no small part due to the fact that it reduces the resting respiratory rate, thus stimulating the parasympathetic nervous system (Joshi et al., 1992; Zucker et al., 2008). Most interestingly, Segal and colleagues (2002) found that breath control (pranayama) enables people to identify negative thoughts as they arise and to distance themselves from them in order to evaluate the accuracy of their content. Practising pranayama while looking into the mirror, therefore, might allow distancing from negative thoughts about one's appearance and a re-evaluation of their accuracy.

Excitingly, pranayama has also been found to increase neuroplasticity, which describes the brain's ability to reorganise itself by forming new neural connections throughout life (Brown & Gerberg, 2005). We touched upon this potential in Chapter Seven when we looked at how it is possible to emerge beyond attachment patterns set in childhood. The simple act of conscious breathing can enhance our brain's ability to literally rewire itself, thus facilitating a move beyond our restrictive cognitive schemas and habitual thought and behavioural processes.

Breathing practices are a vital element of the practice of yoga, which has massively grown in popularity in recent years. The word "yoga" is derived from the Sanskrit *yuj*, meaning to yoke, or to bind. It is an ancient practice, originating in India, which involves physical, mental, and spiritual disciplines comprising three elements: gentle stretching (*asana*), exercises for breath control (*pranayama*), and meditation practices (Ernst, 2001). According to van der Kolk (2009), yoga teaches us that there are things we can do to change our brainstem arousal system, our sympathetic and parasympathetic nervous systems, and to quieten the brain. Regular yoga practice in typical adults has been shown to increase GABA levels (which have a calming effect on the nervous system) in the brain and to improve both mood and anxiety (Streeter, 2010).

Throughout our lives, our identities and sense of self are embedded to a significant degree in the sensations and awareness of the body (Hagglund & Piha, 1980). The practice of yoga postures (*asana*), "often provides a radical form of engagement with the body, which can prove deeply influential on the practitioner's understanding of their embodied selfhood" (Smith, 1997, p. 37). People engaged in appearance battles frequently feel painfully disconnected from their bodies while concurrently placing heightened amounts of importance on the physical over the emotional and spiritual. Yoga can exquisitely provide a lived sense of connection between the physical and spiritual aspects of the Self and offer a profound experience of embodiment. My personal practice of yoga certainly bears testimony to this. When immersed in the practice of *asana* and *pranayama*, I begin to both feel and view my body in radically new ways, moving away from a focus on appearances and judgements and towards a sense of wonder at my physical and spiritual being. Van der Kolk's example of Annie echoes my own experience poignantly:

> "Some thoughts during and after my yoga today. It occurred to me how disconnected I must be from my body when I cut it. When I was doing the poses I noticed that my jaw and the whole area from where my legs end to my bellybutton is where I am tight, tense and holding the pain and memories. Sometimes you have asked me where I feel

things and I can't even begin to locate them, but today I felt those places very clearly and it made me want to cry in a gentle kind of way." (van der Kolk, 2014, p. 271)

People struggling with appearance distress frequently display strong self-objectification, predominantly focusing on the appearance of the body above other aspects of their personhood. Fredrickson and Roberts (1997) offered objectification theory almost two decades ago as a formal socio-cultural analysis of the mental health consequences of being a woman in a culture that sexually objectifies the female body. Research has shown that through a predominant focus on appearance, the central tenet of objectification, individuals might eventually separate themselves from their bodily functioning, with a move away from the consideration of how they feel and what they are capable of towards a focus on physical appearance alone (Moradi & Huang, 2008). This is an important shift, since unobservable dimensions of the body, such as health and physical fitness, form a significant part of the overall experience of the body. Moreover, as Augustus-Horvath and Tylka (2009) reason, people lose touch with their internal cues to the extent that they experience body shame.

Research by Avalos and Tylka (2006) demonstrated that focusing on body functionality (in the case of this research, on how the body functions and feels internally through the practice of intuitive eating), as opposed to a focus on bodily appearance, was related to more positive feelings in relation to the body and to greater body appreciation. A focus on bodily functionality through exercise has also been shown to produce improvements in body satisfaction, which are unrelated to changes in physical fitness (Campbell & Hausenblas, 2009). In terms of yoga, it has been theorised by Boudette (2006) that it teaches people to focus on how the body feels internally, thus promoting the skill of interoception, rather than on how the body looks. Prichard and Tiggemann (2008) found, for example, that participation in yoga classes was related to lower levels of self-objectification and greater levels of body satisfaction.

Yoga has also been shown to be a useful tool for people engaging in binge eating episodes. In one study, which asked women who regularly binged to keep a journal throughout the yoga practised during the course of the study, one woman wrote in an early entry,

I hate what I'm doing to myself. I recognise it as self-punishment/ mutilation but my intellect and emotions aren't communicating with each other. The urge to overeat is overriding all other considerations . . . even vanity . . . Body feels awful. Aches and pains all over, bloated, constipated, flatulent, headaches, nausea, puffy ankles. Can no longer see stomach. Body full of air. I really hate feeling this way and cannot see that it's ever going to change. (McIver et al., 1999, p. 1239)

Then, towards, the end of the study, the same woman wrote,

I feel peaceful and hopeful. I'm eating like a normal person, enjoying what I eat and not obsessing like usual. I'm really enjoying eating fresh fruit and veggies, grainy bread, soy products. I'm cooking regularly and I'm not afraid of feeling hungry. (McIver et al., 1999, p. 1239)

In their discussion of the study, McIver and colleagues explain, "A connection to the body augmented feelings of ease, whereas disconnection perpetuated an ongoing paradigm of force, resistance and struggle" (McIver et al., 1999, p. 1239).

In *Yoga and Body Image*, Melanie Klein and Anna Guest-Jelley interview Alanis Morrisette, poetic songwriter–performer and a personal hero of mine. Having struggled with disordered eating for many years, Morrisette found a path beyond her over-identification with her body through a regular yoga practice. She explains:

I like my own quiet experience and the kind of practice my body dictates that day. I have a new sense of insight, awareness, and curiosity about my body . . . each time I'm on the mat, it's a different experience . . .

Yoga is an approach to life for me. It's multifold. How can yoga not include everything? Because it is everything—my perfectionism that day, my exhaustion, my prowess, the gymnast in me—and it includes all the shadows. The evidence of whether I am forcing anything, or overly flexible, or attempting to ignore pain, or nurturing my body. Yoga is physical and spiritual. It's an attunement to all parts of me; it's the unity of being a whole person from my bones, muscles and ligaments to my heart and intellect. (Klein & Guest-Jelley, 2014, p. 168)

My own personal practice of yoga has enabled me to experience my wholeness viscerally and to learn to love again the body I have spent decades starving into submission. As I move my body and breathe mindfully, I sense a flow of energy beyond my flesh, my thoughts, or my life story. This energy, or *prana* (meaning life force in Sanskrit), feels timeless and connects me to a truth so much greater than my thighs and my acne, so much deeper than society's message of self-worth and physical appearance. I am lifted beyond my physical appearance, catapulted beyond my mind and taken beyond my identification with these things. As I move on the mat, I also feel calcified fears and emotions move and dissipate. It is as though I am stretching and breathing myself free of years of stored-up suffering.

Body psychotherapists, such as Babette Rothschild (2000), would also argue that our habitual posture—the way in which we hold ourselves when standing, sitting, walking, and so on—grows out of and reflects our early history. In the early years of our lives, we learn to hold ourselves in particular ways that help us to cope with the world around us. Yoga, Qigong, the Rosen Method, the Alexander Technique, ecstatic dance, and other mindful movement practices can bring us back into the body and allow us to notice and challenge any habitual patterns, perhaps for the first time. In one of my very first yoga classes it was pointed out to me that I always hold my arms very close to my body. I wonder if I was afraid to reach out, fearful of taking up too much space, petrified of allowing myself to be seen. It is my personal postulation that people engaged in appearance battles feel sincerely unsafe in their own bodies, which is often physically evident through their shallow "chest" breathing. Their habitual posture often reflects this and the resumption of a sense of safety can thus be promoted by an exploration and enablement of emotions and exercises that elucidate and alter these habitual postures. Since adopting the practice of yoga, a close friend of mine has noticed that I no longer hang my head and look down at the ground when I walk. This has been coupled with an altered understanding of myself that I am worthy to be seen and have every right to live with my head held high.

Mindfulness practices, therefore, may be astonishingly useful and life-giving to people experiencing appearance distress. We must be mindful of the danger, however, of all the shame and blame being laid at a single person's feet, discounting the need for remedial action both within the family and within society as a whole. In this way, mindfulness practices may be partnered with family therapy, for example, and with a sincere look at unrealistic societal expectations and demands. Indeed, mindfulness can help us to see and, therefore, address these wider systemic issues in fresh and authentic ways. Some suggestions for societal and family interventions can be found in Appendices I and II of this book.

As with all things, each of us will find different practices helpful in different ways and to differing degrees. Forcing yourself to meditate for extended periods of time if you feel intensely adverse to such practice, for example, is extremely unlikely to be useful to you. A family member of mine feels most aware and in the present moment when he is on his motorbike. While his wife goes to her yoga class, he engages in some motorbike meditation. At its core, mindfulness is concerned with following your internal cues and listening to your heart. Your body, psyche, and spirit will soon let you know if something is not right for you, perhaps through feelings of discomfort, agitation, physiological unsettledness, and so on. There might be times when we feel particularly called to conversation with others, to dancing, to reading a novel, to browsing the shops, and a whole host of other activities, all of which can, of course, be done mindfully. If you reside in awareness, you will recognise the difference between a level of discomfort you are called to sit with and subsequently move beyond and a level of discomfort that is calling you to another practice at that particular time. Non-judgement is key here, alongside a willingness to truly listen to your Self, which holds an expansive knowledge of what you need at each moment of your beautiful life.

> Generally, by the time you are Real, most of your hair has been loved off, and your eyes drop out and you get loose in the joints and very shabby. But these things don't matter at all, because once you are Real you can't be ugly, except to people who don't understand. (Williams, 2007)

CHAPTER ELEVEN

Wholeness through an embrace of the darkness

"The hero, whether God or Goddess, man or woman, the figure in a myth or the dreamer of a dream, discovers and assimilates his opposite (his own unsuspected self) either by swallowing it or by being swallowed. One by one the resistances are broken. He must put aside his pride, his virtue, beauty, and life, and bow or submit to the absolutely intolerable. Then he finds that he and his opposite are not of differing species, but one flesh"

(Campbell, 2008, p. 89)

"The black moment is the moment when the real message of transformation is going to come. At the darkest moment comes the light"

(Campbell & Moyers, 1989, p. 44)

As we have seen, appearance struggles are a metaphor for our time, are external manifestations of a collective brokenness often rooted in our very early life experiences. We have starved, sliced, and segmented our physical bodies as "a defence against further trauma [which] now becomes itself destructive in a variety of ways: The person survives but cannot live creatively" (Kalsched, 1996, p. 4). Jung explained that when trauma strikes the developing psyche of a child, a fragmentation of consciousness occurs in which the different pieces (which Jung called splinter-psyches, or complexes) organise themselves into typical patterns. Ordinarily, one part of the ego regresses to the infantile period and another part progresses and grows up too fast, becoming adapted to the outside world as a false self. The progressed part of the personality then takes on the care of the regressed part of the ego.

In the case of appearance battles, the regressed part of the self is protected by a progressed personality that uses self-destruction as its protective mechanism. By physically harming the self, the progressed personality shields the regressed infantile fragments from external harm; it pre-empts and staves off any impending injury from outside agencies, thus remaining in control, feigning the retention of owner-ship over what will happen and when. The progressed and regressed parts of the psyche become organised thus into a self-care system. All relations with the outside world are then screened by the self-care system, becoming a force of major resistance to unguarded, sponta-neous expressions of the self. The true Self becomes hidden and the false self takes centre stage. For all intents and purposes, the true Self appears to have been annihilated.

As many people who are entrenched in appearance struggles will attest to, the self-destructive behaviours, which were originally a part of the self-care system, frequently end up taking on a life of their own. This is often truer the longer and the deeper one becomes immersed. The person might cease to feel in control, instead experiencing the terrifying sense of being ruled by his behaviours. Those who inten-tionally starve themselves may speak of being compelled to exercise, despite extreme tiredness and a deeper desire to lie down and rest. Those who purge may speak of an inexorable compulsion to vomit, of a strong force that seems to take over their mind and capacity for logic. Others may agonise over their inability to pull themselves away from the mirror, while others lament their lack of command over when they cut and how deep they go. At this point, the progressed part of the personality has taken over to such an extent that the once protective mechanism becomes truly dangerous, potentially fatal.

It is only possible for our physical bodies to become endangered because the progressed fragments of our psyche were never con-cerned with protecting us from physical death, but from psychologi-cal death, from loss of the self. Our starving and skin picking, our purging and muscle pumping are methods of self-preservation and, as such, serve as desperate bids for survival. Returning to my own experience, I look back now and realise that I would have crumbled into a million tiny pieces had I not found a way to explore and express my uncontainable, yet carefully hidden, emotions. My self-starvation, while almost killing my physical body, achieved what my psyche needed. My anger and pain were expressed and I was simultaneously soothed and numbed emotionally. If safer ways of managing and displaying my inner turmoil were known and available to me, I would have used them. As it was, I turned to starvation, using my body to say what I felt unable, and perhaps even forbidden, to say. Despite the painful, dark depths of appearance battles, they serve to take us into our own little world, somehow cocooning us from the traumas lurking in our external reality. The internal devastation that ensues then facilitates a suspension from life.

Moving beyond appearance struggles, or beyond any kind of emotional distress, requires a death—the death of the false self. We have perhaps come to fear the darkness, to be literally terrified of our own shadow, instead of seeing this very darkness as the path to our wholeness, as the path to the light. Jung wrote extensively about something he called the "black sun" in his alchemic writings. The black sun emits black rays and yet illuminates. The central idea is that the darkness *is* the light. Some of us have attempted to escape our pain by creating more pain: instead of immersing ourselves in our authentic sadness, we have created a decoy, an alternative form of suffering. The metaphor of the black sun is the image of entering fully into what terrifies us the most and finding our wholeness in this very place. We then find that everything, even the darkness, illuminates the path back to our true Selves. As Jung explains,

> If you will contemplate (your nothingness), your lack of fantasy, of inspiration, and of inner aliveness which you feel as sheer stagnation and a barren wilderness, and impregnate it with the interest born of alarm at your inner death, then something can take shape in you, for your inner emptiness conceals just as great a fullness, if you allow it to penetrate into you. (Jung, cited by Marlon, 2005, p. 179)

When we stop distracting ourselves from our deepest fears, from our darkest pain, we find that the true Self begins to rise up and, with this, a rupturing of the false self occurs. This severance, this death of

the false self, can ignite tremendous pain since we have come to identify our false selves with who we are. We fear that the death of our
false self will mean the death of us, so we cling mercilessly to our
purging and our razor blades. We believe ourselves to have *become* our
so-called eating disorders, our body dysmorphia, and our self-created
scars. We fear that if we lose these things we will lose our very selves
completely. The irony is that this death of our false self which will
allow us to live fully from the true Self once more.

Marianne Williamson, the popular commentator on *A Course in
Miracles*, writes that "our deepest fear is not that we are inadequate.
Our deepest fear is that we are powerful beyond measure. It is our
light, not our darkness that most frightens us" (Williamson, 1996,
p. 190). Our reliance on achieving beauty and power keeps us focused
on our shortcomings, on what is seemingly imperfect about us, thus
holding us back. Rather conveniently for consumerism, it also
prompts us to continue buying products in order to achieve the
beauty and power we are told we should crave. Yet, our greatest fear
is not that we are not good enough, but that we are. The idea that we
are good enough, just as we are, tips just about every capitalist myth
on its head. It also comes with massive responsibility. If we do not
have to wait to be beautiful or rich, muscular or societally powerful in
order to go out and live boldly and fearlessly, we can consequently
start living life vibrantly right now. We no longer have any excuses to
be ashamed of ourselves, to hide or to hold back. This is a truth some
of us might not yet feel brave enough to hear. Maslow puts it another
way, in what he calls the "Jonah Complex":

> We are generally afraid to become that which we can glimpse in our
> most perfect moments, under the most perfect conditions, under
> conditions of great courage. We enjoy and even thrill to the godlike
> possibilities we see in ourselves in such peak moments. And yet we
> simultaneously shiver with weakness, awe, and fear before these very
> same possibilities. (Maslow, 1973, p. 37)

Jung spoke of the collective subconscious. So, too, do we carry a
collective shadow. This shadow comprises wider beliefs we have
assimilated into our psyche and have taken on almost unthinkingly as
our own. Every war that has ever been fought has sprung from this
collective shadow, a shadow with a rhetoric something like "God is on
our side". When George W. Bush began his war on terror, he claimed

he had experienced a clear message from God to do so. Hitler's systematic annihilation of six million Jews, not to mention other minority groups, was executed under the belief that pure Aryans were God's chosen people, the worthy and superior race. Our collective shadow's theme is one of superiority and ultimately, therefore, of separateness. With appearance battles, we have decided that we ourselves are the "inferior race", that it is we who are to be annihilated. As Pogo, the cartoon possum, once exclaimed, "we have met the enemy and he is us" (Walt, 1972). We have bought into the myth that beautiful people are superior people and have deemed ourselves to be unworthy on account of the appearance of our bodies. Then we punish ourselves, beat ourselves into submission, declare not a war on another, but on our own flesh.

Freedom from appearance difficulties necessitates a decisive stride away from this notion of superiority, this myth of separateness. Freedom is synonymous with an embrace of equality, with a firm claim on our right to be on an equal footing with everyone else. This also requires a letting go of our need to be superior, to be special. A massive element of my own personal battle with disordered eating was the pursuit of specialness. I wanted to be really good at something, recklessly craved acceptance through praise, and was desperate to be noticed despite behaving as though I wished to hide. I thought that making myself "beautiful" and "thin" would set me apart, would prompt people to notice me and, therefore, love me. Part of the process of my recovery was to realise two truths tangentially: that I was as good as everyone else, and that I would never be better than anyone else. Each and every human is as special and as worthy as the next. The deep penetration of this understanding, which had only been a surface-level notion up until that point, freed me both to love myself again and to understand how life actually works, to let go of my rigid and perfectionistic tendencies, to realise that every single person is good, exactly as they are. I came to realise that I am good, too.

Appearance battles are always, in part, an attempt to prove to the world that we are worthy. Yet, the truth is that we have absolutely nothing to prove.

There will always be someone seemingly more intelligent, more physically attractive, thinner, yet these external forms have nothing to do with our true Selves, with who we are at our core. When we move our gaze from the world of form to the world of being, everything changes. We relax. We no longer need to prove ourselves. We realise that we are no better than anyone else . . . and no worse, either. Any belief or attempt to be otherwise is futile. And we let it go.

We see the world that we have made, yet we do not see ourselves as the image-makers. The mirror does not make the image. Our size, the state of our skin, or our perceived level of beauty does not create our pain. If you listen closely to your thoughts you may notice that a surprising proportion are the voice of society, or voices of adults from your childhood, not the convictions of your true, deeper Self. Recovery from any appearance struggle is a move towards this Self, a move towards wholeness. Appearance struggles quite literally dismember us as human beings. The call back to life is a call to gather those divided parts and to become re-membered once more.

For Maslow, as for transpersonal theorists in general, human development is ultimately a spiritual realisation that goes beyond even humanness and self-actualisation. Perhaps Maslow's greatest contribution was his emphatic view that spiritual experience is a potentiality of human nature that belongs inherently to us all as a biological species (Maslow, 1997). Spirituality is innate and intrinsic to the human experience and life crises and struggles are seen in this way as avenues of transformation that provide powerful opportunities for growth, development, and healing.

Part of this journey is, as Jung puts it, to integrate our shadow-side. Each of us has such a shadow-side, a seeming darkness within, which is neither good nor bad but has been rejected by us outright nevertheless. That which we dismiss as "bad" becomes our shadow and this shadow is always seeking reintegration, no matter how desperately we might strive for its demise. As Jesus explains in the Gnostic Gospels, "there is nothing hidden that won't become exposed, and nothing buried that won't be raised" (Valantasis, 1997, p. 35). Appearance battles are a manifestation of this shadow. Robin Robertson, author of *The Shadow's Gift*, invites us initially to think of the shadow as an equal and opposite reaction to the face we show to the world (Robertson, 2001). If we desperately struggle to uphold, for example, our good-girl image to others then any aspect of the self that is considered to be in opposition to this image will be driven underground, becoming our shadow-side.

The more we seek out the light, the more the darkness, or the shadow, will present itself in order to return us to wholeness. This is a beautiful process and nothing to be afraid of. Yet many of us are terrified of our shadows, projecting our worst fears about ourselves on to people and objects and rejecting entire facets of our selfhood and experience in the process. Appearance struggles are perhaps even more complex, since we project our greatest fears on to our bodies, thus becoming completely fragmented in the process. Yet, to face our own darkness, to reach out and embrace those rejected aspects of ourselves, is to once again move towards wholeness, or, more correctly, to move once again towards remembering that we are already whole and always have been. As T. S. Eliot explains, ". . . the end of all our exploring will be to arrive where we started. And know the place for the first time" (Eliot, 1963, p. 208).

Some shadow aspects are denied existence and rejected so completely that they form separate identities. We see this, for example, in a person who was always expected to be perfect as a child and later develops external personalities for his rejected lack of perfection in the form of self-destructive urges, voices, disordered eating, and so on. Our egos cannot face that which does not have form. By giving our shadow aspects a form, the psyche is given an opportunity to face and, ultimately, reintegrate these aspects, which would otherwise remain cut off, leaving us in tatters. The shadow aspect, once externalised, can then be faced and finally embraced. Unfortunately, the current medical model is overwhelmingly one of rejecting or suppressing such externalisations of the shadow with pathologisations and medication. New approaches, however, are beginning to recognise the validity of fully addressing these shadow aspects as fragments of the person's own being, working not towards obliteration of the shadow but towards reintegration and wholeness.

Our shadow is the part of ourselves we have disowned and is, in truth, a projection. The poet Robert Bly (1988) presented us with the five stages of projection. These projections are nothing other than disowned and discarded aspects of ourselves on their way home. The first of these stages, according to Bly, is that of identifying a person or object to hold our projection. If we have disowned our anger, for example, we might find it difficult to be in close proximity with someone who expresses their anger freely. It is my personal belief that the majority of people with appearance-focused distress have denied their own anger at some level. At this stage, therefore, such an individual might project their disowned anger on to her body, providing the perfect conditions for an appearance battle to ensue.

The next stage is that the projection may begin to slip. At this point, we might begin to notice that our attempts at body perfection do not quite live up to our expectations. Those of us who starve our bodies, for example, realise that we do not become happier as we become thinner, as we had hoped we would. We are not ready at this stage, however, to let our projections go, so we rationalise these conflicts, making excuses such as that we are not yet happy because we are not yet thin enough. We could remain at this stage of justification for a long time, perhaps indefinitely (thus continuing to lose more and more weight), unless we begin to move on to the third stage.

At the third stage, the projection totally falls off. At this point, we begin to see beyond the image we have projected and become infuriated that things have not worked out as we had hoped they would. We feel disappointed and let down, cheated and bemused. At this vital and pivotal stage, we have a choice. We can either move on to stage four or transfer our projection on to another object, perhaps spending our whole lives tragically transferring from one self-destructive behaviour to another. To return to our example, we might realise that starvation has not delivered the promised goods: it does not appear to have made others accept and love us more and has not promoted greater self-love and esteem. There is a feeling of being let down and cheated by the whole escapade. The master plan has failed to deliver. We might, at this point, transfer the projection, the anger, to something else. Starving becomes purging, skin picking becomes hair pulling, muscle building becomes starving, and so on, *ad infinitum*. We might stagger ill-fatedly from one form of projection to another for the rest of our lives unless we find the courage to move on to the fourth stage.

At the fourth stage we finally recognise the projection. At this point, we see the projection for what it really is, realising that it has nothing to do with the object and everything to do with our own inner pain. We come to understand that the projection is a lost and rejected part of ourselves, begging frantically for reintegration. This stage often brings with it an immense, heaving grief. We mourn for the lost part of ourselves and lament over having been entrenched in destructive ways of being for so long. For the person engaged in a battle with her body, the grief is often centred on the realisation that her inner pain has nothing to do with her body, but has been suppressed from another source. This grief, when embraced and accepted, leads organically on to the fifth and final stage, during which we have compassion for the projection and begin the process of reintegration. Our compassion, at this stage, extends to others and ourselves in equal measure. We begin to live out the qualities we have projected, owning that which we have previously disowned. If we have disowned our anger, for example, this stage brings acceptance of our capacity for anger, enabling us to express our feelings as opposed to hiding and rejecting them. We may find ourselves speaking out authentically when our boundaries are crossed, as opposed to outlawing any difficult feelings and ultimately projecting them onto our bodies.

A useful exercise for recognising and acknowledging our shadow aspects is offered in Table 1 on the following page. The initial step in this shadow reintegration process is to write down a list of personality or behavioural aspects we find difficult in others. We then relate each item on the list to a rejected aspect of ourselves. The third step is to identify from where or whom this self-belief came (this is virtually always rooted in childhood: if an adult relationship is the first to come to mind, the reason this incident or comment affected us so deeply might be due to a similar message from childhood. It is often useful, therefore, to trace back a little further). The final step is to identify the shadow aspect which is on its way home. Table 1 contains a condensed example of this exercise, which could perhaps be undertaken after a time of mediation/yoga in order to come into a place of open awareness.

For Jung, the Self can neither be limited to images of light nor split off from its shadow. The Self is a "transcendent concept . . . that . . . expresses the sum of the conscious and unconscious contents" and, as such, "can be described only in the form of antimony" (cited by Marlon, 2005, p. 150). For this reason, the process of shadow integration is a *mysterium coniunctionis* (a mysterious conjunction of opposites) in that the Self is experienced in a union of opposite halves. Michael Washburn describes it as a wedding of the ego (as lesser self) to spirit (as greater Self) (Washburn, 1995). This conjunction of opposites is a "monstrosity almost unbearable for the ego to tolerate" (cited by Marlon, 2005, p. 151), yet we must face such an experience if we are to have any genuine recognition of the Self. The result of this union of

Table 1.   An exercise to facilitate recognition and acknowledgment of our shadow aspects.

Difficulty with another	Mirror aspect of Self	Where this came from	Specific incidents	Aspect of Self on its way home
Arrogance	Assertiveness	Primary carer	Stood on stage to sing and was deemed to be an embarrassment	Self-confidence and self-esteem
Selfishness	Self-care	Primary carer	Admonished for not sharing biscuits and called "greedy" for eating them	Compassion, generosity, recognition of own needs
Lack of commitment	Independence	School teachers	Called "strange" for choosing to spend so much time alone	Self-efficacy, charisma
Emotional weakness	Self-protection	Primary carer	Called "weak" repeatedly	Strength and courage
Aloofness	Empathy	Family member	Called "a complicated child" and labelled as "difficult to understand"	Ability to connect with and understand others

opposites is that we are simultaneously destroyed and reborn, broken and brought to life, obliterated and returned to authenticity, to the true Self.

This union of opposites is also expounded by Patanjali (2009, I.33), compiler of the yoga sutras, who prompts us to live beyond a binary reality of good and bad, pleasure and pain, joy and sorrow, and move towards a lived reality within which no experience is denied or pushed away. Embedded within this understanding is the belief that seeming opposites cannot be separated. We are called, rather, to develop our capacity for experiencing things the way they are, thus making a conscious choice for all of life, as opposed to constantly judging and cherry-picking emotions and human experiences with our minds. In the context of appearance battles, this means *choosing* those painful emotions and memories, actively engaging with them and, through this non-judgemental embrace, finding that they are intrinsically part of our wholeness and, therefore, not to be feared or rejected.

In the same way in which we, as individuals, have rejected our shadow side, so, too, has society spurned its collective shadow. The huge increase in appearance struggles in recent years is symptomatic of such rejected shadow aspects, which are aching imploringly to be reintegrated. In society's pursuit for achievement and power, it has denied its gentleness, its desire for connection, its selflessness, and its love. When we return once again as a society to these person-centred traits and begin to embed our lives in them, we may no longer have any need to prove ourselves through the manipulation of our bodies and the denial of our true Selves. Instead, there is a hope of becoming a society that lives from the heart as opposed to the head. This change begins with a resolute decision made by each of us to live from our own deeper authenticity and truth.

Matthew Sanford writes beautifully about this move towards wholeness in *Waking: A Memoir of Trauma and Transcendance: A Passage into the Body* (Sanford, 2006). Matt's life and body were shattered at the age of thirteen when his family car skidded off a snowy Iowa over-pass, killing his father and sister and leaving him paralysed from the neck down. From that moment onwards, Matt's life was set on a completely new course, leading him to become a yoga teacher and founder of a non-profit organisation. Matt poignantly describes the movement away from an understanding of himself as a mind and a body towards a notion of himself as pure awareness, which was only made possible by a full embrace of the darkness. Implored by doctors and nurses to fight against the darkness he found himself immersed in, Matt retaliated: "But what if I really wanted to be whole? If I wanted to work with the darkness rather than against it?" (Sanford, 2006, p. 128). He likens this darkness to a silence, to a soundless move towards true wholeness. He explains,

> Silence is what remains when mind becomes separated from body. My most basic unknown is how I will interact with this silence. The

medical model's answer is that I won't interact with it at all. I am, instead, led to ignore it and to give up my paralysed body as lost. Rather than working to integrate any residual silence that I might experience into who I am, I am urged to overcome it, to step over my paralysis with a courageous exertion of will. The medical model deems the air of this silence as too cold for me to breathe . . .

The relevance of this book turns on a simple thought. My traumatic experience of a spinal cord injury and its resulting paralysis has made more tangible a silence that exists in everyone's consciousness, a silence than can be experienced in the gap between mind and body. How we relate to this silence, how we process it, is a fundamental issue presented by our consciousness. (Sanford, 2006, p. 98)

All ancient religions, myths, and traditions encapsulate this understanding in some form, describing a silence and a darkness that begs assimilation and a death that must occur in order for new life to emerge. I turn now to Joseph Campbell, American mythologist and author of many volumes, including my favourite, *The Hero with a Thousand Faces*. He writes,

Everywhere, no matter what the sphere of interest (whether religious, political, or personal), the really creative acts are represented as those deriving from some sort of dying to the world; and what happens in the interval of the hero's nonentity, so that he comes back as one reborn, made great and filled with creative power. (Campbell, 2008, p. 28)

While it might be difficult to see our appearance battles in this way, they are, in fact, a call to adventure, with this adventure being the journey of reintegration of our shadow and a return to the true Self. This is the first stage of the hero's journey in myths and religions across the expanse of time. Campbell explains,

The herald or announcer of the adventure, therefore, is often dark, loathly, or terrifying, judged evil by the world; yet if one would follow, the way would be opened through the walls of day into the dark where the jewels glow. (Campbell, 2008, p. 44)

If our appearance battles have emerged as agents of safety and self-care, as we have previously discussed, then we will need to face any perceived dangers if we are to hope for a "birth in the world without". For most of us, this will mean facing the perceived dangers within our own family and societal units. We shall also have to confront our identity projects, many of which would have seemed to be most vital and virulent in adolescence and early adulthood. The mental ego is invisible to itself in introspection and, therefore, needs to give itself some kind of recognisable form. It responds to this need by creating an identity for itself that, as it is recognised by others, provides a sense of worldly existence. We tend to experiment with a plethora of identity possibilities in adolescence, later committing ourselves to a long-term identity project in early adulthood. As we have seen, appearance-focused identity struggles often emerge at this very time and could be said, therefore, to be one such identity project that later, sadly, becomes a longer-term sense of who we are. Giving up our appearance battles can be so very painful, as we must abandon part of our created identity in the process. We have frequently muddled up these identities in our minds with who we intrinsically are.

Part of the relinquishment of our created ego identities is the call to face the fear of not being good enough, of being rejected and, ultimately, of not being loved. We are invited to take this risk, much as it pains us, by following our bliss, as Campbell put it, by laying aside our false self, as Winnicott would have said. If we quieten the chatter of people-pleasing, of conforming, of following a path we think *they* want us to take, we can begin to remember what we really love to do, what we are really about. When we stop desiring "this man's gift and that man's scope" (Eliot, 1950, p. 60), we come to a place of knowing what it is we are personally called to do with our lives. These can be explosive realisations that might necessitate changing our careers, moving homes, letting go of relationships, and, perhaps, changing every aspect of our lives completely. We may fear these changes, yet they are exactly what are necessary for the next stage of our hero journey to take place. Campbell describes it thus:

> It cannot be described, quite, as an answer to any specific call. Rather, it is a deliberate, terrific refusal to respond to anything but the deepest, highest, richest answer to the yet unknown demand of some waiting void within: a kind of total strike, or rejection of the offered terms of life, as a result of which some power of transformation carries the problem to a plane of new magnitudes, where it is suddenly and finally resolved. (Campbell, 2008, p. 53)

The passage of the threshold between our false self and true Self is the passage of "a form of self-annihilation" (Campbell, 2008, p. 77). Here, "instead of passing outward, beyond the confines of the visible world, the hero goes inward, to be born again" (Campbell, 2008, p. 77). In mythology and religion, the hero might actually be slain, as in the case of the Egyptian saviour Osiris, who was murdered by his brother before returning from the dead, or the incidence of the crucifixion and rising from the dead of Jesus Christ. Once the death and rebirth have taken place, a transfiguration occurs: "the myths do not deny this agony [the crucifixion]; they reveal within, behind and around it essential peace" (Campbell, 2008, p. 288). Our appearance battles take us to the eye of the storm, to the very heart of the darkness we have been rallying against. If we surrender and allow our false selves to perish, the true Self is enabled to rise up and our lives are utterly transfigured. Again we return to Campbell:

> The individual, through prolonged psychological disciplines, gives up completely all attachment to his personal limitations, idiosyncrasies, hopes and fears, no longer resists the self-annihilation that is prerequisite to rebirth in the realisation of truth, and so becomes ripe, at last, for the great at one-ment. His personal ambitions being totally dissolved, he no longer tries to live but willingly relaxes to whatever may come to pass in him. (Campbell, 2008, p. 204).

Throughout the ages, the great sages and mystics have repeatedly emphasised the need to pass through the darkness and surrender our false self in order to become truly alive. Such surrender is not to be confused with defeat. We do not lay down our battle armour because we believe ourselves to have been defeated. Rather, we wave our white flag in recognition of the futility of the fight. In order to reach this place of surrender, we must first enter into the dark night and engage with our pain. As Marcel Proust teaches us, "we are healed of suffering only by experiencing it in the full" (cited by Chang, 2006, p. 679).

Many of us want to recover from our appearance battles without having to converse with the darkness. We might, indeed, have spent much of our lives dodging the shadows at every turn, doing everything in our power to avoid having to acknowledge certain painful events and emotions. While we may understand that failing to address our deeper issues might result in longer-term and potentially graver suffering, we wish, nevertheless, to negate any suffering in the here-and-now by avoiding our fears and difficult emotions.

In order to move beyond our appearance distress, we are called to enter into our pain in the present moment by allowing our emotions to be deeply felt and heard. This involves an exploration of the multitude of sensations, impressions, and images associated with these emotions and, as such, necessitates an active engagement with the body and its signposting stirrings. Part of this process is an acknowledgement that our emotions spring from desires that run much deeper than any attachment to the appearance of our physical bodies. The tears we must cry are not tears for the way we look, but tears for the ways others have treated us and the ways in which we have treated ourselves. It is at this point that the compulsion to run in the opposite direction might be the most compelling, as we might experience these emotions as too intense and heart-rending to sit with. As Portia De Rossi writes in her beautiful memoir, *Unbearable Lightness*, "Recovery feels like shit. It didn't feel like I was doing something good; it felt like I was giving up. It feels like having to learn to walk all over again. I felt pathetic" (De Rossi, 2011, p. 280).

The emotions that emerge as we face our appearance struggles can, indeed, for many of us, feel overpowering. We are then faced with the choice, as was Shakespeare's Hamlet, of whether to feel these emotions or distract ourselves from them. Overwhelmed by the assassination of his father, Hamlet famously pondered whether he should manage his emotions by continuing to engage the "slings and arrows of outrageous fortune" or by disengaging from his "sea of troubles" through sleep or death (Shakespeare, 1982 (reprint)). As our emotions are allowed to rise to the surface, they typically involve experiential, behavioural, and physiological responses, which can take the form of a seemingly all-consuming whole-body response. At this often terrifying stage, we can either suppress our reactions or trust in the wisdom behind them. Frequently, our body-mind may feel as though it is being obliterated under the weight and intensity of our emotions, a hugely intimidating and engulfing experience. It is, however, as we have seen, exactly this grinding down which needs to take place in order for the true Self to re-emerge.

Of all of the emotional states that constellate around appearance difficulties, shame is often the hardest to acknowledge and enter into. The existence of shame brings with it the sense of a secret, which is often deeply buried, resulting in some form of a withdrawal from others and even from life itself. This withdrawal, which John Steiner (1993) referred to as a psychic retreat, can result in a lifelong cut-offness, bringing with it all manner of emotional suffering. This suffering, for some of us, takes the form of an appearance battle, which itself can become a psychic retreat from the painful reality of our lives. A focus on the appearance of the physical body can serve to numb shameful feelings and memories and give a sense of "fixing" or "redeeming" oneself. Guilt itself can act as a defence against shame, with such guilt then adding further fuel to this fire of self-destruction.

Shame as an emotion is closely enmeshed with identity and experiences of the self. When we truly enter into any sense of shame or, indeed, enter into any emotion instead of engaging in distractive behaviours, our lives can often feel as though they are getting worse before they begin to get better. We are finally coming face to face with that which terrifies us the most. Support for people fighting against their bodies, therefore, should *increase* when the external behaviours such as the skin picking, the starving, the bingeing, and so on are laid aside. In tandem with such support, it is precisely at this stage that we are called to share and express our fears and emotions unreservedly. Unfortunately, many treatment centres and protocols withdraw their support as the external behaviours decrease. As the self-starver's weight goes up and the skin-picker's wounds begin to heal, it is decided that they must be doing well and are a pleasing way into the healing process. It is at this point, however, that the real work begins and the most courage is needed. When we stop hiding behind our behaviours, the rawness of our fear and pain can erupt to the surface and take us into the dark night of the soul St John of the Cross wrote so compellingly about. This might not feel good . . . but it is! Finally, we are coming face to face with our shadows. Finally, we have arrived at the precipice.

Despite the plundering nature of the pain and darkness we must inevitably move through, we are not swallowed up, as we feared we might be. As Mooji explains, "the one who is on fire is not you, it is your self-image. And it is this self-image that is somehow eclipsing the recognition that you are the freedom itself" (Mooji, 2012). As our false selves burn in the fire of our awareness, they might shriek and gnash their teeth, igniting immense amounts of psychological and emotional pain. Yet, this pain cannot swallow us up, and will pale in comparison to the pain we have inflicted on ourselves in our attempts to run away. As this pain is acknowledged and given the chance to tell its story, the true Self is finally provided with the space within which to resurface. When we then decide to say a resounding "yes" to life, whether we succeed or fail in any or all of our endeavours, we enter into the heart of our fears and emerge into a new life, which we no longer measure by societal standards, but by our own. It is, essentially, a full and unapologetic embrace of the totality of who we are. As Marya Horbacher, author of the poignant memoir *Wasted*, explains,

> What all this grandiosity covers—and not very well, I might add—is a very basic fear that the real world will gobble you up the minute you step into it. Obviously, the fear is incredibly large or you wouldn't go to all the trouble of trying to leave it, and certainly not in such a long, drawn-out manner. The fear too, is a fear of yourself: a completely dualistic and contradictory fear. On the one hand it is a fear that you do not have what it takes to make it, and on the other hand, a possibly greater fear that you do. (Hornbacher, 2009, p. 281)

When we step out into the world as our true Selves, we find that it does not gobble us up at all. We find, rather, that whereas love and acceptance might have been difficult to assimilate in the past (on account of its offer having been made towards the false self), we are now able to trust in the authenticity and deservedness of the embrace and accept it fully. All it really requires is a leap of faith:

> Looking back, I see that what I did then was pretty basic. I took a leap of faith. And I believe that has made all the difference. I hung on to the only thing that seemed real to me, and that was a basic ethical principle: if I was alive, then I had a responsibility to stay alive and do something with the life I had been given. And though I was not at all convinced, when I made that leap of faith, that I had any sensible reason for doing so—though I did not fully believe that there was anything that could possibly make as much sense as an eating disorder—I made it because I began to wonder, in the same way I had wondered what would happen if I began to lose weight, what would happen if I stopped. It was worth it. (Hornbacher, 2009, p. 280)

Freedom begins with a willingness to imagine that life can be another way. When we are entrenched in our appearance battles, our ability to imagine a better life can be heavily marred by our behaviours and desperate ideals. The leap of faith Hornbacher speaks of is, at its heart, a profound act of surrender. It is a falling backwards into unseen arms, a blind dive towards a depth we have no hope of estimating. When this surrender is absolute, there is instantly the sense that life will never be the same again, a deep understanding that there is nothing left to fear.

Living and dying occur simultaneously. (Sanford, 2006, p. 154)

CHAPTER TWELVE

From false selves to true Selves: returning home

"Go, go, go said the bird: human kind cannot bear very much reality"

(T. S. Eliot, 1988, p. 205)

I had reached the depths of the ocean
where all was silent, white.
I spoke but couldn't hear myself
as I waited for the night.
The darkness fell just when it should
and caught hold of my hand,
I told it why I trembled and
it seemed to understand.
'Please leave my mind' I whispered,
it nodded its shadowy head,
'then surrender your mind' it pleaded
'and invite me in instead'.

I closed my eyes and took a breath
and opened all to the black.

197

After endless years of running,
I stood still

and found my way back.

(N. Schnackenberg)

An appearance battle does not just appear one day like the chicken pox. It begins slowly, insidiously. Nobody notices what is happening at first, least of all yourself. Later, it might be hard to trace it back. Everyone may have a different suggestion, an alternative take on things. The truth is, nobody really knows.

Many times, in the early years, I would try to remember how and why my appearance struggle began and end up getting lost in the world of mirrors and self-hatred instead. This is what such a civil war pitted against the Self does, acting as an agent of perfect distraction, reducing the whole world down into an internalised binary vacuum of good and bad, fat and thin, beautiful and ugly, worthy and achingly unlovable.

Yet, it is possible to feel and survive the true source of our suffering and assimilate the seeming darkness to once again become whole. To live from such wholeness is to truly live. Anything less will only ever be a half-life, a mere semblance of an existence.

This is not a chapter focused on my personal descent into an appearance battle or the messy depths of the thick of the drama. This is not a chapter about calories or skin picking or jutting bones. We have heard, and lived, enough of all that. This is a chapter that looks the "why" directly in the face, that muses upon a roadmap, a way back.

It is extremely difficult to pinpoint exactly how much each of the elements of my journey had an impact on my gradual return to my true Self. Over the years, I have had individual therapy, family therapy, inpatient and outpatient treatment, in addition to the uncountable number of kindnesses shown to me by friends and family and the support I have received from every imaginable quarter. I have had art therapy, spent hours meditating and practising yoga, been hypnotised, had CBT, been prayed over, and read every book on the subject of psychological distress I could lay my hands on. I have no doubt that every element played a part in my healing while some things, of course, were far more helpful than others. The aspects that helped me might be very different to the ones you find the most supportive. Yet, the message for us all, perhaps, is that we should not give up, but, rather, keep exploring and embracing the hand offered to us in its many guises.

It would seem to me that we only enter into an over-identification with our bodies if we have hidden or denied who we are. Without an external manifestation of our pain, of which an appearance struggle can be one form, our true Self would, in all probability, have continued to be relinquished increasingly further into the shadows. Our true beingness will always rally against such dismissal, since it is not our deeper nature to be squashed, to be restricted, to be hemmed in. Our innate nature is unbridled and knows itself to be so. At our core, we are completely and beautifully free.

Donald Winnicott, upon whose intensely insightful ideas the title and central tenet of this book rest, focused on how an infant moves from an illusory sense of merged existence with the mother or primary caregiver to a secure and separate sense of self. Within the space between these two self-experiences, the infant often uses what Winnicott called transitional objects, which typically come into play from about four to twelve months old and are the infant's first "not me" possessions. While they are commonly physical objects, such as a blanket, a teddy, or a thumb, they are thought to symbolise a third reality in between subject and object: in between that which is merged with the mother and that which is separate to her. Such transitory objects are thought to preserve the illusion of connection with the mother while also mediating the process of establishing the difference between the inner and the outer life and between the "I" and the "Thou" or "Other". According to Winnicott, these objects facilitate the growth of the infant's potential to experience and convey her true Self (Winnicott, 1965).

It is my postulation that appearance-focused identity struggles, or, perhaps more accurately, the objectified body, comprise one such potential transitional object. Winnicott's transitional object might continue to play out for some of us in adult life in the form of clinging to perceived sources of comfort with the hope of transitioning towards, or, more accurately, back to our true Selves. A child reaches out for a blanket, dummy, teddy, and so on as that which has previously been offered to him as a source of comfort in his distress. This object is, henceforth, perceived as soothing and, thus, becomes the soother, the go-to entity when the child longs for her carer and cannot access him or her, either physically or emotionally. Appearance struggles, as we have seen, most commonly emerge during times of transition, such as the transmutation to adolescence, motherhood, and so on, necessitating a rearrangement of the gap between ourselves and an important other. At this point, it would seem that we scan our periphery looking for something stable, something solid, something soothing to hold on to. As a child, I once reached for my stuffed toy elephant. I later reached for my protruding hipbones and bathroom scales. Both had been offered to me as a potential source of comfort, the first by my parents and the second by society at large.

Thinness was the first "not me" possession to emerge in my transition to adolescence. It separated me from my mother (my thinness was "mine" and nobody else's) and yet gave me some sense of continued symbiosis, a psychic necessity given my insecure attachment to her. As I staved off the bodily changes of adolescence, I remained a small and needy child. As I became physically weaker, my mother was called once again to take care of me as though I was still a tiny baby. The breast milk that had rapidly dried up due to intense anxiety and postnatal panic became, many years later, the milky, high-calorie formula she syringed and, later, pumped into my stomach via a nasogastric tube. As Winnicott explained, in some cases only a regression to dependence is sufficient to break through the false self system so that one can begin to exist as a person again (Little, 1990; Winnicott, 1975). As much as I needed to separate from my mother, I would have given my life to remain connected to her. I was, however, acutely unaware of this at the time.

The stage had been set by my own mother's painfully traumatic childhood and attachment difficulties with her own mother through the process of intergenerational transmission of trauma. Early ground-breaking work by Fraiberg and colleagues (1975), entitled "Ghosts in the nursery", described how unresolved past traumatic experiences may compromise a parent's ability to offer adequate physical and emotional caring. Fraiberg suggested that specific vulnerabilities, such as the trauma of abandonment or domestic violence, might limit a parent's ability to understand and respond sensitively to her infant, thus resulting in the repetition of her own anguished past. My mum and dad were immensely dedicated parents, continuously putting myself and my siblings at the very centre of their world. Their own early life experiences, however, which would need a book of their own to go into a just amount of detail, naturally had a massive impact on their adult lives. For now, suffice to say that between them they experienced multiple and acute traumas, layered on to their own deep attachment-based struggles, a description that says little about the depth of pain they experienced nor the sheer magnitude to which they suffered. These kinds of trauma can take a lifetime to process, yet my parents were only in their early twenties when they had me, their first and much-longed for child.

I was not born, therefore, into the most emotionally secure environment nor the most stable of marriages, although there was never any lack of love and affection in our home. When I was born, it now seems to me that I became the container for my mum's unresolved pain and her "saviour" simultaneously, a rather tall order for a tiny baby. Consequently, there were no clear lines between my own self and that of my mother and we became truly enmeshed in every sense of Minuchin's explanation of the word (Minuchin, 1974). I became the surrogate for her sense of identity, well-being, safety, security, and self-worth, and she subsequently became such a substitute for me. Our sense of wholeness came to be largely embedded in one another.

If I had been born in another century, I might have found a less life-threatening transitional object to provide me with a much needed soother, a less dangerous bid for separateness and psychological survival. As it was, I had been drip-fed the myth that you can enhance your happiness and well-being and please the people around you by losing weight and, in fact, even secure people's love by becoming a bit thinner, a trifle more beautiful. I was so achingly desperate to be loved, particularly by my mother, but also by the line of children who bullied me in cruel and confusing ways. My low self-esteem and withdrawn nature seemed to make me a prime target for this bullying, which only compounded the sense of my own badness. If I had lived in another era, I might have found another way to self-soothe and secure love, another method to make sense of my pain. As it was, self-starvation was quite literally handed to me on a plate.

Ideally, my chosen transitional object would have provided me with the platform to leap beyond my enmeshment and towards a sense of my own, separate wholeness. However, by choosing a starving body for comfort as I did, a whole host of biological factors very rapidly came into play that made it seemingly impossible to escape the vortex I felt enticingly sucked into. Initially, my body responded to the food restriction by increasing my appetite and reducing my satiety, or fullness, levels. Driven by my quest for psychological survival and powered by my perfectionism, I ignored these signals and continued to deny myself adequate nourishment. All the while, my disrupted sleep and intense sadness were, in all probability, compounded by my elevated cortisol levels. My drive towards physical activity increased and my appetite for food (despite my hunger) eventually decreased, which is unlikely to have been helped by my plummeting neuropeptide Y levels. My feelings of well-being and ability to relax both decreased, as did my levels of mood-enhancing beta-endorphin. This all happened alongside my energy uptake regulation going awry, including disturbances in my appetite and metabolism becoming intensified by my unstable leptin levels. Simultaneously, my brain began to shrink, with my cortex, the diligent regulator of my emotions, diminishing in size and heightening my growing sense of feeling alternately numb and overwhelmed by my feelings. Thus, the wheels were set in motion, the conditions for a precarious spiral of self-destruction rapidly taking a compelling hold.

Starvation led me to near-insanity. But the beauty myth gave me the keys to the vehicle I used to drive myself there. Part of the pursuit of my thinness was the belief that losing weight was the good and acceptable thing to do. This corrosive thinness took me from the arms of my family and locked me in multiple general and psychiatric wards. It stole my adolescence and early twenties. It hurt beyond compare just about every person who loves me. It made me immeasurably sad and often suicidal. It isolated me and destroyed my ability to enjoy, to learn, and to grow. It gave me polycystic ovaries, a heart murmur, and osteoporosis. If I fall on my coccyx, I have been told that my spine might shatter like glass. This is not a cosy possibility to be walking around with. Was being thin worth it? I do not think the question even merits an answer.

I never intended or imagined that things would go so far. Yet, the battle for life, which is exactly what this was, can never be a quiet, half-hearted affair. I could only push my true emotions down for so long before they began to seep out of every orifice. It is so often assumed that the person starves themselves, and the cutter slashes into their flesh, in a quest for a way out. I was looking for a way *in*. To live as a false self is no life at all. Eventually, the masquerade may disintegrate you, unless something or someone steps up to save you. My starving and cutting, strange as this might sound at first impression, were the forces that rose up to save my life. They were my soothing transitional object, my attempt to resolve the cavernous expanse between my false self and true Self, between my symbiosis with my mother and a sense of my own edges. My bony frame and self-inflicted gashes screamed what I could not say. They flaunted the pain I was too suppressed to share.

It was around the age of ten or eleven, as far as I can remember, that the world started to gradually became darker and darker. It was a slow and slippery slope, which seemed to gather momentum as the years passed and I collected more proof for my supposed badness. Around the time of my fourteenth birthday, I landed myself in a psychiatric hospital. Many of the weeks and months preceding this are a bit of a blur, a muddled mass of gaping contradictions and desires cut off at the knees.

Each of the treatment centres I attended brought one main agenda to the table: the annihilation of my so-called anorexia. They told me to fight it, to get rid of it, to ignore it, and to hate it with all of the passion I could muster. In the early years, I resisted and fought this annihilation as though my very life was being attacked in every quarter. And, indeed, it was. Taking a child's transitional object away from them in the midst of a tantrum is a heartless and provocative act, often igniting a sense in the child that they themselves are under threat of harm and even dissolution. As the doctors, the nurses, and my family tried to tear my "anorexia" away from me, I felt as though my very identity and sense of self were being ripped from the centre of my chest. The natural response to such intense threat is to cling on all the more virulently. So I ate even less, cut and purged even more, put up a metaphorical middle finger and exclaimed with my behaviours "You aren't going to take this away from me. This *is* me. This is the only way the world and I make any sense".

Eventually, utterly exhausted by the battle, wrenched apart by the unthinkable pain of my family, and devastated by a life wholly consumed by locked hospital doors, I began to follow the doctor's orders and fight this "anorexia" with all the strength I could muster. I tried this for many, many years. It never really got me very far. This seemingly destructive force had come to deliver a message and was not going away until it was heard. It represented a shadow side which needed integration, not relinquishment, and a darkness that was part of the light, not a threat to it. What I really needed was for my family and the professionals to cease their attempts at "curing" me and start listening to the message and metaphor behind my self-starvation. What was this inner force really trying to say when it told me to starve, purge, and punish myself into oblivion?

Through the denial and destruction of my body I was screaming out a single, clear, and unyielding message: "I want to live as my true Self. I want to be treated kindly. I want to find my own edges. I want you to love me for who I am".

I had, it seems, taken the drama of my external reality and created a meticulous replica inside my head, a perfect microcosm of pain. All the roles were there and I played all the parts. I was persecutor, victim, and rescuer all at one and the same time. I drove myself close to insanity, then invented ways to bring myself back again. I had no need now for anyone else to take my world and tear it unceremoniously apart. I was doing that perfectly well all by myself, thank you very much. The split, the part of myself everyone else called anorexia, among other things, was the part crying out to be heard. The problem was that nobody knew what they were listening to. It was as though they had tuned into the wrong radio station, the frequency blurred and the voices speaking a foreign language. They thought they had tuned into *Pursuit of Beauty FM*, with a young girl wanting to lose some weight to fit in. They had actually caught the tail-end of *I'm Losing my Self and Don't Know What to Do About it FM*. Starve myself, maybe? Given the societal acceptance of such an act, it seemed like a feasible option.

I am convinced now that I began to starve and hurt myself because *I just didn't know what else to do*. My sense of self was spinning off its axis and I absolutely needed to find something I could use to stabilise it, something I could hold on to when everything else seemed to be falling apart. I yearned desperately to be accepted for who I truly was, with my sometimes less-than-the-best grades, my unruly hair, my cheeky and irreverent nature. Instead, unrealistic heights of perfection were perpetually demanded of me and I always felt like the "bad" girl, a feeling that gradually morphed into the sense that I was some kind of monster. I hated this monster and longed desperately to be a "real person", without a cause for feeling ashamed and guilty so much of the time. I covered myself up so expertly in a bid to hide this monstrousness that I almost lost myself completely. Thankfully, just before my true Self disappeared into a puff of thin air, another force in the form of an appearance battle rose up to stand my ground. I hated this seemingly destructive impulse for many years. Now I understand that I actually owe it my life.

It was not an easy journey. I only narrowly outwitted death and felt as though I almost lost my tentative grip on sanity many times. Although my body did not die, there was a death that took place, a death of the kind Joseph Campbell writes about so profoundly. In my late teens I descended to such depths that I did not have the presence to keep the false self going any more. The charade seemed to detonate inside of me, making it impossible to pretend any longer. I could not smile. I could not say "I am all right". I could hardly say anything at all.

I did not have the strength to hold on to anything. So I let go. I entered into the darkness I had been running away from for so very many years. I gave up the façade of coping and let myself cry for hours and hours. Sometimes, I would cry so hard that my chest would rattle for days afterwards, reverberating all over the house. In those weeks and months of relaxed-guard of myself and my emotions, just a little bit of my true Self began to seep through. I realised that I had absolutely no idea what I actually liked, what I really enjoyed, who I really was.

My initial desire was not to starve myself. It was to find a way to cope with life and a means by which I could become a good girl so that I would be worthy of love. In many ways, it was the internalised voice of both external commands and subsequently self-created unrealistic demands, nothing more sinister than that. I then scanned my surroundings looking for a way to be good. Society told me that being thin would be good. Society told me that I had the power to manipulate and gain mastery over my flesh. I had swallowed the myth that a person's measure of perfection increases as their weight decreases. I had assimilated the message that I needed to be perfect. At any cost.

The call, perhaps, then, is to stop hating and blaming the self-starvation, the mirror gazing, the cutting, the hair pulling, and the skin picking. These are not illnesses in the way the *DSM* would have us believe. Rather, they are a cluster of metaphorical behaviours that beg existence until the metaphor has been understood. When I understood that I was ultimately trying to make myself lovable by starving my body, I could then address that need. I came to view my self-harming behaviours both as a rebellion against the systematic destruction of my true Self and as a desperate call to be loved by the people I loved the most. The great tragedy in families is that, despite the very best of intentions, we can only relate to each other from where we are. Our greatest responsibility, then, is to take care of our own stuff. We can smile our own traumas away and cover them up, but until they are dealt with there may always be marred interactions, unhelpful projections, selves unscrupulously picked apart at the seams.

Emerging from my appearance battles was the most difficult experience of my life, even darker than the self-destruction itself. I would inch forwards and leap backwards, afraid to fully let go and terrified of losing my faltering grip on sanity. Most of my twenties were spent in a kind of grey twilight. Life was so much better, yet I was still afraid of my own shadow, still terrified to let my true and unadulterated Self shine through for all the world to see. Then something happened that I would never have guessed would tip my whole world upside down all over again, something so seemingly innocuous that had anybody told me it would have been so heart-wrenching I would have almost certainly dismissed them outright. I got acne. A case of what I now understand to have been mild acne, which became severe when I began to pick at it and assail it with every chemical I could lay my hands on. Eventually, it became infected and crawled unabashedly across my face, concurrently nullifying my scraps of self-esteem all over again. Although I had refrained from actively starving myself for some years, I clearly had not yet worked through my underlying need to be perfect. In this way, my skin problems were another invitation from life towards wholeness, in a similar way that the metaphor of my self-destructive behaviours had been.

I believed my chin and jaw to be smothered in red lesions, though when I look at pictures now I can see that it was not nearly as bad as I thought it was at the time, another trick of my skewed perception. Nevertheless, I was mortified. I scrubbed at my skin and spent hours in front of the mirror covering up the blemishes. This only made matters much, much worse. Then I began to cut out whole food groups again, believing I might have developed a food allergy. I took a ridiculous amount of supplements, spent every evening desperately reading skin care blogs, and was prescribed endless rounds of creams and antibiotics by various doctors after much begging. I became deeply consumed, enormously obsessed.

The fear I felt at this time was indescribable. The unpredictability made the whole thing so incredibly unbearable for me. Controlling everything I put into my mouth for so many years had given me a false sense of control over my body and, therefore, my life in general, yet now I was waking up each morning to new blemishes without having any way of thwarting them. My self-control had been another of my transitional objects, a sort of lifejacket, and it now felt as though my means of survival was being taken from me as I drowned inexorably in my own fear. I tried to control the eruption of my pimples by controlling what I ate but still they came, stubbornly emerging no matter what I did or refrained from doing. As I lost control over my appearance, I felt as though I was losing control over my life and sense of self, which is how I felt as a young child before I turned to self-starvation in a desperate survival bid. My identity had remained so strongly wrapped up in my physical appearance that I lost myself all over again when my face changed.

The people who love me became particularly frustrated with me at this time. "A few spots won't kill you", I was told again and again when I would cry over the state of my skin, yet, ironically, my suicidality meant that they almost did.

We are never upset for the reasons we think we are. Over the course of almost two years, and having exhausted the "if I just clear my skin up I will be okay" manifesto, I slowly began to consider what might be underlying my dark distress. Was it really my skin that was causing me to enter into such a tailspin? Or was this just a surface battle, a metaphor, as my self-starvation had been, and, therefore, an invitation to address deeper issues and longer-standing hurts?

I began to realise that despite maintaining a safe-ish weight for many years, I had never really addressed the underlying root of my disordered eating. Rather, I had been living a muted semi-existence, within which I still felt ashamed of who I was as a person while concurrently understanding that starving myself was not the answer to my problems. I had set myself up for an endless string of sufferings, which were all facets of the same problem: my disordered eating, self-mutilation, skin obsession, body dysmorphia, perfectionism, workaholism, self-deprecation, and people-pleasing tendencies, among other things, were just different colours on the same canvas, were all aspects of my inability to love and embrace myself fully. My continuous oscillation between one behaviour, one obsession, and another was a clear indication that I had not yet fully undergone the death Joseph Campbell speaks of. I had not yet been courageous enough to fling myself headlong into the very centre of Jung's black sun.

I still believed that I was fundamentally unlovable and that my physical appearance was a core measure of my lovability. I still had not worked through my pain. Not really. I was still pirouetting in that space between enmeshment with my mother and a separate sense of self. I had allowed a small part of my true Self to come to the surface, maintained some semblance of a socially acceptable weight, and enjoyed my life to a certain extent—yet I had not managed to let go of my fear of being unlovable. I still believed that I needed to present a pristine image to the world if I had any hope of being accepted. I still clung to the notion that life was impossible if certain others did not love me. It was hard to admit after so many years, decades really, of pain and self-rejection that I had not come as far as I thought I had. In many ways, I was still merely existing. I had not remembered how to live at all.

The knowledge of this sent me spiralling into the darkest place I had ever known. It was not over. All the years of starving and screaming, all those many months of being hidden away in hospitals and tearing my family apart . . . and here I was, still standing at square one, terrified of food, petrified of my body, scared to death by life. What had been the point? I began not only to wish that I could die, but also to believe I should have died many years ago.

I went down so low that I literally had nowhere else to go. My back was against the wall and any semblance of hope was completely absent. I could not imagine the shattering pain ever going away, that I would ever be acceptable, that I could ever be anything other than hideous and unlovable. Yet, a small part of me knew that I had to feel this darkness. I had to trust and somehow find a way to let go.

The lowest moment is a moment of few possibilities. The only thing left to do was to walk headlong into everything I was afraid of. There was nowhere else to go. So I entered into the pain of facing people with what I considered to be a wholly unacceptable face instead of hiding away from the world. It felt as if my heart was breaking. I would look people in the eye and concurrently feel as though I was dying inside. I kept repeating Mooji's words to myself over and over again: "The one who is on fire is not you. It is your self image. And it is this self-image that is somehow eclipsing the recognition that you are the freedom itself" (Mooji, 2012). It was not me who was dying, but my false self, my belief that I needed to be perfect in order to be worthy of love.

In many ways, I intuitively put myself through some exposure therapy. I threw my concealer in the bin and faced the world without make-up. I gradually stopped covering up the mirrors in the house, but also set a timer to stop me spending too long in front of them. I began, courtesy of Louise Hay, to look myself in the eye in the mirror and say "I love you Nicole". I began to eat from every food group again and stopped obsessively reading labels and checking my skin after every morsel. I went to social occasions, even if I spent the whole time suppressing an overwhelming sense of panic. None of this was easy, and it took time and huge amounts of patience with myself. Sometimes, I would take a massive step forwards and half a step back, or would spend a few days back in the silence of a mirror-covered house again before finding the strength to continue the journey. Many times I felt as though I did not have the courage to live another second . . . yet I always did.

I also made the decision to use the hours upon hours of time I had spent obsessing over my skin to enter fully into my emotions. For me, this meant sitting with myself for extended periods of time and allowing the feelings of shame, guilt, and safe-hatred to come to the surface without distracting myself from them, pushing them away, or escaping into the plethora of self-harming behaviours I had built up over the years. I cried endlessly. The pain of my existence had never been so stark nor so strong. Yet, something was slowly beginning to shift inside. As I described in Chapter Eight, by fully embracing my emotions, I rediscovered that they find a safe equilibrium organically and fail to overwhelm me. I re-learnt that my challenging feelings only become unbearable when I push them away, with such rejection consequently fostering their growth and revisitation. I remembered that difficult emotions depart very quickly once their message has been heard.

The only things that have any power to hurt us are the things we identify with. When I invited my feelings in as guests and began to see them as separate to myself and intrinsically ephemeral, they were no longer distressing and became stripped of their ability to disturb my peace of mind. For many, many years my appearance had been my identity. As I gradually welcomed my emotions and allowed my true

Self to re-emerge, I awoke to the knowledge that my identity was not to be found in my thighs or on my face, or even in the stories I told myself about who I was. I began to feel as though I was gradually being stripped of each of layer of misplaced identity: *Nicole the monster*, *Nicole the "bad" daughter*, *Nicole the anorexic*. The deeper I went, the more feathers of my identity were gently plucked out, culminating in the relinquishment of the identity of *Nicole the body*. It is no exaggeration to call this an existential and truly transpersonal awakening, which stunningly dawned on me as I was practising self-enquiry (a description of which can be found in Appendix III) and could not find my true Self in any of the places I had believed it to be. My true Self was not my perceived appearance, my credentials, my personality, my abilities, or my thoughts. These facets comprised my false self, which had been nurtured and encouraged from my earliest days by my conditioning and, ultimately, by my decision to buy into the myths I had been fed from birth. My true Self, rather, is, and always has been, nothing less than pure love, total awareness, wild acceptance, and an unconditional embrace of the entirety of life without judgement, without fear, just as the true Selves of us all so beautifully are.

When I understood this, not just logically, but deeply experientially, there was no longer any need to battle against my physical body. Throughout the years of my self-starvation, I believed that if I just became small enough, then people would accept and love me, and throughout my skin battles I believed that everything would be all right when my skin cleared up. The truth is, it was neither my flesh nor my blemishes that were causing my pain. My suffering had only ever emerged in response to living as a false self. I oscillated back and forth on this one in the early stages, spending a few hours on the Internet researching acne or cutting out yet another food group before remembering that these things were not the real battle and were never, therefore, going to take me beyond my agony. For decades, I had been going about things the wrong way around. I thought that when my physical body changed, I would be content with who I was. In fact, when greater contentment came through living life as my true Self and relinquishing my identification with my appearance, my physical body became wholly acceptable to me, whether it was peppered with acne or was a few pounds heavier or not.

I had already been meditating for years, but began to make it an integral part of my life at this time. I took up yoga, which brought me viscerally back into my body and helped me to connect with the flesh I had tried to beat down and disown for so long. As I woke up to my physical sensations, I realised that I had spent decades feeling constantly afraid and chillingly numb, often wondering if I was actually human at all, since I felt so intensely hollow and lifeless inside. I was consummately cut off from my emotions and unable to orientate myself towards present-moment experience, resulting in a state of almost constant semi-dissociation. When I finally acknowledged each of these aspects, it became very clear to me that I was, indeed, traumatised, and would need to address this trauma in my body, the place where it lives.

Insecurely attached as I already was, an uninvited incident of a sexual nature involving a fellow inpatient on a psychiatric children's ward, which, thankfully, fell considerably short of rape, was, nevertheless, highly traumatic for me, and certainly involved a state of frozen terror during which I was completely unable to move or call out for help in any way. My hospital admissions, a serious suicide attempt, and being repeatedly force-fed were also traumas of their own which layered unapologetically on to my existing attachment-based pain. A vital element in my assimilation of these experiences was the compassionate exploration of the inner landscape of my body through yoga. This exquisite form of mindful movement helped me to relearn acceptance and tolerance of all emotion-based ambiences within my body without becoming engulfed by them. In this way, I reintegrated the disowned sensations of fear, paralysis, shame, and helplessness and, by allowing them to have life, found that I was once again able to have life also. When I managed to reside in this place of aware acceptance, my over-identification with my body hurtled towards even greater evaporation. I increasingly remembered that I am not the seen, or even the seer, but the awareness behind both.

I found myself writing a lot of poetry at this time, which was wonderfully cathartic and incredibly healing. I entitled one later such poem simply *Mother*:

> I am thirty-one
> and sometimes in the night I call for my mother.
> I am dreaming.

A narrow staircase, woollen socks
scratching at the ankle
where my birthmark sits,
shaped like the wing of a bird.
I climb and I wonder where I am going to,
so tired, one metal leg
in front of the other,
aching for the end.

I am climbing and I am lying,
face pressed hard against the pillow,
hair stuck to my forehead, feet peeping out
from below the covers,
each foot in a different world.
Then I hear it; a voice,
my voice,
shrill and frightened like a bird clipped of its wings
in mid-flight.
I am calling,
calling for her.
'Mummy' I weep, like a tiny child.
'Mummy'.

The duvet is tumbling down on me, the whole world
tumbling down on me
and all I want are her arms,
wrapped tightly around my shoulders
to hold the pieces of me together.

She does not come.

I wake and my husband is holding me.
'I am here', his voice is gentle as the moon.
I clasp his silent back and breathe in
his solid heartbeat, his steady frame.
'You were calling for your Mother'
he says.

'I know'.

I look over his shoulder
for her.

I have spent endless hours saturated in total self-hatred and suffocating guilt over the myriad of self-destructive behaviours I have engaged in over the years. I had such an idyllic childhood in so many ways, and parents who would have turned the whole world upside-down for me. My mother and father are the most loving people I have ever known. Yet, I have gradually come to understand that, regardless of the degree, any suppression of the true Self is enough to devastate us, particularly in early childhood when we so often ill-fatedly accept as truth close to everything we are told and assimilate unthinkingly the subtle messages permeating the ways in which we are treated.

The process of allowing and embracing my emotions was not enough in and of itself. I could only move fully beyond the battle against my body when I finally let go of the belief that I am somehow innately bad and intrinsically unlovable. It was as simple and as complex as this. When I fully understood that I am inherently good as I am and ultimately only responsible for my own self-worth, I was able to transition into the world as a person in my own right, as a woman who knew she had nothing to prove and everything to live for. Only then was I able to fling off the cultural myth that beauty is needed in order to gain the love of those around us. Only then did I realise that unconditional self-love was the only true lack in my life. My mum has always loved me an inordinate amount and I, in turn, have always loved her intensely. Yet, when false self meets false self eye-to-eye, this love can get scrambled, lost, and sometimes even forgotten. Now, as true Self more regularly meets true Self, my mum and I are gradually remembering how to love each other and ourselves again. Bit by bit, we are learning how to be with one another without muddling our needs up with this love. These days, we are beginning to own our own wholeness and are increasingly aware of where each one of us ends and the other begins.

I now know that I have played a part in my mum's healing, as she has, indeed, been a central driving force in mine. When we remember and return to our true Selves, we can go back to the people with whom we have struggled armed with a liberating message to share with them. We can serve as eloquent reminders to our loved ones that they have nothing to prove and are inherently good and always have been. Thus, the student becomes the teacher. And both are set free.

When I entered fully into my pain and allowed my emotions to surface, the darkness did not consume me as I feared it would, but instead wrapped itself around my false self until it could barely be seen. I stopped trying to impress people. I heard the voices of my childhood and the beckonings of society imploring me to be one way and thanked them for their suggestion before exploring my own heart's deepest desire and following that, even if it meant going against everyone's expectations. I truly began to follow my bliss and slowly relearn what moves, inspires, provokes, and delights me. As I entered my thirties, I took the career ladder down from the wall and gave up my well-paid but stifling job, retrained as a therapeutic yoga practitioner, wrote poetry in the middle of the night, set up my own little mindfulness business, made authentic connections by finally letting down my previously impenetrable guard, studied psychology and spirituality, collected beautiful pieces of fabric and sewed them together simply because it pleased me, and generally tried to do the opposite of whatever fear told me to do. I also began to eat what I fancied as opposed to what I had pre-determined was "allowed" and rediscovered the absolute joy of sharing a slice of cheesecake with someone you love. At first, this kind of Self-listening and spontaneity felt like an ill-fitting dress, yet, over time, it began to become second nature, as, indeed, it would have been when I was a young child.

The true Self has no need of fulfilling other people's expectations. It has no desire to prove itself or to be anything it is not. The true Self knows itself as the one who listens to the mind but is vaster than the mind, as the one who observes the appearance of the body but is not this appearance. A beautiful practice is to look at oneself in the mirror and seek the "I" perceiving the reflection. If the body is being perceived, the body itself cannot be the perceiver. If the mind is being perceived, the mind itself cannot be the perceiver. Where, then, is this perceiver? Who is it? If we reside in this place of awareness, we often find that our identification with the appearance of the body melts away. We may then come to an experience of ourselves as someone infinitely greater than anything that can be seen. We may remember that we are not the object but the perceiver of the object. We are the awareness itself.

When I was personally able to sense this (aided greatly by some of the practices suggested in Appendix III), I no longer felt the need to battle against my mind and body, since I no longer ascribed any of my identity there. I passionately believe that we can stop our suffering right now, if we are only willing to let go of the false selves we have so carefully manufactured in the quest to secure the love of those around us. Picture yourself at the end of your life and ask yourself if covering up and despising your true nature was a good use of your time here on earth. Ask yourself if you wish to go to your grave, as Henry David Thoreau lamented, with your song still in you. Ask yourself if those lonely hours in front of the mirror, those gnawing days of hunger, that rejection of love and of people and of life was worth it. Then come back to the present day and give yourself a hug. You are good as you are. You always have been, from the moment you were born. You were only ever called to be your true Self and to live life fully and vibrantly as this Self. Is there any other way to live?

> The time will come
> when, with elation
> you will greet yourself arriving
> at your own door, in your own mirror
> and each will smile at the other's welcome,
>
> and say, sit here. Eat.
> You will love again the stranger who was your self.
> Give wine. Give bread. Give back your heart
> to itself, to the stranger who has loved you
>
> all your life, whom you ignored
> for another, who knows you by heart.
> Take down the love letters from the bookshelf,
>
> the photographs, the desperate notes,
> peel your own image from the mirror.
> Sit. Feast on your life.
>
> (Walcott, 1962, p. 328)

PART III
APPENDICES

"Identity is a set of beliefs, not the immutable contents of a person's soul. Personal and social transformation requires us to claim our identities fully and proudly and to cast off piece by piece any ways the identities have limited what we believe to be possible for ourselves and other(s)"

(Shuster, 1992, p. 148)

Taking action

"Caring for myself is not self-indulgence, it is self-preservation, and that is an act of political warfare"

(Lorde, 2009 p. 81)

W e have considered how returning to an awareness of our true Selves can help us to move beyond appearance struggles and embrace the knowledge that we are good as we are. Armed with this knowledge, we are better equipped to address the systemic elements of our appearance distress. Until we remember that we are so much more than our bodies, we cannot really implore society convincingly to do the same. Until we are willing to face the pain inside of us, we cannot really hope to address the pain in our families, societies, and culture at large. On a practical level we are also unlikely to have the energy to ignite social change if all of our energies are wrapped up in vicious circles of appearance battles.

Nutrition

"If you don't look after your body, where are you going to live?" (Anon)

The first step in the process of addressing appearance difficulties at a systemic level is to become a living, breathing example of un-abashed self-care. I spent many years at a chronically low weight trying to help others to move beyond their appearance distress. I was, in short, a terrible example and did not provide the beacon of hope so many people entrenched in appearance battles so desperately crave. When I achieved a healthy weight, stopped self-harming, and began to nurture and nourish my physical body, other people began to sit up and pay attention to what I had to say. Only then was I truly able to provide support from an authentic place of self-love, as opposed to a place of confused desperation. Only then was I able to dependably call upon society to address its own appearance-based obsessions.

Our first responsibility, then, is always to ourselves. When we reside in a place of awareness, we are likely to be naturally compelled to take better care of our bodies, to listen to its cues and to understand the deeper yearnings beneath our self-destructive behaviours. This will manifest in different ways for different people . . . because we are all unique! What is the best course of action for one person will be unhelpful to another. We cannot hope for rule books or recovery maps, therefore, but can only return to the innate wisdom of our own awareness, of our own bodies. I write from experience when I say that trying to make recovery follow one particular path might lead to extended pain.

Nourishing and embracing our bodies is the most effective way of igniting change in the area of appearance-focused struggles in our family systems and in society as a whole. Gandhi implored us to "be the change you want to see in the world". If we want the world to become a place in which people respect and celebrate their own bodies, then we must first respect and love the body that has been given to us.

Our bodies have some basic requirements. They need to be ade-quately nourished in order to function effectively. We saw in Chapter Three what huge ramifications a semi-starvation diet had on the psychologically robust men selected for the Minnesota Study, a diet which, incidentally, was based on the daily consumption of around

1,800 calories, a figure far above what some of us on diets and/or engaged in disordered eating behaviours allow ourselves. As Janet Treasure, a British psychiatrist and one of the world's leading experts on eating disorders, explains, the brain alone needs at least 500 calories a day to function, never mind the requirements of other body systems. Without this baseline amount of nutrition, the brain begins to shrink, with areas such as the cortex (which regulates emotions and enables empathy) becoming diminished (Laird-Birmingham & Treasure, 2010). These brain changes can cause a person to become very focused on minute detail, often losing sight of the bigger picture, with tendencies towards perfectionism becoming even more rigid.

We need to deem ourselves worthy before we can help others return to their own worthiness. We declare this worthiness by refusing to diet, to restrict, to control, and to fear our food and our bodies. We assert this worthiness by relinquishing our constant quest for the supreme diet and, instead, return to the wisdom of our own physiologies. We accept that our particular body will have particular needs and will not be shy in telling us. My body personally told me in no uncertain terms that I needed fat and protein. I only wish I had not ignored it for so many years.

If we have engaged in dieting practices for any length of time, it can be difficult to return to a more intuitive way of eating. Within any emergence from a period of self-starvation, the question of "What should I eat?" can become all the more confusing. It might take time to tune into our body signals again. As we saw in the Keys study, it took an average of five months for the men to experience normal hunger and satiation signals after the semi-starvation diet had ended.

In time, it is indeed possible to remember how to listen and respond to the body's signals. In the interim, dieticians, nutritionists, and naturopaths might be able to offer advice and support around meal-planning and so on. It is important to be honest with these professionals about any disordered eating history and continuing appearance distress.

Cosmetics

"Beauty is not in the face; beauty is a light in the heart" (Kannings, 2015, p. 1)

The sister of the dieting industry is surely the cosmetics industry. We can become further advocates, therefore, of the true Self beyond the physical body by also rejecting societal ideals and expectations on this front. This does not have to mean relinquishing make-up and other associated practices entirely. For some of us at least, applying and wearing cosmetics can be fun, playful, and a means of self-expression. It might serve us, however, to be honest about how attached to cosmetics we might have become, particularly if we have been experiencing appearance-related distress. As I explained in Chapter Twelve, I became hugely reliant on my concealer at one point, which only served to further heighten my focus on my physical appearance. The more time I spent in front of the mirror applying my concealer, the more blemishes I discovered and the bigger and more distressing they seemed to become. When I finally threw my concealer in the bin, I negated this daily battle and finally felt as though people were responding to the real me, as opposed to a carefully airbrushed version of me created by layers of concealer and hours of doctoring in front of the looking glass.

It is certainly important to our health and well-being to exercise some discrimination when selecting cosmetic products, many of which contain extremely toxic and harmful substances. The whitening mercury soaps we discussed in Chapter Six are only the tip of the iceberg and many everyday chemist-shelf products are laced with chemicals we would not ordinarily dream of slathering on our bodies. The skin is our largest organ and is highly permeable, with the body absorbing about 60% of whatever we apply to it. The majority of synthetic chemicals contained within cosmetics have not been adequately tested and can potentially wreak all manner of havoc on our internal systems. A good rule of thumb is not to put anything on your skin that you would not put into your mouth. The Campaign for Safe Cosmetics (www.safecosmetics.org) is an outstanding resource for checking the safety of your chosen cosmetic products and finding safer alternatives. The website also contains opportunities for involvement including a range of online petitions.

I decided, as an experiment, to forgo my make-up, which mostly only ever consists of mascara and occasional eye-liner, for the forty days of Catholic Lent in 2013. I thought my endeavour would be a walk in the park, yet was surprised at the plethora of emotions and niggling discomforts such a simple relinquishment brought up: *Did I look feminine enough? Would people think I wasn't "making an effort" at social occasions? Did I look too young to be teaching teenagers? Did my husband find me less attractive?* When I allowed myself to feel and move through these fears, I, too, experienced a great sense of liberation at not having to apply mascara each morning and a surprising depth of peace related to leaving the house as "me as I am" as opposed to "me as I have created myself to be". These days, I feel much less attached to my eye make-up and feel equally at ease leaving the house with or without it.

Exercise

"A strong body makes the mind strong". (Jefferson, 1785)

We can also practise and inspire self-respect by providing our bodies with the physical activity they need and crave. The human organism was not designed to sit all day in front of a computer screen, yet this is exactly what a significant proportion of jobs in the modern-age demand. We can choose to centre our exercise-related goals around weight loss, body perfection, and other similar strivings (goals which will do nothing to challenge beauty stereotypes or shake up society in any way), or we can choose to exercise for reasons of enjoyment, increased functionality, and self-care. Such exercise not only benefits our bodies, but can also have a profound impact on our sense of well-being and aid in community building.

Recently, I had the absolute pleasure of attending the "Eat Breathe Thrive" training with Chelsea Roff, which aims to explore how yoga, service, and community can be used to cultivate a healthier relationship to food, body, and self. Chelsea Roff, the impassioned and highly dynamic founder, has personally moved beyond years of body battles. 'At the height of her struggle she was offered weekly therapy by a psychologist, who suggested that she try yoga. By her own admission, Chelsea agreed to the idea as a bid to burn more calories, but her yoga practice very quickly became so much more than this. She explains,

> I hated my body because I hated myself, not the other way around. And much as I wish it could have, inpatient treatment alone couldn't change that. Treatment, in many ways, put a Band-Aid on a wound too deep to see from the surface. I was taught to eat when I wasn't

hungry, to think rationally rather than give in to my feelings, to stop looking in the mirror altogether so I wouldn't sabotage myself. To survive, I had to disconnect from my body and my emotions, because at the time I didn't have the inner-resources to cope with them.

Treatment did indeed save my life. But to move beyond merely surviving—to thrive, to live fully, to be happy—I had to integrate my body in the healing process. That, for me, is where yoga was an absolute godsend. Yoga taught me to relate to my body as an ally rather than an enemy, as a gateway to intimacy and connection with others and, perhaps most importantly, it helped me cultivate the skills I needed to be with emotions I'd nearly killed myself trying to stave off. (Roff, 2015a).

Assured of her own goodness, Chelsea reached out to others with similar experiences and stands as a beacon of hope for people entrenched in their appearance battles. She went on to set up a clinical programme offering "Yoga for Eating Disorders" in hospitals, treatment programmes, and community settings. For Chelsea, community building is a core factor in recovery from appearance struggles. She explains,

In many ways, yoga saved my life. The practice gave me a reason to feed my body, taught me to recognise and respond to its needs, provided a safe space where I could learn to be with emotions that I'd almost killed myself trying to stave off. More importantly though, yoga brought me back to people. The desire to practice forced me to leave the house and interact with others, and the community I discovered became a source of support and connection far beyond anything I ever imagined. (Roff, 2015b)

I think every person on this planet would benefit from taking Chelsea's training, which is exquisitely focused on connecting us all to the light of our true Selves. Some example exercises from the "Eat Breathe Thrive" programme can be found on the outstanding "Eat Breathe Thrive" app, which is completely free to download.

Movement can take many forms and we will all inevitably enjoy different types in different ways. As with all things, it makes more sense to go with what we enjoy and with what our heart is calling us towards most convincingly. If we are experiencing muted energy and low mood, more stimulating forms such as running or trampoline-bouncing might be more useful, while a state of anxiety might benefit from more parasympathetic-enhancing and calming practices such as tai chi. Team sports and community exercise classes, as Chelsea has explained, have the additional benefit of creating a sense of belongingness.

For some people experiencing appearance distress, exercise can become an addiction. Returning to more mindful, gentler forms of exercise might help if we find ourselves hurtling down this particular path. I would argue that excessive exercise practices will only occur if we ignore our pain and squash down our emotions instead of inviting and observing them without identification and judgement. If we allow our emotions to surface while we swim/run/dance and so on, we will be less likely to feel compelled to exercise to excess.

A cautionary note should be added here. If there is any active engagement in disordered eating behaviours such as restricting, purging, or laxative abuse, then exercise should be approached with serious caution. Such behaviours can throw our electrolytes completely off balance, thus putting a massive strain on our heart. Exercise, which usually results in an increased heart rate, can be dangerous and even fatal. This is not to say that we should refrain completely from engaging in any movement-based recreation. Rather, we should take great care in the types of exercise we choose and listen closely to our bodies as we engage in such exercise, ideally also taking the time to consult with a healthcare practitioner. Most yoga asanas, for example, can be moved through slowly while lying supine; a practice which, when engaged with alongside conscious breathing and focused attention, can have just as many benefits as upright forms of yoga.

Supporting and overcoming as a family

"One of the most disturbing aspects of the thin-obsessed beauty culture is that it hits children and teens hard—maybe even harder than it hits adults . . . we had to try to find a way to teach our daughters to live with the flood of messages that they weren't thin enough, beautiful enough, smart enough—an impossible task in a culture that routinely tells women that our main (or only) value lies in how we look"

(Brown, 2015, p. 142)

We are wired biologically to care for and protect our offspring. Human evolution, more than any other species, has led to incredible amounts of time and energy being invested in the safety of our young. As we have seen, however, this innate drive to care for and protect is not always as straightforward as we might hope it to be. Parents have difficulties of their own, can be faced with threats to their own security and safety, and might experience challenging life events that have an impact on their children in ways they could have never foreseen. While we have explored attachment issues and early childhood trauma, we have also discussed how appearance difficulties are more complex than being attributable to singular events or relationships. Appearance battles are situated within both a social and societal context which all too frequently fears difference and places unrealistic demands on the physical appearance of our bodies.

As families we are called to take some collective responsibility without shouldering all of the blame and guilt ourselves. Families have been struggling with various issues across the ages, yet appearance difficulties have only emerged in such dramatic numbers fairly recently in human history. As family and friends of people experiencing appearance struggles, therefore, we might also wish to address some of the wider societal issues, perhaps by using some of the suggestions in the previous appendix.

Mindfulness practices and techniques can also be adopted on a whole-family level to soothe and address appearance distress. According to Fletcher and Hayes (2005), change can be fostered by six highly interrelated processes: acceptance, defusion, contact with the present moment, self-as-context, and committed action. We shall now take each of these in turn and consider how they could be utilised systemically.

Acceptance

Acceptance is the moment-by-moment process of actively embracing every occurrence without unnecessary attempts to change anything. When we refuse to accept that an appearance battle is taking place, an unfortunate by-product is that we might also fail to accept intrinsic elements of the person. Far too frequently, we throw the baby out with the bathwater. An appearance struggle is not an external demon that needs to be exorcised, as is so very often the stance taken by the psychiatric community. As we have seen, any appearance distress is a metaphor for the person's experiences and feelings and, as such, is fundamentally a part of them at the time. Both the metaphor and the person's story require airtime and acceptance before we can move on to unpicking and tackling the deeper wounds.

We begin to accept an appearance difficulty when we stop burying our heads in the sand and take a long, unflinching look at what is taking place. If our brother is starving himself, we observe as he piles his plate with only lettuce for lunch and refrain from averting our gaze from his increasingly jutting bones. If our daughter is picking her skin, we admit to ourselves that she is spending longer and longer in front of the mirror and that her skin looks raw and sore. It never fails to amaze me just how effectively so many of us manage to fool ourselves and how emphatically we refuse to see what is happening in front of our very eyes. The earlier appearance battles are noted and addressed, the more positive the long-term trajectory tends to be. Recovery from diagnosed anorexia, for example, becomes much less likely the longer the associated behaviours persist (van Holle et al., 2008).

Once we have been courageous enough to truly see what is happening, acceptance then implores us to *talk about it*. The importance of this seemingly simple step cannot be over-emphasised. It is impossible to estimate how much pain and anguish could have been avoided in so many families if we had only found the strength to discuss openly what was going on. The sooner we can have these frank discussions, the more unlikely an appearance difficulty is to erupt into a full-scale disaster. This involves talking about what is happening openly and non-judgementally within our families and also within wider connections, such as our extended families and friendship circles. The temptation can be, often due to shame and guilt, to both ignore and deny what is happening and to work very hard at keeping the appearance battle a "family secret". Such secrets can only ever serve to make everyone involved feel increasingly shameful and even stigmatised on account of their struggles.

Defusion

Defusion techniques stem from the idea that we have a tendency to over-identify with our thoughts and amplify them to become the "truth". In becoming so attached, or fused, to our thoughts, they become extremely powerful. Defusion is the process of understanding (or, more accurately, remembering) that our thoughts are just thoughts. Thoughts only hold the reality we give them. Harris (2009) describes defusion as: looking *at* thoughts rather than *from* thoughts; noticing thoughts rather than becoming caught up in thoughts; letting thoughts come and go rather than holding on to them.

Defusion can be most effectively accomplished by creating contexts that reduce the stimulus functions transformed by thought. For example, we might give our thoughts a shape, colour, and weight; listen to them as though listening to the radio; label the ongoing process of thinking itself (e.g., "I am having the thought that I am ugly") or repeat a word many times, rather like a mantra (Masuda et al., 2004). Rather than attempting to get rid of thoughts or attack their form logically, these techniques aim to reduce their literal believability.

Supporting someone engaged in an appearance battle can be extremely stressful and we could have become caught up in unhelpful thinking patterns ourselves, giving our own thoughts too much power. When we engage with the appearance battle with increased clarity of thought (perhaps through the adoption of some of these defusion techniques), we are in a better to position to offer useful support. We can then model these processes explicitly within our families: for example, "I am having the thought that you are touching your skin too often", as opposed to a more "attacking" exchange such as "You are making me really angry when you keep touching your face so much".

Another useful defusion technique is that of mirroring. The discovery of mirror neurons has greatly aided our understanding of empathy, which is the experience of entering into the feelings and experience of the other. When we mirror the words and actions of another, we validate the other person's beingness and, thus, provide a forum for their true Self to be present in the interaction. We mirror by entering into the world of our loved one, repeating their utterances back to them (in their own words) and allowing our movements and expressions to follow theirs. Part of this process is necessarily the relinquishment of over-identification with our own thoughts and opinions. The key is to become solely focused on the reality of the other person as opposed to our own ideas and judgements. You might be surprised at the depth of connection felt by both parties when such mirroring becomes part of the interaction and by how quickly conflict situations can be defused.

Contact with the present moment

Contact with the present moment involves moving one's attention to what is happening in the here-and-now. This includes contacting both internal stimuli, such as bodily sensations, thoughts, and feelings, and external stimuli coming in through our senses. Ideally, we observe the reactions that emerge from these stimuli as continuously changing experiences in an ongoing process of knowing ourselves, without attaching any judgements to them. This contact can be practised by ourselves individually and also within our families by refusing to get lost in fears about the future and ruminations over the past. While the past may almost certainly need to be addressed in some way, it can be very unhelpful to become stuck as family units in vicious circling around past events. It is important as a family to engage in the present moment and to notice and acknowledge anything that might be currently feeding into any struggles.

Returning to the present moment when family conflicts emerge can also be incredibly healing. In practice, we could try the following:

- Putting small silences in-between our exchanges (following the example of the Quakers). When one person has finished talking, the listener or listeners agree to hold a minute's silence, for example, before they respond to what has been said. This minute is used to come back into the body, into the room, and become grounded in the present moment, perhaps by noticing inner bodily sensations, practising deep breathing, and so on.
- Practising seeing and hearing the other person as if for the first time. Throughout our lives, we are constantly interacting with others through the smog of our past experiences with them, thus losing sight of the totality of who they are in the moment. When we see a person afresh with each and every word they speak, we enter into a full and authentic experience of them, enabling us to respond with greater compassion.
- Halting an argument or difficult discussion to engage in a mindful activity together. This could involve a breathing exercise, some yoga asanas, or even taking a mindful walk. Depending on your relationship with the other person, mindful touch can be particularly valuable here, which should again ideally be conducted in silence in order to transmute the modality of communication. Massage, hair-brushing, or a gentle foot-rub are just a few possibilities. Agree to put the discussion on hold for the next ten minutes, for example, while you engage in this silent activity, after which time the conversation may be resumed if you still feel there is more to be said.

- Practise eye gazing. When we are locked in conflict with another, we cease to truly see them as we become so entrenched in our own frame of reference. Again, take a break from the verbal exchange, sit opposite the other person, and take at least three minutes to do nothing other than gaze into their eyes as they gaze into yours. Do not look around the room, fiddle, or distract in any way. Focus fully on the other person and keep your mind particularly absorbed in the similarities between you. Allow yourself to feel a sense of connection to this person beyond any of your conditioning and egoic ideas.

Self as context

We have explored a notion of the Self as something transcending thought, feeling, and even time. This Self, the true Self, is vaster than our experiences and thoughts and is completely peaceful and accepting at its core. In some spiritual circles, it has been described as nothing/everything. If we can retain this sense of a transcendent Self within our families, we are less likely to identify with a conceptualised self (e.g., "I am a bad mother"; "I am the black sheep of the family") or as a conceptualised family-self (e.g., "We are a dysfunctional family"; "We are a high-achieving family"). The self-concept of the family as a unit is very likely to strongly feed into the self-concept of each member individually. Within my own family unit, for example, we had built up a collective self-concept that could be described as "We are an exemplary family". An element of my appearance battles was indeed about becoming an exemplary person in some way in order to fit in and obtain their love.

If we are able to return to an open and fluid family-self, we can encourage and more easily invite each family member to do the same. I personally found it much easier to accept my true Self when my family as a collective had taken on the new stance of "We are good as a family as we are".

Values

According to Fletcher and Hayes (2005), values are chosen life directions that differ from goals in that they are not objects to be attained, but, rather, ongoing patterns of purposeful action. If we are able as families to choose life directions that are meaningful, we are more easily able to disengage from behaviours based on social compliance and avoidance, both of which are frequently rife in someone with appearance distress. How often do we stop to consider what our family values are and take time to think about how we can live them out? If you had asked my family about their values, they would have almost certainly spoken about happiness and self-fulfilment, yet the patterns we were caught up in were hurtling us in the opposite direction. We had not actively identified, as a family, which actions we would need to take in order to facilitate such values. These might have included:

> Giving equal time and importance to academia and hobbies.
> Holding different preferences in equal esteem.
> Promoting self-expression through dialogue, family activities, enablement of free-expression and so on.

Committed action

Once we have identified our value-consistent desires as a family, we can then move towards committed action, which involves the creation of concrete and attainable short-, medium- and long-term goals. If our value is open communication, for example, two avenues of committed action might be expressing our emotions regularly and making time each day to listen to one another. It is useful to explicitly discuss both our values and the actions we can employ to this end as a family, perhaps within a family meeting. As we support a family member engaged in an appearance battle, these values and actions are likely to be helpful regardless of whether or not they are explicitly linked to the appearance struggle. In my own family, for example, making the decision to value each person's interests in equal measure to their academic achievements was actioned by arranging leisure pursuits. I chose to continue my earlier piano lessons, which I had given up in favour of excessive homework. The piano had always been, and once again became, a great source of self-esteem for me. Committed action might also involve accessing outside help, such as family therapy.

* * *

The importance of non-judgement is embedded within each of these areas. Appearance battles are centred around an individual who, for whatever reasons, has judged themselves to be inadequate in some way. The more non-judgement we can exercise as families, the more space we provide for each member to fully accept himself. Such non-judgement also extends to the appearance battle itself, which we may have judged as being abhorrent and despicable. Not only could the person with the appearance-related distress view any such judgement as a direct attack on herself, but, furthermore, as we have seen, the appearance struggle is not bad in and of itself but, rather, a messenger to deeper processes within. If we destroy the messenger without hearing the message, the truth will find another way to be heard and one battle is likely to be replaced with another. In this way, we might end up watching one presentation and one diagnosis stumble haplessly into another.

A battle against the body delivers a clear message in no uncertain terms. We are invited to ask ourselves as families how we can heed this message and work together towards a future within which each person is valued, esteemed, understood, and unconditionally loved.

> I find that when I am closest to my inner, intuitive self, when I am somehow in touch with the unknown in me, when perhaps I am in a slightly altered state of consciousness, then whatever I do seems to be full of healing. Then, simply, my presence is releasing and healing to the other. (Rogers, 1980, p. 129)

Mindfulness and body awareness practices for appearance struggles

"You have to ask yourself the question 'Who am I?' This investigation will lead in the end to the discovery of something within you, which is behind the mind. Solve that great problem and you will solve all other problems"

(Sri Ramana Maharshi, 1988, p. 60)

"Who says 'I' inside this body? Does it have an age, a size, a gender? Find this out with full devotion and attention. Now is the auspicious moment for this discovery"

(Mooji, 2014, p. 27)

I deally, we would live in a society less obsessed with external appearances. Since we do not, these mindfulness exercises may support you in living beyond the beauty myths we are fed so prolifically. When we step outside of these societal untruths and return to the awareness of our own goodness, we are also more likely to be able to tackle any systemic issues, perhaps by exploring family-related matters or campaigning for more realistic beauty standards in wider society.

Basic awareness mediation: Self-enquiry

Sri Ramana Maharshi, widely acknowledged as one of the most inspiring Hindu gurus of modern times, maintained that Self-realisation can be brought about by giving up the idea that there is an individual self which functions through the body and the mind. When asked to prescribe a spiritual practice that would facilitate such Self-awareness, Maharshi recommended a technique he called Self-enquiry, which became the cornerstone of his practical philosophy.

Self-enquiry is concerned with separating the subject "I" from the objects of thought it has identified with. Since the individual I-thought cannot exist without an object, if attention is focused on the subjective feeling of "I" or "I am", then the thoughts "I am this" or "I am that" will not arise. If this awareness of "I" is sustained, the individual I-thought will disappear and will be replaced with a direct experience of the Self. Sri Ramana Maharshi advised maintaining awareness of the "I"-thought until it dissolves in the source from which it came. He explained,

> From where does this "I" arise? Seek for it within; it then vanishes. This is the pursuit of wisdom. When the mind unceasingly investigates its own nature, it transpires that there is no such thing as mind. This is the direct path for all. The mind is merely thoughts. Of all thoughts, the thought 'I' is the root. Therefore the mind is only the thought "I". (Sri Ramana Maharshi, 1988, p. 50)

> . . . After the "I"-thought has arisen, the wrong identity with the body arises. Get rid of the "I"-thought. So long as "I" is alive there is grief. When "I" ceases to exist there is no grief. (Sri Ramana Maharshi, 1988, p. 51)

To engage in Self-enquiry, find a quiet space and put your full attention on the inner feeling of "I". Hold on to this feeling for as long as possible. If your attention is distracted by other thoughts, gently bring your attention back to the awareness of "I". To aid in this process, you might want to ask yourself "Who am I?", or "Where does this 'I' come from?" In the early stages, it might feel as though the practice of attention to the "I" is a mental activity which takes the form of a thought. As the practice develops, however, the thought "I" gives way to a subjective feeling. When this feeling ceases to identify with thoughts and objects, it disappears. What is then likely to remain is an experience of the Self as pure awareness. Repeated experience of this state is said to weaken the mental tendency to identify with the mind and the body, resulting in a state of deep Self-realisation.

If this still feels a little complicated, perhaps this simple explanation of Self-enquiry by Mooji might help:

> Begin like this: I am. I exist. This is the most natural recognition and knowledge. The sense of existence is spontaneously felt in you as "I am". No one taught this to you. Be aware of this simple intuition, without associating it with other thoughts. Feel how it is to be simply present in this instant, without holding onto any intention. Don't touch any thought of doing something special. Keep inwardly quiet. If suddenly a wave of thoughts should come, don't panic. There is no need to control or suppress them. Simply let them play without your involvement. Observe with detachment. Remain empty of intention. Keep quiet.
>
> . . . Now observe the observer. "Who am I?" Check inwardly but remain quiet with alert attention. Don't collect any answer or clues; an answer would and could only be an opinion, an idea or another concept. Don't tie yourself to any concept. Turn the attention away from objects towards the viewing subject. What and where is the seer? Remain silent and neutral. There should now be an increased strength of focus in the looking.
>
> Now, again, watch the sense "I am". What is "I"? From where does it arise? Watch. What do you find?
>
> It cannot be found. It does not exist!
>
> It cannot be found objectively. Nevertheless, the "I" sense or intuition continues to be present. It is the non-finding of "I", phenomenally, that proves its non-objective existence.
>
> "I" or "I am" is found to be without form, an intuition arising from, in, and as emptiness. Without focused inquiry, "I" appears to be an entity comprised of body and conditioned mind. When searched for as a form, it is found to be merely a thought; the form of "I" is thought. Formless, it arises from emptiness as the intuitive sense of subjective presence.
>
> Now that "I" is found to be formless presence, what recognises this? Does this possess form?
>
> Inquire like this. (Mooji, 2014, p. 1)

Breathing exercises (Pranayama)

The word "spirit" comes from the Latin *spiritus*, meaning "breath". In India, the breath is known as *Brahmachaitanya*, meaning "the breath of God". Breath is our connection to life, to spirit, and to Self, as we explored in Chapter Ten. Connecting to the breath is an important method for becoming present. When we breathe consciously, we activate the more evolved areas of the brain in the cerebral cortex that balance our emotions, with the slowing of breath having a soothing effect on our emotional state. The length and quality of our breath, as we have seen, also affects our vagus nerve, which sits just behind the throat, and acts as a "switch" between our sympathetic ("fight or flight") and parasympathetic ("rest and digest") autonomic nervous systems.

With all breathing exercises, it is recommended to sit with an upright spine, in a comfortable position. Alternatively, one can lie flat on the ground or bed, with the head lightly supported and the spine straight. Despite these recommendations, these breathing exercises can, in fact, be done anywhere and in all manner of positions.

Long, deep breathing

In yoga, breathing exercises are known as pranayama, a word comprising two roots: prana, meaning vital energy or life force, and yama, meaning regulation, extension, expansion. Thus, pranayama means to regulate, extend, and expand the dimension of vital energy.

With long, deep breathing, the whole breath is done very slowly and consciously, solely through the nose. Inhale, and slowly move your belly outwards, thus drawing your diaphragm down. Allow first your lower ribs and then your upper ribs to expand, filling the lungs to their full capacity with air.

Now, exhale, slowly moving your belly in. Contract your lower ribs and then your upper ribs for a full exhalation. Then slowly and mindfully repeat. Ensure that the length of your exhale is about the same length as your inhale, although make the in-breath longer if you want to stimulate the sympathetic nervous system (useful for low-mood, lethargy, etc.), or the out-breath longer if you wish to promote parasympathetic activity (useful for anxiety, etc.). Some people find it helpful to count or repeat a mantra on each inhalation and exhalation.

Ujjayi breathing

Ujjayi breath is commonly translated as "victorious breath", but is sometimes called "ocean breath" because the sound created by the gentle contraction of the laryngeal muscles and partial closure of the glottis is reminiscent of the sound of the sea. This slow breath technique (ideally, two to four breaths per minute) has a balancing effect on the entire cardio-respiratory system, thus aiding the release of anxiety.

Begin by taking an inhalation that is slightly deeper than usual. With your mouth closed, exhale through your nose while constricting, or "valving", your throat muscles. It might help to imagine that you are steaming up a mirror as though your mouth were open. If done correctly, your breath should indeed sound rather like the waves of the ocean. Once you have mastered this on the exhale, use the same method for the inhale.

Three-part breath

Three-part breathing is like filling your lungs as you fill a glass of water, from the bottom up, and is helpful for bringing yourself into a state of relaxation. You begin by breathing slowly into the low belly (just below the belly button), then into the low chest (lower part of the rib cage) and finally into the low throat (just above the top of the sternum). The exhalation then begins in the low throat, moves to the low chest and finishes in the low belly. This breath can take a little practice and it might be helpful at first to rest your hands on the individual positions on your body to feel the breath rising and falling in each place.

Alternate nostril breathing

Alternate nostril breathing is thought to harmonise the two hemispheres of the brain, resulting in a balanced physical, mental, and emotional state of well-being. First, block your right nostril with your right index finger and take a long, slow inhale through your left nostril. Then block your left nostril with your left index finger and exhale slowly through your right nostril. Now breathe in from your right nostril, block and breathe out from your left. Continue inhaling and exhaling from alternate nostrils, remembering to breathe in from the same nostril from which you just exhaled. You can also take a particular hand gesture, or *mudra*, such as *Vishnu mudra*, to facilitate the passage of air through the nostrils. For *Vishnu mudra*, bend the first two fingers of the right hand into the palm, using the thumb to control the passage of breath through the right nostril and the ring (third) finger to control the passage of air through the left nostril. As you become more experienced, it is also possible to practise the breath without the use of your fingers, simply blocking off alternate nostrils at will.

Kapalabhati

This is a rapid, rhythmic, and continuous breath which is excellent for lifting mood and energy levels. It is equal on the inhale and exhale with no pause in between, practised solely through the nostrils with the mouth closed. Begin on an exhale, expelling the breath powerfully through the nose by pressing the naval point back towards the spine. To inhale, the upper abdomen muscles relax, the diaphragm extends down and the breath will come in naturally. This breath should ideally contain around 2–3 cycles per second.

Yoga

It took me a long time personally to engage in a yoga practice, despite having read about it copiously and having meditated for years, because I wrongly assumed that the practice would largely focus on the correct form of the asanas. I feared I would be compromised in achieving the physical elements of yoga due to poor flexibility and brittle-bone-related effects. I am, sadly, not alone in such fears and assumptions, yet the practice of yoga is concerned neither with flexibility nor physical exercise. It is not the movement itself, but the attention we bring to the movement which transforms the asanas into yoga, particularly the attention we bring to the breath. There are many forms of yoga and I would highly recommend trying a number of different disciplines to find a practice best suited to you and your needs. Some forms of yoga are more calming and promote the activity of the parasympathetic nervous system, while others are highly stimulating and kick-start sympathetic arousal. I personally find that Kundalini yoga suits me very well most of the time as I am prone to low mood and energy. My body, therefore, revels in the repetitive, stimulating practices of Kundalini and the balance of my nervous system is thereby tipped from a parasympathetic predominance towards more sympathetic activity. The flow of Vinyasa is also a very beautiful and lifting practice for me. When I find myself in high states of arousal and anxiety, however, I have learnt over time that a Kundalini class is far from being useful, at which times I benefit much more from a gentle practice such as Yin or a slow-paced Hatha class.

A specialist yoga institute for the health of the mind also exists, the Minded Institute (www.themindedinstitute.com), which is based in London. The Minded Institute offers both online and face-to-face classes, workshops, and teacher trainings in the applications of yoga for mental health. Special Yoga Foundation (www.specialyoga. org.uk), while primarily a charitable organisation for the training and delivery of yoga therapy for children with special needs, also offers training and workshops in yoga and mental health.

Mindfulness meditation

Self is the awareness of everything that is arising. Becoming mindful can enable us to reside in this awareness instead of identifying our true Selves with external phenomena such as the appearance of the physical body. Mindfulness meditation can take many forms and is always steeped in the physical sensations of the body, since, for each of us, our earliest perceptions and imaginings would have been sensory in content. Here are a few of my favourite such practices.

Mantra meditation

Sit or lie down comfortably with the spine straight. Bring your attention gently to your breathing. Use your breath as your anchor. You may silently repeat a mantra on the inhalation and exhalation. Each time a thought arises, watch it non-judgementally and then bring your attention back to your breathing and/or mantra. I personally have used both *Maranatha* from the Christian tradition, meaning "come

Lord Jesus" and *sa ta na ma* from the Kundalini Yoga tradition, meaning "birth, life, death, re-birth".

Body scan/progressive muscle relaxation

Sit or lie down comfortably, ensuring that your spine is straight. Cover yourself with a blanket if available (our body temperature tends to drop when we enter a state of relaxation) and close your eyes.

Take a few moments to notice the movement of your breath. Deepen your breath, perhaps practising long, deep breathing, ujjayi, or the three-part breath.

When you are settled, bring your attention to the physical sensations in your body, noticing where your body is in contact with the floor/bed/chair and how this feels.

Now bring your attention to your toes. Become aware of each toe and of the space between them. Then continue to move your awareness slowly through your feet and up through your legs. Take the time to become aware of any sensations in your feet and legs, being particularly mindful of any tension you are holding there. Now inhale deeply and imagine the breath passing down from the nostrils and into your legs and feet. On the exhalation, feel the breath move up through your feet and legs and out through the nose. On each exhalation, release any discomfort or tension.

Continue to bring awareness to each part of the rest of your body in turn, working from the tips of your toes up to the top of your head. As you leave each area, inhale and exhale into it and let any discomfort or tension go.

Once you have moved through the entire body (perhaps spending longer on those areas within which you notice the most unease) return again to the sensation of the body as a whole and assess how you are feeling.

Mindful eating

For those of us with a difficult relationship with food, this meditation can be particularly moving. Choose a small morsel of an enjoyed food (for example, a raisin) and take it gently into your hands. Look at it with fresh eyes, as though you have never seen such a food before. Notice its colour, its texture, its temperature, the way it feels against your skin. How heavy is it? Does the light catch it in any particular way?

Explore the raisin like a geologist exploring a newly discovered mineral formation. Roll it gently in your fingers, perhaps squeezing it a little or stroking its surface. Next smell the raisin, taking long deep breaths as you hold it mindfully underneath your nose.

Take the raisin and bring it slowly up to your lips. Notice how it feels next to your lips before putting out your tongue and making contact with it. What sensations do you notice? Do you experience it differently on your tongue than in your fingers? How does your tongue react? Do you notice any reactions in other parts of your body?

Now slowly place the raisin in your mouth, noticing how it feels, how much space it takes up and how it moves in your mouth before taking a mindful bite. Sense the flavours that are released and how these are responded to in your mouth. Do any particular thoughts or sensations come up? Slowly chew your raisin, noticing any changes in consistency and texture.

Next, swallow your raisin and follow it as it moves down your oesophagus. Can you detect the moment of its arrival in your stomach? How does your tongue feel now?

Thank all the occurrences that made it possible for this raisin to come into your hands. Extend gratitude to the ground that nourished the grapevines, the sun that shone down upon it as it grew and those who planted, tended to, and harvested the grapes. Consider the journey this small raisin has made in order to get to you. Bring your attention back to your body now and offer thanks for the simple fact that you can nourish your body and charge it with the energy to live your precious life.

Compassionate visualisations

Visualisations can be incredibly powerful. They are frequently preceded by a progressive muscle relaxation/body scan. I recommend assuming a comfortable seated or supine position, with your spine straight, and completing a full body scan, which will ease you into a heightened state of relaxation, before engaging in any of the following visualisations.

Compassionate self-imagery

Find somewhere peaceful to sit or lie down, where you will not be disturbed. Focus on a few minutes of long, deep breathing or complete a full body scan.

In your mind's eye, see yourself as a deeply compassionate person. Think of all the qualities you have as this compassionate person. See yourself thinking, acting, and feeling compassionately, both towards yourself and towards others. Focus on each quality/facet of this compassion. You might choose kindness, for example, and focus on this sense of kindness which comes from the nature of our lives, of our minds, and of our bodies, which includes a deep knowledge of the nature of suffering. Then move on to other qualities such as strength, empathy, sensitivity, strength, openness, and so on, spending a generous amount of time on each. Explore your body posture and facial expressions as a person with each of these qualities and allow yourself to feel any associated emotions and sensations without judgement.

Finally, move into the sense of a feeling of responsibility. Immerse yourself in the sense of having lost interest in condemning, blaming, and criticising. Hold on to your compassionate facial expression, your relaxed body posture, and your inner warmth.

Compassionate imagery using memory

Seek out somewhere peaceful to sit or lie down, where you will not be disturbed. Focus on a few minutes of long, deep breathing or complete a full body scan.

Focus on allowing your body posture and facial expression to become compassionate. This might involve a relaxed posture and a gentle smile. You might want to try out different facial expressions until you find one that feels warm and natural to you. When you feel ready, bring your mind to the memory of a time when someone was kind to you. Spend some time gazing at the facial expression of the person who was kind to you. Focus on the things the person said and the tone of their voice before immersing yourself in feeling of the emotion within that person. Finally, focus on the entire experience and notice your sense of gratitude and pleasure at being treated in this kind and compassionate way. Spend liberal time with this memory and allow the sense of warmth and of being held and validated to grow.

Mindful writing

I explained in Chapter Twelve how important poetry writing was for me in the assimilation of my rejected emotions. Any form of writing, particularly when undertaken in an aware, mindful state, can open us up to new realisations and aid the integration of past wounds in such a gentle, encompassing way. I have found the following exercise extremely transformative in my own relationship with my body and deeper Self.

Letter to your body

(Adapted from an exercise in the "Eat Breathe Thrive" programme.) After a time of mediation or deep relaxation, take a pen and some paper and find a place where you will not be disturbed for at least half an hour. At the top of your paper write "To my body" and then begin a letter to your body, explaining how you have struggled with it over the years, how it has let you down or betrayed you in any way, and, finally, how it has pleased and served you. Sign off the letter however you feel moved to do so. Hold the letter in your hands and take a few moments to engage in long, deep breathing before reading the letter through again, slowly. When you are ready, take another piece of paper and respond to the letter (i.e., "Dear Nicole" . . . "With love from your body"). Move through any sense of resistance by continuing to write, allowing your thoughts to flow completely uncensored through your hand and on to the paper. You can type on a computer if this is easier and feels more natural to you. Here is a shortened example of such an exchange, but I encourage you to take adequate time over this—the full extent of this exercise for me personally, although it will be different for everyone, spanned almost ten pages.

To my body,

Writing to you is rather painful for me because I have struggled to even look at or acknowledge you for so long. I have wanted you to be different, to be quiet, to disappear. I always yearned for you to be taller and leaner, firmer and less "obvious", but you are so stubborn and have refused to bend to my relentless will. For many years I hated you. I wanted you to look more like my mother's, which always received so many compliments, but you maintained your sturdy legs no matter how hard I tried. I have ignored your needs in my attempts to mould you to look a certain way. For so long I couldn't find any level of contentment with you, no matter how much weight you lost or how much effort I put in to making you look "good".

I marvel at the fact that you have never given up. You are so strong! I have treated you in ways I would never so much as dream of treating another, almost starving and cutting you into complete oblivion. Yet your heart has miraculously continued to beat throughout it all. As much effort as I have ploughed into subduing you, you have plunged an exponentially grander resolve into keeping me alive. You have continuously held me up with those consummately berated legs and taken me everywhere I have wanted to go.

I am so sorry I have hurt you so much. I choose to listen to you and to give you all that you so rightfully deserve. This life is the one time we will be together and this time will be short. I choose to enjoy you, to nourish you, to take care of you and to give you my unconditional attention. Thank you for being with me and for being my wise and beautiful ally.

With love and deep affection,

Nicole

Dear Nicole,

Thank you for your letter. I have waited a very long time to hear such words from you. It was incredibly hard for me to survive with such inadequate nourishment for so many years but I wanted you to live! It has been inordinately hard work just keeping your basic functions going sometimes, let alone giving us the energy to swim and ride your bicycle, to dance and to love. We have been living less than a half-life and have missed out on so much.

It feels so good to finally have the energy to explore and enjoy life and all the magnificent things it has to offer. This is all I ever wanted. I was never interested in how I looked, only in how effectively I could serve you to live the highest version of your true Self. I am structured in a very unique way, just as every single body on this planet is, and it has been incredibly painful to be pushed and constricted into something I am not. These legs are here to walk you to every place you wish to go, not to scrutinise in the mirror and cry over. This belly exists to receive nutrition and provide us with the vitality to do all that we wish to, not there to be sucked in, pinched and derided. Don't you understand? Your life is not about me but about expressing and being through me. You are so much more than this flesh and these bones, which, never-theless, are ingeniously and exquisitely made.

Please listen to me when I tell you what you need. I know when it would be good for you eat, to rest, to move, to be alone and to seek company . . . I know everything really! And I will not be shy in telling you these things, which are only ever for your highest good. Please listen without judgement and root your awareness in me. You will rediscover an inner compass with which you can never really go wrong.

Please trust me.

With joy and in solidarity,

Your body.

While each of these exercises have been included in the hope that they may be useful to you, it is also important to remember that we can bring mindful awareness into each and every moment of our lives. When we begin to bring our awareness into the present moment as we wait for the train, iron our clothes, type on the computer keyboard, cook our meals and every other activity and occurrence we are brought into a beautiful engagement with our bodies and our true Selves. From this place, truly spontaneous and authentic lives are given a stage upon which to emerge organically and effortlessly.

> One must be clear about one's real position. Once it is irrefutably clear that I am that in which witnessing of the world takes place, that I am not that which is perceived, that I am beyond all forms and modifications, the effect of the seeing will follow spontaneously . . .
>
> You are the eternal being, beyond becoming—witnessing but not a witnesser. Let all come and go. One day this body also will go, and that too you will witness. (Mooji, 2014, pp. 24, 26).

Useful apps for mindfulness practices

Breathe2Relax provides guided breathing sessions.

Eat Breathe Thrive. If you get one app, please make it this one! It is a truly outstanding resource, is completely free and will take you through a number of mindful body awareness exercises including the stunning "Tracking of Needs" meditation.

The Mindfulness App provides guided meditation sessions that can last anywhere from three to thirty minutes. Meditation sessions can be personalised.

Yoga Studio provides sixty-five ready-made yoga and meditation classes ranging from ten to sixty minutes. Customised classes can also be created from the apps library of yoga asanas, to which music and ambient sounds can be added.

Avenues of support and further reading

Disordered eating

www.b-eat.co.uk: Beat provides helplines, online support, and a network of self-help groups to assist young adults and people in the UK engaged in disordered eating practices. Helplines are for anyone who needs support and information: Parents and Teachers helpline: 0845 6341414. Helpline for sufferers: 0845 6347650.

www.eating-disorders.org.uk: The National Centre for Eating Disorders offer treatment both in person and over the phone and via Skype. They also provide a database of specialist counsellors. The website contains a broad range of information on disordered eating and training materials/courses for professionals.

www.mengetedstoo.co.uk: Men Get Eating Disorders Too is a national charity offering peer support, advice, and workshops specifically for men.

Garrett, C. (1998). *Beyond Anorexia: Narrative, Spirituality and Recovery.* Cambridge: Cambridge University Press.

Johnston, A. (2000). *Eating in the Light of the Moon: How Women can Transform their Relationship with Food through Myths, Metaphors and Storytelling.* California: Gurze Books.

Roth, G. (2004). *Breaking Free from Emotional Eating.* New York: Plume.

Perceived ugliness

www.bddfoundation.org: the Body Dysmorphic Disorder Foundation offers support to individuals and their families in the form of face-to-face and Skype support groups. Their website is a rich source of information and contains personal stories of people diagnosed with BDD and their family members.

www.ocdaction.org.uk/support-info/related-disorders/body-dysmorphia: OCD Action offers advice and support for people with obsessive–compulsive tendencies. They also provide information and advice about compulsive skin picking and hair pulling.

www.skinpick.com: Skin Pick is an online resource and community for people who compulsively pick their skin. Their website contains a forum, blog, articles, and an online treatment programme.

Phillips, K. (2005). *The Broken Mirror: Understanding and Treating Body Dysmorphic Disorder*. Oxford: Oxford University Press.
Veale, D., & Neziroglu, F. (2010). *Body Dysmorphic Disorder: A Treatment Manual*. New York: John Wiley.
Veale, D., Wilson, R., & Clarke, A. (2009). *Overcoming Body Image Problems Including Body Dysmorphic Disorder*. Quincym, MA: Robinson Press.

Visible differences

www.changing faces.org.uk: Changing Faces offers self-help guides, support services, and workshops for people with visible differences. There is also a designated support helpline: 0300 012 0275.

www.britishskinfoundation.org.uk: The British Skin Foundation.

www.eczema.org: The National Eczema Society.

www.psoriasis-association.org.uk: The Psoriasis Association.

www.vitiligosociety.org.uk: The Vitiligo Society.

Go to www.changingfaces.org.uk/show/feature/CST-Condition-specific-organisations-IS to find a wider range of condition-specific organisations for visible differences.

www.katiepiperfoundation.org.uk: The Katie Piper Foundation supports burns victims in gaining access to rehabilitation and psychological support. They also offer a peer support programme.

Partridge, J. (1990). *Changing Faces: The Challenge of Facial Disfigurement.* London: Penguin

Piper, K. (2011). *Beautiful: A Beautiful Girl. An Evil Man. One Inspiring True Story of Courage.* London: Ebury Press.

Rumsey, N., & Harcourt, D. (2005). *The Psychology of Appearance.* Oxford: Open University Press.

Self-harm

www.harmless.org.uk: Harmless is a user-led organisation that provides support, information, training, and consultancy to people who self-harm, their friends and families, and professionals.

www.nshn.co.uk: The National Self Harm Network provides a closely monitored online support forum for people who self-harm and their friends and families.

Robson, A. (2007). *Secret Scars: One Woman's Story of Overcoming Self Harm.* Franklin, TN: Authentic.

Shapiro, L. (2008). *Stopping the Pain: A Workbook for Teens who Cut and Self-Injure.* Oakland, CA: New Harbinger.

Strong, M. (2005). *A Bright Red Scream: Self Mutilation and the Language of Pain.* London: Virago.

Gender identity

www.gendertrust.org.uk: The Gender Trust provides support and an information centre for anyone with any question or problem concerning their gender identity, or anyone whose loved one is struggling with gender identity issues. They offer help to people who might be transgender, transsexual, people who do not identify with the gender they were assigned at birth, or those who are simply unsure.

www.mermaidsuk.org.uk: Mermaids offers family and individual support for teenagers and children with gender identity issues. They also offer support groups, training, and separate mailing lists for young people, parents, and professionals.

Bernstein Sycamore, M. (2006). *Nobody Passes: Rejecting the Rules of Gender and Conformity.* New York: Seal Press.
Brown, M., & Rounsley, C. (2003). *Understanding Transsexualism—For Families, Friends, Co-workers and Helping Professionals.* San Francisco, CA: Jossey-Bass.
Dececco, J., & Atkins, D. (1998). *Looking Queer: Body Image and Identity in Lesbian, Bisexual, Gay, and Transgender Communities.* London: Routledge.
Weise, E. (Ed.) (1992). *Closer to Home: Bi-sexuality and Feminism.* Washington, DC: Seal Press.

Variations of sex development

www.dsdfamilies.org: DSD Families provides an online information and support resource for families with children, teenagers, and young adults who have sex chromosomes and an internal and/or external genital anatomy that are unexpected for a boy or girl.

www.oiiuk.org: Organisation Intersex International (OII) is devoted to systemic change to end the fear, shame, secrecy, and stigma experienced by children and adults through the practice of non-consensual normalisation treatments for people born with atypical anatomy. It provides online support groups in many languages and information about intersex on its website.

www.ukia.co.uk: The UK Intersex Association runs a website which contains information about all aspects of intersex and is intended to inform and educate. It also provides links to other websites and avenues of support.

Callahan, G. (2009). *Between XX and XY: Intersexuality and the Myth of Two Sexes.* Chicago, IL: Chicago Review Press.
Ezekiel, J., & Preves, S. (2003). *Intersex and Identity: The Contested Self.* New Brunswick, NJ: Rutgers University Press.

Trauma

www.mankindcounselling.org.uk: Mankind offers specialist support services for men who have experienced childhood sexual abuse and/or sexual assault at any time of their lives. They offer one-to-one counselling and therapeutic support groups.

www.mybodybackproject.com: My Body Back runs a variety of services in London for women who have experienced sexual violence in order to support them to love and care for their bodies again. They run specialist services including cervical screening clinic and an STI self-testing clinic specifically designed for women who have been raped. They also run Café V, which is a quarterly session for women to learn about loving their bodies after violence.

www.thesurvivorstrust.org: The Survivors Trust is a national umbrella agency for over 135 specialist rape, sexual violence, and childhood sexual abuse support organisations throughout the UK and Ireland. They offer a comprehensive database of avenues of support for survivors and their families.

www.traumaclinic.org.uk: The Trauma Clinic offers advice and treatment to people experiencing stress, anxiety, and depression in relation to past trauma.

Emerson, D., Hopper, E., Levine, P., & Cope, S. (2012). *Overcoming Trauma through Yoga: Reclaiming Your Body*. Berkeley CA: North Atlantic Books
Herman, J. (1998). *Trauma Recovery: From Domestic Abuse to Political Terror*. London: Pandora Press.
van der Kolk, B. (2014). *The Body Keeps the Score: Mind, Brain and Body in the Transformation of Trauma*. London: Allen Lane.

Attachment

www.pipuk.org.uk: The mission of Parent and Infant Partnership (PIP) UK is to make psychotherapeutic support available to all families who are struggling to form a secure relationship with their baby. They offer qualified attachment therapists and a range of support services for parents and their babies.

www.thebowlbycentre.org.uk: The Bowlby Centre offers a referral system for attachment-based psychodynamic psychotherapy in North London and can make referrals to attachment-based therapists delivering the service from their centre or from other locations across

London and elsewhere. They also run outreach and development activities.

Gerhardt, S. (2004). *Why Love Matters; How Affection Shapes a Baby's Brain*. London: Routledge.

Seidenfaden, K., Draiby, P., Soborg Christensen, S., & Hejgaard, V. (2011). *The Vibrant Family: A Handbook for Parents and Professionals*, M. Davidsen & R. Draper, R. (Eds.). London: Karnac.

Join the community and continue the conversation at:

www.facebook.com/falsebodiestrueselves

BIBLIOGRAPHY

Mindfulness

Jays, J. (2011). *Mindful Eating: A Guide to Re-discovering a Healthy and Joyful Relationship with Food*. Boston, MA: Shambhala.

Kabat-Zinn, J. (2004). *Wherever You Go, There You Are: Mindfulness Meditation for Everyday Life*. London: Piatkus.

Thich Nhat Hanh (2014). *The Miracle of Mindfulness: The Classic Guide to Meditation by the World's Most Revered Master*. London: Ebury Digital.

Self-enquiry

Adyashanti (2004). *Emptiness Dancing*. Louisville: Sounds True.

Godman, D. (1991). *Be As You Are: The Teachings of Sri Ramana Maharshi*. London: Penguin.

Mooji (2014). *Before I Am* (2nd edn). London: Mooji Media.

Self-compassion

Brown, B. (2013). *Daring Greatly: How the Courage to Be Vulnerable Transforms the Way We Live, Love, Parent, and Lead*. London: Penguin.

Germer, C. (2009). *The Mindful Path to Self-Compassion: Freeing Yourself from Destructive Thoughts and Emotions.* New York: Guildford Press.

Neff, K. (2011). *Self-Compassion: Stop Beating Yourself Up and Leave Insecurity Behind.* New York: Harper Collins.

Yoga

Cope, S. (2001). *Yoga and the Quest for the True Self.* New York: Bantam.

Desikachar, T. K. V. (1999). *The Heart of Yoga: Developing Personal Practice.* Vermont: Inner Traditions Bear.

Klein, M., & Guest-Jelley, A. (2014). *Yoga and Body Image: 25 Personal Stories about Beauty, Bravery and Loving your Body.* Minnesota: Llewellyn.

Miller, R. (2010). *Yoga Nidra: A Meditative Practice for Deep Relaxation and Healing.* Louisville, CO: Sounds True.

Sanford, M. (2006). *Waking: A Memoir of Trauma and Transcendence: A Passage into the Body.* New York: Rodale.

REFERENCES

Aas, K. (2006). The body does not lie: identity, risk and trust in techno-culture. *Crime Media Culture*, 2(2): 143–158.

Abalos, D. (2002). *The Latino Male: A Radical Redefinition*. Boulder, CO: Lynne Rienner.

Ackard, D., Neumark-Sztainer, D., Hannan, P., French, S., & Story, M. (2001). Binge and purge behaviour among adolescents: associations with sexual and physical abuse in a nationally representative sample: The Commonwealth Fund survey. *Child Abuse & Neglect*, 25: 771–785.

Adami, G., Gandolfo, G., Campostano, A., Meneghelli, A., Ravrea, G., & Scopinaro, N. (1998). Body image and body weight in obese outpatients. *International Journal of Eating Disorders*, 24(3): 299–306.

Adebajo, S. (2002). An epidemiological survey of the use of cosmetic skin lightening cosmetics among traders in Lagos, Nigeria. *West African Journal of Medicine*, 21(1): 51–55.

Adyashanti (2006). *Emptiness Dancing*. Louisville, CO: Sounds True.

Aharon, I., Etcoff, N., Ariely, D., Chabris, C., O'Connor, E., & Breiter, H. (2001). Beautiful faces have variable reward value. fMRI behavioural evidence. *Neuron*, 32(3): 537–551.

Al-Abadie, M., Kent, G., & Gawkrodger, D. (1994). The relationship between stress and the onset and exacerbation of psoriasis and other skin conditions. *British Journal of Dermatology*, 130(2): 199–203.

All Party Parliamentary Group (APPG) on Body Image (2012). *Reflections on Body Image*. London: APPG and Central YMCA.

American Psychiatric Association (2013). *Diagnostic and Statistical Manual of Mental Disorders* (5th edn). Arlington, VA: American Psychiatric Association.

American Psychological Association (2007). *Report of the APA Task Force on the Sexualisation of Girls*. Washington, DC: APA.

Andersen, A., & Holman, J. (1997). Males with eating disorders: challenges for treatment and research. *Psychopharmacology Bulletin, 33*(3): 391–397.

Anderson, C., Robins, C., Greeno, C., Cahalane, H., Copeland, V., & Andrews, R. (2006). Why lower income mothers do not engage with the mental health care system: perceived barriers to care. *Qualitative Health Research, 16*(7): 926–943.

Andrews, B. (1998). Shame and childhood abuse. In: P. Gilbert & A. Andrews (Eds.), *Shame: Interpersonal Behaviour, Psychopathology and Culture* (pp. 176–190). Oxford: Oxford University Press.

Anschutz, D., Engels, R., & Becker, E. (2008). The bold and the beautiful. Influence of body size of televised media models on body dissatisfaction and actual food intake. *Appetite, 51*(3): 530–537.

Aristotle (2001). *The Basic Works of Aristotle*, R. McKeon (Ed.). New York: Modern Library.

Ashikari, M. (2005). Cultivating Japanese whiteness: the 'whitening' cosmetics boom and the Japanese identity. *Journal of Material Culture, 10*(1): 73–91.

Aspell, J., & Heydrich, L. (2013). Turning body and self inside out: visualized heartbeats alter bodily self-consciousness and tactile perception. *Psychological Science, 24*(12): 2445–2453.

Atkins, D. (Ed.). (1998). *Looking Queer: Body Image and Identity in Lesbian, Bisexual, Gay and Transgender Communities*. New York: Haworth.

Augustus-Horvath, C., & Tylka, T. (2009). A test and extension of objectification theory as it predict disordered eating: does women's age matter? *Journal of Counselling Psychology, 56*(2): 253–265.

Avalos, L., & Tylka, T. (2006). Exploring a model of intuitive eating with college women. *Journal of Counseling Psychology, 53*(4): 486–497.

Averill, J. (1982). *Anger and Aggression: An Essay on Emotions*. New York: Springer.

Azrin, N., & Nunn, R. (1973). Habit reversal: a method of eliminating nervous habits and tics. *Behaviour Research and Therapy, 11*(4): 619–628.

Baard, E. (2003). New science raises the spectre of a world without regret: the guilt-free soldier. *The Village Voice*, January 22–28. Accessed at: www.villagevoice.com/issues/0304/baard.php on 13 July 2015.

Backless, M., Charuvastra, A., Derryck, A., Fausto-Sterling, A., Lauzanne, K., & Lee, E. (2000). How sexually dimorphic are we? Review and synthesis. *American Journal of Human Biology*, 12(2): 151–166.

Bahrke, M. (2007). Muscle enhancement substances and strategies. In: J. K. Thompson & G. Cafri (Eds.), *The Muscular Ideal: Psychological, Social and Medical Perspectives* (pp. 141–160). Washington, DC: American Psychological Association.

Bakermans-Kranenburg, M., & van Ijzendoorn, M. (2009). The first 10,000 adult attachment interviews: distributions of adult attachment representations in clinical and non-clinical groups. *Attachment & Human Development*, 11(3): 223–263.

Balconi, M., & Mazza, G. (2009). Brain oscillations and BIS/BAS (behavioral inhibition/activation system) effects on processing masked emotional cues. ERS/ERD and coherence measures of alpha band. *International Journal of Psychophysiology*, 74(2): 158–165.

Baldwin, J. (1902). *Social and Ethical Interpretations in Mental Development* (3rd edn). New York: Macmillan.

Balogun, O. (2012). Cultural and cosmopolitan: idealised femininity and embodied nationalism in Nigerian beauty pageants. *Gender and Society*, 26(3): 357–381.

Barlett, N., Vasey, P., & Bucowski, M. (2000). Is gender identity disorder in children a mental disorder? *Sex Roles*, 43(11–12): 753–785.

Barnes, R., & Tantleff-Dunn, S. (2010). Food for thought: examining the relationship between food thought suppression and weight-related outcomes. *Eating Behaviours*, 11(3): 175–179.

Bashir, M. (1995). Interview with Princess Diana. *Panorama*. Broadcast in November 1995. Available at: www.bbc.co.uk/news/special/politics 97/diana/panorama.html. Accessed on 2 July 2015.

Baumrind, D. (1971). Current patterns of parental authority. *Developmental Psychology Monographs*, 4(1): 1–103.

Beardslee, W., Versage, E., & Gladstone, T. (1998). Children of affectively ill parents: a review of the past 10 years. *Journal of the American Academy of Child & Adolescent Psychiatry*, 37: 1134–1141.

B-EAT (2015). *The Costs of Eating Disorders: Social, Health and Economic Impacts*. London: B-EAT.

Becker, A., Burwell, R., Herzog, D., Hamburg, P., & Gilman, S. (2002). Eating behaviours and attitudes following prolonged exposure to television among ethnic Fijian adolescent girls. *British Journal of Psychiatry*, 180(6): 509–514.

Beddoe, A., & Murphy, S. (2004). Does mindfulness decrease stress and foster empathy among nursing students? *Journal of Nursing Education*, 43(7): 305–312.

Bell, C. (1914). *Art*. London: Chatto & Windus.

Bell, S. (2015). https://usodep.blogs.govdelivery.com/2015/06/12/my-experience-living-with-syndactyly-fusion-of-fingers/. Accessed on 7 August 2015.

Benjamin, A. (2007). Image conscious: an interview with James Partridge. *Guardian*, 2nd May.

Benoit, P., & Parker, K. (1994). Stability and transmission of attachment across three generations. *Child Development*, *65*(5): 1444–1456.

Ben-Tovim, D., & Walker, M. (1995). Body image, disfigurement and disability. *Journal of Psychosomatic Research*, *39*(3): 283–291.

Bermúdez, J. (2009). Self-consciousness. In: T. Bayne, A. Cleermans, & P. Wilken (Eds.), *The Oxford Companion to Consciousness* (pp. 577–579). Oxford: Oxford University Press.

Bhugra, D., Bhui, K., Desai, M., Singh, J., & Baldwin, D. (1999). The Asian cultural identity schedule: an investigation of culture and deliberate self-harm. *International Journal of Methods in Psychiatric Research*, *8*(4): 212–218.

Bigler, R., & Liben, L. (1993). A cognitive–developmental approach to racial stereotyping and reconstructive memory in Euro-American children. *Child Development*, *64*: 1507–1518.

Birnie, K., Speca, M., & Carlson, L. (2010). Exploring self-compassion and empathy in the context of mindfulness-based stress reduction (MBSR). *Stress and Health*, *26*(5): 359–371.

Blair, R., Morris, J., Frith, C., Perrett, D., & Dolan, R. (1999). Dissociable neural responses to facial expressions of sadness and anger. *Brain*, *122*(5): 883–893.

Blake, W. (1788a). Auguries of Innocence. In: D. V. Erdman (Ed.), *The Complete Poetry and Prose of William Blake* (revised edn) (pp. 490–496). New York: Anchor Doubleday.

Blake, W. (1788b). London. Songs of Innocence and of Experience. In: D. V. Erdman (Ed.), *The Complete Poetry and Prose of William Blake* (revised edn) (pp. 7–32). New York: Anchor Doubleday.

Blanchard, M. (1994). Post-bourgeois tattoo: reflections on skin writing in late capitalist societies. In: L. Taylor (Ed.), *Visualising Theory: Selected Essays from V.A.R., 1990–1994* (pp. 287–301). New York: Routledge.

Blanke, O., & Metzinger, T. (2009). Full-body illusions and minimal phenomenal selfhood. *Trends in Cognitive Sciences*, *13*(1): 7–13.

Blanke, O., Landis, T., Spinelli, L., & Seeck, M. (2004). Out-of-body experience and autoscopy of neurological origin. *Brain*, *127*(2): 243–258.

Blashill, A., & Hughes, H. (2009). Gender role and gender role conflict: preliminary considerations for psychotherapy with gay men. *Journal of Gay & Lesbian Mental Health, 13*(3): 170–186.

Blowers, L., Loxton, N., Grady-Flesser, M., Occhipinti, S., & Dawe, S. (2003). The relationship between sociocultural pressure to be thin and body dissatisfaction in preadolescent girls. *Eating Behaviours, 4*(3): 229–244.

Bluhm, R. (2009). Alterations in default network connectivity in posttraumatic stress disorder related to early-life trauma. *Journal of Psychiatric Neuroscience, 34*(3): 187–194.

Bly, R. (1988). *A Little Book on the Human Shadow*. Australia: HarperCollins.

Body Modification Ezine. www.bme.com. Accessed on 2 April 2015.

Bonafini, B., & Pozzilli, P. (2010). Body weight and beauty: the changing face of the ideal female body weight. *Obesity Reviews, 12*(1): 62–65.

Boni, F. (2002). Framing media masculinities: men's lifestyle magazines and the biopolitics of the male body. *European Journal of Communication, 17*(4): 465–478.

Boon, S., & Sinclair, C. (2009). A world I don't inhabit: disquiet and identity in Second Life and Facebook. *Educational Media International, 46*(2): 99–110.

Bordo, S. (2003). *Unbearable Weight: Feminism, Western Culture, and the Body: Tenth Anniversary Edition*. Berkeley, CA: University of California Press.

Borges, J. (1957/ 2006). Fauna of mirrors. In: *The Book of Imaginary Beings*, A. Hurley (Trans.) (pp. 81–85). London: Penguin Classics.

Borkovec, T., & Costello, E. (1993). Efficacy of applied relaxation and cognitive behavioural therapy in the treatment of generalized anxiety disorder. *Journal of Consulting and Clinical Psychology, 61*(4): 611–619.

Boroughs, M., Cafri, G., & Thompson, J. (2005). Male body depilation: prevalence and associate features of body hair removal. *Sex Roles, 52*(9–10): 637–644.

Botvinick, M., & Cohen, J. (1998). Rubber hands 'feel' touch that eyes see. *Nature, 391*: 756.

Boudette, R. (2006). Question and answer: yoga in the treatment of disordered eating and body image disturbance: how can the practice of yoga be helpful in recovery from an eating disorder? *Eating Disorders, 14*(2): 167–170.

Bovensiepen, G. (1995). Suicide and attacks on the body as a containing object. In: M. Sidoli & G. Bovensiepen (Eds.), *Incest Fantasies and Self-Destructive Acts* (pp. 43–54). New Brunswick, NJ: Transaction.

Bowlby, J. (1951). *Maternal Care and Mental Health: A Report Prepared on Behalf of the World Health Organization as a Contribution to the United Nations Programme for the Welfare of Homeless Children.* Geneva: World Health Organisation.

Bowman, G. (2007). *Thin.* London: Penguin.

Boyd, D. (2006). Friends, friendsters, and MySpace top 8: writing community into being on social network sites. *First Monday, 11*(12): 4 December.

Breen, A., Lewis, S., & Sutherland, O. (2013). Brief report: non-suicidal self-injury in the context of self and identity development. *Journal of Adult Development, 20*: 57–62.

Brennan, K., & Shaver, P. (1995). Dimensions of adult attachment, affect regulation, and romantic relationship functioning. *Personality and Social Psychology Bulletin, 21*(3): 267–283.

Briere, J., & Gil, E. (1998). Self-mutilation in clinical and general population samples: prevalence, correlates, and functions. *American Journal of Orthopsychiatry, 68*(4): 609–620.

Briere, J., & Scott, C. (2006). *Principles of Trauma Therapy: A Guide to Symptoms, Evaluation, and Treatment.* Thousand Oaks, CA: Sage.

Broberg, A., Hjalmers, I., & Nevonen, L. (2001). Eating disorders, attachment and interpersonal difficulties: a comparison between 18- to 24-year-old patients and normal controls. *European Eating Disorders Review, 9*(6): 381–396.

Brogaard, B. (2011). Are there unconscious perceptual processes? *Consciousness and Cognition, 20*(2): 449–463.

Brown, H. (2015). *Body of Truth.* Boston, MA: Da Capo Press.

Brown, L. (1987). Lesbians, weight, and eating: new analyses and perspectives. In: Boston Lesbian Psychologies Collective (Eds.), *Lesbian Psychologies. Explorations & Challenges* (pp. 294–310). Chicago, IL: University of Illinois Press.

Brown, R., & Gerbarg, P. (2005). Sudarshan Kriya Yogic breathing in the treatment of stress, anxiety, and depression: part II–clinical applications and guidelines. *Journal of Alternative and Complementary Medicine, 11*(4): 711–717.

Brown, S., & Shalita, A. (1998). Acne vulgaris. *Lancet, 351*(9119): 1871–1876.

Bruch, H. (1962). Perceptual and conceptual disturbances in anorexia nervosa. *Psychosomatic Medicine, 24*: 187–194.

Bruch, H. (1985). Four decades of eating disorders. *Handbook of Psychotherapy for Anorexia Nervosa and Bulimia, 7*–18.

Buhlmann, U., Cook, L., Fama, J., & Wilhelm, S. (2007). Perceived teasing experiences in body dysmorphic disorder. *Body Image, 4*: 381–385.

Buhlmann, U., Mara, J., Rupf, L., Zschenderlein, K., & Kathmann, N. (2011). Modifying emotion recognition deficits in body dysmorphic disorder: an experimental investigation. *Depression and Anxiety*, *28*(10): 924–931.

Buri, J., Louiselle, P., Misukanis, T., & Mueller, R. (1988). Effects of parental authoritarianism and authoritativeness on self-esteem. *Personality and Social Psychology Bulletin*, *14*(2): 271–282.

Burke, E. (1757). *A Philosophical Enquiry into the Origin of our Ideas of the Sublime and Beautiful*. London: R. & J. Dodsley.

Burns, E., Fischer, S., Jackson, J., & Harding, H. (2012). Deficits in emotion regulation mediate the relationship between childhood abuse and later eating disorder symptoms. *Child Abuse & Neglect*, *36*: 32–39.

Burrows, R., Slavec, J., Nangle, D., & O'Grady, A. (2013). Severe BDD, ERP, medication, and brief hospitalisation in the treatment of an adolescent with severe BDD. *Clinical Case Studies*, *12*(1): 3–21.

Butler, J. (1990). *Gender Trouble*. New York: Routledge.

Cahners, S. (1992). Young women with breast burns, a self-help group by mail. *Journal of Burn Care and Rehabilitation*, *13*(1): 44–47.

Campbell, A., & Hausenblas, H. (2009). Effects of exercise interventions on body image: a meta-analysis. *Journal of Health Psychology*, *14*(6): 780–793.

Campbell, J. (2008). *The Hero with a Thousand Faces*. Novato, CA: New World Library.

Campbell, J., & Moyers, B. (1989). *The Power of Myth*. New York: Bantam Doubleday Dell.

Campos, P., Saguy, A., Ernsberger, P., Oliver, P., & Gaesser, G. (2006). The epidemiology of overweight and obesity: public health crisis or moral panic? *International Journal of Epidemiology*, *35*(1): 55–60.

Capriotti, M., Ely, L., & Snorrason, I. (2014). Acceptance-enhanced behaviour therapy of excoriation (skin picking) disorders in adults: a clinical case series. *Cognitive and Behavioural Practice*, *22*(2): 1–10.

Cash, T. (1990). The psychology of physical appearance: aesthetics, attributes and images. In: T. Cash & T. Pruzinsky (Eds.), *Body Images* (pp. 51–79). New York: Guilford Press.

Cash, T., Theriault, J., & Annis, N. (2003). Body image in an interpersonal context: adult attachment, fear of intimacy, and social anxiety. *Journal of Social and Clinical Psychology*, *23*(1): 89–103.

Castells, M. (2000). *The Rise of the Network Society* (2nd edn). Oxford: Blackwell.

Champagne, F., & Curley, J. (2009). Epigenetic mechanisms mediating the long-term effects of maternal care on development. *Neuroscience and Bio-behavioural Reviews*, *33*(4): 593–600.

Chang, L. (Ed.) (2006). *Wisdom for the Soul*. Washington: Gnosophia.

Chapman, A., Gratz, K., & Brown, M. (2006). Solving the puzzle of deliberate self-harm: the experiential avoidance model. *Behaviour Research and Therapy*, 44(3): 371–394.

Chase, C. (1998). Hermaphrodites with attitude. *GLQ*, 4: 189–212.

Chasseguet-Smirgel, J. (1990). On acting out. *International Journal of Psychoanalysis*, 71(1): 77–86.

Cheng, H., & Malinkcrodt, B. (2009). Parental bonds, anxious attachment, media internalization, and body image dissatisfaction: exploring a mediation model. *Journal of Counselling Psychology*, 56(3): 365–375.

Chernin, K. (1985). *The Hungry Self: Women, Eating and Identity*. New York: HarperCollins.

Chiesa, A., & Serretti, A. (2009). Mindfulness-based stress reduction for stress management in healthy people: a review and meta-analysis. *Journal of Alternative and Complementary Medicine*, 15(5): 593–600.

Clark, A. (2002). Language of self-harm is somatic and needs to be learnt. *British Medical Journal*, 324(7340): 788–789.

Clarke, J. (1999). The sacrificial body of Orlan. *Body and Society*, 5(2–3): 185–207.

Cline, A. (2014). Defining my identity through the outside from the inside. *Body Modification Ezine*. Accessed at www.bme.com on 21 May 2014.

Coates, A., Abraham, S., & Kaye, S. (1983). On the receiving end—patient perception of the side-effects of cancer chemotherapy. *European Journal of Cancer Clinical Oncology*, 19(2): 203–208.

Cochrane, V., & Slade, P. (1999). Appraisal and coping in adults with cleft lip: associations with well-being and social anxiety. *British Journal of Medical Psychology*, 72: 485–503.

Cogan, J. (1999). Lesbians walk the tightrope of beauty: thin is in but femme is out. *Journal of Lesbian Studies*, 3(4): 77–89.

Colton, C. C. (1820). CXXX. In: *Lacon: or Many Things In Few Words* (p. 75). London: Longman. Hurst, Rees, Orme, and Brown.

Cook, M., & Mineka, S. (1989). Observational conditioning of fear to fear-relevant versus fear-irrelevant stimuli in rhesus monkeys. *Journal of Abnormal Psychology*, 98(4): 448–459.

Cooper, L., Shaver, P., & Collins, N. (1998). Attachment styles, emotional regulation and adjustment in adolescence. *Journal of Personality and Social Psychology*, 74(5): 1380–1397.

Cope, S. (2001). *Yoga and the Quest for the True Self*. New York: Bantam.

Corbin, J., (2007). Reactive attachment disorder: a biopsychosocial disturbance of attachment. *Child and Adolescent Social Work Journal*, 24(6): 539–552.

Cotterill, J. (1996). Body dysmorphic disorder. *Dermatology Clinics, 14*: 457–463.

Coyle, C., & Enright, R. (1997). Forgiveness intervention with post-abortion men. *Journal of Consulting and Clinical Psychology, 65*(6): 1042–1046.

Craig, M. (2006). Race, beauty, and the tangled knot of a guilty pleasure. *Feminist Theory, 7*(2): 159–177.

Creighton, S. (2004). *Prevalence and Incidence of Child Abuse: International Comparisons.* London: NSPCC Information Briefings.

Cromby, J., & Nightingale, D. (1999). What's wrong with social constructionism? In: D. J. Nightingale & J. C. Cromby (Eds.), *Social Constructionist Psychology: A Critical Analysis of Theory and Practice* (pp. 1–21). Buckingham: Open University Press.

Crossley, M. (2003). Would you consider yourself a healthy person? Using focus groups to explore health as a moral phenomenon. *Journal of Health Psychology, 8*(5): 501–514.

Curiel-Levy, G., Canetti, L., Galili-Weisstub, E., Milun, M., Eitan, G., & Bachar, E. (2012). Selflessness in anorexia nervosa reflected in the Rorschach comprehensive system. *Rorschachiana, 33*(1): 78–93.

Cvajner, M. (2011). Hyper-femininity as decency: beauty, womanhood and respect in emigration. *Ethnography, 12*(3): 356–374.

Dalai Lama (1995). *The Power of Compassion.* London: HarperCollins.

Dalai Lama & Vreeland, N. (Eds.) (2001). *An Open Heart: Practising Compassion in Everyday Life.* London: Hodder & Stoughton.

Damasio, A. (2000). *The Feeling of What Happens: Body, Emotion and the Making of Consciousness.* London: Vintage Books.

Das, L. (1997). *Eight Steps to Enlightenment: Awakening the Buddha Within: Tibetan Buddhism for the Western World.* New York: Broadway Books.

D'Augelli, A., Pilkington, N., & Hershberger, S. (2002). Incidence and mental health impact of sexual orientation victimization of lesbian, gay, and bisexual youths in high school. *School Psychology Quarterly, 17*: 148–167.

Davidson, S. (2009). Mouths wide shut: gender-quiet teenage males on gender-bending, gender passing and masculinities. *International Review of Education, 55*(5–6): 615–631.

Davis, S. (1985). Interview with Michael Jackson by first editor of *Moonwalk.*

De Berardis, D., Carano, A., Gambi, F., Campanella, D., Giannetti, P., & Ceci, A. (2007). Alexithymia and its relationships with body checking and body image in a nonclinical female sample. *Eating Behaviours, 8*(3): 296–304.

De Mello, A. (1990). *Awareness*. New York: Doubleday.

De Rossi, P. (2011). *Unbearable Lightness: A Story of Loss and Gain*. New York: Simon and Schuster.

De Young, M. (1982). Self-injuries behaviour in incest victims: a research note. *Child Welfare, 61*: 577–584.

Dececco, J., & Atkins, D. (1998). *Looking Queer: Body Image and Identity in Lesbian, Bisexual, Gay and Transgender Communities*. London: Routledge.

Deckersbach, T., Wilhelm, S., Keuthen, N., Baer, L., & Jenike, M. (2002). Cognitive–behaviour therapy for self-injurious skin picking. *Behaviour Modification, 26*(3): 361–377.

DeGroot, T., & Motowidlo, S. (1999). Why visual and vocal interview cues can affect interviewers' judgments and predict job performance. *Journal of Applied Psychology, 84*(6): 986–993.

Del Guidice, P., & Yves, P. (2002). The widespread use of skin lightening creams in Senegal: a persistent public health problem in West Africa. *International Journal of Dermatology, 41*(2): 69–72.

Depue, R., & Morrone-Strupinsky, J. (2005). A neurobehavioral model of affiliative bonding. *Behavioural and Brain Sciences, 28*: 313–395.

Devor, H. (1987). Gender blending females: women and sometimes men. *American Behavioural Scientist, 31*(1): 12–40.

Devor, H. (1997). *FTM: Female-to-Male Transsexuals in Society*. Bloomington, IN: Indiana University Press.

Dewey, J. (1928). Body and mind. *Bulletin of the New York Academy of Medicine, 4*(1): 3–19.

Diamond, G., Siqueland, L., & Diamond, G. (2003). Attachment-based family therapy for depressed adolescents: programmatic treatment development. *Clinical Child and Family Psychology, 6*(2): 107–127.

Didden, R., Korzilius, H., & Curfs, L. (2007). Skin-picking in individuals with Prader–Willi syndrome: prevalence, functional assessment, and its comorbidity with compulsive and self-injurious behaviours. *Journal of Applied Research in Intellectual Disabilities, 20*(5): 409–419.

Didie, E., Tortolani, C., Pope, C., Menarda, W., Fay, C., & Phillips, K. (2006). Childhood abuse and neglect in body dysmorphic disorder. *Child Abuse and Neglect, 30*(10): 1105–1115.

Diedrichs, P., Paraskeva, N., & New, A. (2011). *Quick Fixes and Appearance Concerns among Men and Women in Britain*. Bristol: University of the West of England: Central YMCA/Centre for Appearance Research.

Dion, K. (1973). Young children's stereotyping of facial attractiveness. *Developmental Psychology, 9*(2): 183–188.

Doering, R., Zucker, K., Bradley, S., & McIntyre, R. (1989). Effects of neutral toys on sex-typed play in children with gender identity disorder. *Journal of Abnormal Child Psychology, 17*: 563–574.

Dossey, L. (1989). *Recovering the Soul.* New York: Bantam.

Drogosz, L., & Levy, P. (1996). Another look at the effects of appearance, gender, and job type on performance-based decisions. *Psychology of Women Quarterly, 20*(3): 437–445.

Dyer, C. (2000). Surgeon amputated healthy legs. *British Medical Journal, 320*: 332.

Eagly, A., Ashmore, R., Makhijani, M., & Longo, L. (1991). What is beautiful is good, but: a meta-analytic review of research on the physical attractiveness stereotype. *Psychological Bulletin, 110*(1): 109–128.

Edwards, S. (2005). A psychology of breathing methods. *International Journal of Mental Health Promotion, 7*(4): 28–34.

Eisenberg, M., Neumark-Sztainer, D., & Story, M. (2003). Associations of weight-based teasing and emotional well-being among adolescents. *Archives of Paediatrics and Adolescent Medicine, 157*(8): 733–738.

Eliot, T. S. (1950). Ash Wednesday. In: *The Complete Poems and Plays.* Orlando, FL: Harcourt Brace.

Eliot, T. S. (1963). *Collected Poems 1909–1962.* London: Faber and Faber.

Eliot, T. S. (1988). *T. S. Eliot: The Poems*, M. Scofield (Ed.). Cambridge: Cambridge University Press.

Emmons, R. (2000). Personality and forgiveness. In: M. McCullough, K. Pargament, & C. Thoresen (Eds.), *Forgiveness Theory, Research and Practice* (pp. 156–179). New York: Guilford Press.

Enright, R., & Fitzgibbons, R. (2000). *Helping Clients Forgive.* Washington, DC: American Psychological Association.

Ernst, E. (2001). Therapies: yoga (section 3). In: *The Desktop Guide to Complementary and Alternative Medicine: An Evidence-Based Approach* (pp. 355–363). Edinburgh: Mosby.

Espino, R., & Franz, M. (2002). Latino phenotypic discrimination revisited: the impact of skin colour on occupational status. *Social Science Quarterly, 83*(2): 612–623.

Evans, G. (1982). *The Varieties of Reference.* Oxford: Clarendon Press.

Faces (2010). The face equality campaign—the evidence. Accessed at: www.changingfaces.org.uk on 3 April 2015.

Fadiman, J., & Frager, R. (Eds.) (1997). *Essential Sufism.* New York: HarperCollins.

Fairburn, C., Shafran, R., & Cooper, Z. (1999). A cognitive behavioural theory of anorexia nervosa. *Behaviour Research and Therapy, 37*: 1–13.

Farah, M., Tanaka, J., & Drain, H. (1995). What causes the face inversion effect? *Journal of Experimental Psychology: Human Perception, 21*(3): 628–634.

Farrell, C., Shafran, R., & Fairburn, C. G. (2004). Mirror cognitions and behaviours in people concerned about their body shape. *Behavioural and Cognitive Psychotherapy, 32*(2): 225–229.

Fassino, S., Piero, A., Gramaglia, C., & Abbate-Daga, G. (2004). Clinical, psychopathological and personality correlates of interoceptive awareness in anorexia nervosa, bulimia nervosa and obesity. *Psychopathology, 37*: 168–174.

Favazza, A. (1996). *Bodies Under Siege: Self-Mutilation and Body Modification in Culture and Psychiatry*. Baltimore, MD: Johns Hopkins University Press.

Favazza, A. (2005). Introduction. In: Strong, M. *A Bright Red Scream: Self Mutilation and the Language of Pain* (pp. 9–14). London: Virago.

Feldman, R., Greenbaum, C., & Yirmiya, N. (1999). Mother–infant affect synchrony as an antecedent to the emergence of self-control. *Developmental Psychology, 35*(1): 223–231.

Fernández-Aranda, F., Krug I., & Jiménez-Murcia, S. (2009). Male eating disorders and therapy: a controlled pilot study with one year follow-up. *Journal of Behavioural Therapy and Experimental Psychiatry, 40*(3): 479–486.

Ferreira, C., Pinto-Gouveia, J., & Duarte, C. (2013). Self-compassion in the face of shame and body image dissatisfaction: implications for eating disorders. *Eating Behaviours, 14*(2): 207–210.

Festinger, L. (1954). A theory of social comparison processes. *Human Relations, 7*(2): 117–140.

Feusner, J., Bystritsky A., Hellemann, G., & Bookheimer, S. (2010a). Impaired identity recognition of faces with emotional expressions in body dysmorphic disorder. *Psychiatry Research Journal, 179*(3): 318–323.

Feusner, J., Moller, H., Altstein, L., Sugar, C., Bookheimer, S., & Yoon, J. (2010b). Inverted face processing in body dysmorphic disorder. *Journal of Psychiatric Research, 44*(15): 1088–1094.

Finkelhor, D. (1994). The international epidemiology of child sexual abuse. *Child Abuse & Neglect, 18*(5): 409–417.

Finn, R. (2003). Paralysis common among victims of sexual assault. *Clinical Psychiatry News, 31*(1): 1 January, 2013.

First, M. (2005). Desire for amputation of a limb: paraphilia, psychosis, or a new type of identity disorder. *Psychological Medicine, 35*(6): 919–928.

Fisher, J. (2002). Tattooing the body, marking culture. *Body and Society, 8*(4): 91–97.

Fisher, K., & Smith, R. (2000). More work is needed to explain why patients ask for amputation of healthy limbs. *British Medical Journal, 320*: 1147.

Flegal, K., Brian, K., Orpana, H., & Graubard, B. (2013). Association of all-cause mortality with overweight and obesity using standard body mass index categories: a systematic review and meta-analysis. *Journal of the American Medical Association, 309*(1): 71–82.

Flegal, K., Graubard, B., Williamson, D., & Gail, M. (2005). Excess deaths associated with underweight, overweight and obesity. *Journal of the American Medical Association, 293*(15): 1861–1867.

Fletcher, L., & Hayes, S. (2005). Relational frame theory, acceptance and commitment therapy and a functional analytic definition of mindfulness. *Journal of Rational-Emotive and Cognitive-Behaviour Therapy, 23*(4): 315–336.

Fliege, H., Lee, J, Grimm, A., & Klapp, B. (2009). Risk factors and correlates of deliberate self-harm behaviour: a systematic review. *Journal of Psychosomatic Research, 66*(6): 477–493.

Fotopoulou, A., Tsakiris, M., Haggard, P., Vagopoulou, A., Rudd, A., & Kopelman, M. (2008). The role of motor intention in motor awareness: an experimental study on anosognosia for hemiplegia. *Brain, 131*(12): 3432–3442.

Foucault, M. (1979). *Discipline and Punish.* New York: Vintage Books.

Fouts, G., & Vaughan, K. (2000). Television situation comedies: male weight, negative references, and audience reactions. *Sex Roles, 46*(11–12): 439–442.

Fox, C., & Hawton, K. (2004). *Deliberate Self-Harm in Adolescence.* London: Jessica Kingsley.

Fox, J. (2009). A qualitative exploration of the perception of emotions in anorexia nervosa: a basic emotion and developmental perspective. *Journal of Clinical Psychology and Psychotherapy, 16*: 276–302.

Fraiberg, S., Adelson, E., & Shapiro, V. (1975). Ghosts in the nursery: a psychoanalytic approach to the problems of impaired infant–mother relationships. *Journal of the American Academy of Child Psychiatry, 14*: 387–421.

Fraley, R., & Shaver, P. (2000). Adult romantic attachment: theoretical developments, emerging controversies, and unanswered questions. *Review of General Psychology, 4*(2): 132–154.

Frank, P. (2013). Orlan talks plastic surgery. *Huffington Post*, www.huffingtonpost.com/2013/01/29/performance-artist-orlan-interview-beauty surgery_n_2526077.html. Accessed on 29 October 2014.

Frederick, D., Buchanan, G., Sadehgi-Azar, L., Paplau, L., Haselton, M., & Berezovskaya, A. (2007). Desiring the muscular ideal: men's body dissatisfaction in the United States, Ukraine, and Ghana. *Psychology of Men and Masculinity, 8*(2): 103–117.

Fredrickson, B. L., & Roberts, T. (1997). Objectification theory: toward understanding women's lived experiences and mental health risks. *Psychology of Women Quarterly, 21*(2): 173–206.

Freedman, S., & Enright, R. (1996). Forgiveness as an intervention goal with incest survivors. *Journal of Consulting and Clinical Psychology,* 64(5): 983–992.

Freud, S. (1905d). *Three Essays on the Theory of Sexuality. S. E.,* 7: 125–245. London: Hogarth.

Fried, R., & Wechsler, A. (2006). Psychological problems in the acne patient. *Dermatological Therapy, 19*(4): 237–240.

Fuchs, T. (2003). The phenomenology of shame, guilt and the body in body dysmorphic disorder and depression. *Journal of Phenomenological Psychology, 32*(2): 223–243.

Gallup, G. (1970). Chimpanzees: self recognition. *Science, 167*(3914): 86–87.

Garner, D. (1997). The 1997 body image survey results. *Psychology Today, 30*: 30–44, 75–80, 84.

Gerhardt, S. (2004). *Why Love Matters: How Affection Shapes a Baby's Brain.* London: Routledge.

Gibian, R. (1992). Refusing certainty: toward a bisexuality of wholeness. In: E. R. Weise (Ed.), *Closer to Home: Bi-sexuality and Feminism, 3*(5). Washington: Seal Press.

Gibran, K. (1991). *The Prophet.* London: Pan Reprints.

Gilbert, E. (2009). *Eat, Pray, Love: One Woman's Search for Everything.* New York: Bloomsbury.

Gilbert, P. (1997). The evolution of social attractiveness and its role in shame, humiliation, guilt and therapy. *British Journal of Medical Psychology, 70*(2): 113–147.

Gilbert, P. (2009a). Introducing compassion-focused therapy. *Advances in Psychiatric Treatment, 15*(3): 199–208.

Gilbert, P. (2009b). *The Compassionate Mind.* London: Constable & Robinson.

Gilboa-Schechtman, E., Avnon, L., Zubery, E., & Jeczmien, P. (2006). Emotional processing in eating disorders: specific impairment or general distress related deficiency? *Depression and Anxiety, 23*(6): 331–339.

Gill, R. (2009). Beyond the sexualisation of culture thesis: an intersectional analysis of sixpacks, midriffs, and hot lesbians in advertising. *Sexualities, 12*(2): 138–160.

Goldin, P., Manber Ball, T., Werner, K., Heimberg, R., & Gross, J. (2009). Neural mechanisms of cognitive reappraisal of negative self beliefs in social anxiety disorder. *Biological Psychiatry, 66*(12): 1091–1099.

Goldman, L., & Haaga, D. (1995). Depression and the experience and expression of anger in marital and other relationships. *Journal of Nervous and Mental Disease, 183*(8): 505–509.

Goleman, D. (2009). *Emotional Intelligence: Why It Can Matter More Than IQ.* London: Bloomsbury.

Goodale, W., & Milner, D. (2005). *Sight Unseen: An Exploration of Conscious and Unconscious Vision.* Oxford: Oxford University Press.

Gorbett, K., & Kruczek, T. (2008). Family factors predicting social self-esteem in young adults. *Family Journal, 16*(1): 58–65.

Government Equalities Office (2014). *Body Confidence: Findings from the British Social Attitudes Survey.* London: HMSO.

Grant, J., Kim S., & Eckert E. (2002). Body dysmorphic disorder in patients with anorexia nervosa: prevalence, clinical features, and delusionality of body image. *International Journal of Eating Disorders, 32*(3): 291–300.

Grant, J., Menard, W., & Phillips, K. A. (2006). Pathological skin picking in individuals with body dysmorphic disorder. *General Hospital Psychiatry, 28*(6): 487–493.

Gray, J., & Ginsberg, R. (2007). Muscle dissatisfaction: an overview of psychological and cultural research and theory. In: J. K. Thompson & G. Cafri (Eds.), *The Muscular Ideal: Psychological, Social, and Medical Perspectives* (pp. 15–39). Washington, DC: American Psychological Association.

Green, R., & Money, J. (1961). Effeminacy in pre-pubertal boys. Summary of eleven cases and recommendations for case management. *Paediatrics, 27*(2): 286–291.

Grieve, F. (2007). A conceptual model of factors contributing to the development of muscle dysmorphia. *Eating Disorders, 15*(1): 63–80.

Griffin, J., & Wilson, J. (1992). Disorders of sexual differentiation. In: P. Walsh, A. Retick, T. Stamey, & E. Vaughan (Eds.), *Campbell's Urology* (pp. 1509–1537). Philadelphia, PA: Saunders.

Griffiths, R., Beaumont, P., Russell, J., Schotte, D., Thornton, C., & Touyz, S. (1999). Sociocultural attitudes towards appearance in dieting disordered and non-dieting disordered subjects. *European Eating Disorders Review, 7*(3): 193–203.

Groesz, L., Levine, M., & Murnen, S. (2002). The effect of experimental presentation of thin media images on body satisfaction: a meta-analytic review. *International Journal of Eating Disorders, 31*(1): 1–16.

Grogan, S. (2008). *Body Image: Understanding Body Dissatisfaction in Men, Women and Children* (2nd edn). London: Routledge.

Gupta, M., Gupta, A., Schork, N., Ellis, C., & Voorhees, J. (1990). Psychiatric aspects of the treatment of mild to moderate facial acne: some preliminary observations. *International Journal of Dermatology, 29*(10): 719–721.

Gupta, M., Schork, N., Gupta, A., Kirkby, S., & Ellis, C. (1993). Suicidal ideation in psoriasis. *International Journal of Dermatology, 32*: 188–190.

Habyarimana, B. (2013). *Inspirational Quotes for All Occasions.* N. Charleston, SC: CreateSpace.

Hagglund, T., & Piha, H. (1980). The inner space of the body image. *Psychoanalytic Quarterly, 49*: 256–283.

Hanh, T. (1975). *The Miracle of Mindfulness.* Boston, MA: Beacon.

Hankinson, A., Daviglus, M., Van Horn, L., Chan, Q., Brown, I., Holmes, E., Elliot, P., & Stamler, J. (2013). Diet composition and activity level of at risk and metabolically healthy obese American adults. *Obesity, 21*(3): 1–15.

Hanson, N. (1958). *Patterns of Discovery: An Inquiry into the Conceptual Foundations of Science.* Cambridge: Cambridge University Press.

Hardit, S., & Hannum, J. (2012). Attachment, the tripartite model, and the development of body dissatisfaction. *Body Image, 9*: 469–475.

Hargreaves, D., & Tiggemann, M. (2003). The effect of thin ideal television commercials on body dissatisfaction and schema activation during early adolescence. *Journal of Youth and Adolescence, 32*(5): 367–373.

Harlow, H., Harlow, M., & Hansen, E. (1963). *Maternal Behaviour in Mammals.* New York: John Wiley.

Harris, R. (2009). *ACT Made Simple.* Oakland, CA: New Harbinger.

Harrison, A., Sullivan, S., Tchanturia, K., & Treasure, J. (2009). Emotion recognition and regulation in anorexia nervosa. *Clinical Psychology, 16*(4): 348–356.

Harrison, A., Sullivan, S., Tchanturia, K., & Treasure, J. (2010). Emotional functioning in eating disorders: attentional bias, emotion recognition and emotion regulation. *Psychological Medicine, 40*(11): 1887–1897.

Harrison, D. (1997). Cutting the ties. *Feminism & Psychology, 7*(3): 438–440. Also cited in Jeffreys, S. (2000). Body art and social status: cutting, tattooing and piercing from a feminist perspective. *Feminism Psychology, 10*(4): 409.

Harter, S., Marold, D., Whitesell, N., & Cobbs, G. (1996). A model of the effects of perceived parent and peer support on adolescent false self. *Child Development, 67*: 360–374.

Hausenblas, H., Janelle, C., Gardner, R., & Hagan, A. (2002). Effects of exposure to physique slides on the emotional responses of men and women. *Sex Roles, 47*(11–12): 569–575.

Healy, D. (2015). Serotonin and depression. *British Medical Journal, 350*: h1771.

Heatherton, T., & Baumeister, R. (1991). Binge eating as escape from self-awareness. *Psychological Bulletin, 110*(1): 86–108.

Heinberg, L., & Thompson, J. (1995). Body image and televised images of thinness and attractiveness: a controlled laboratory investigation. *Journal of Social and Clinical Psychology, 17*: 1–14.

Herbert, G. (1919). Love. In: A. Quiller-Couch (Ed.). *The Oxford Book of English Verse: 1250–1900* (p. 328). Oxford: Oxford University Press.

Herring, C., Verna, K., & Hayward, D. (Eds.) (2003). *Skin Deep: How Race and Complexion Matter in the "Colour Blind" Era.* Chicago, IL: Institute for Research on Race and Public Policy.

Herskind, A., Christensen, K., Juel, K., & Fogh-Anderson, P. (1993). Cleft lip: a risk factor for suicide. Paper presented at the 7th International Conference for Cleft Palate and Related Craniofacial Anomalies, Australia.

Hildebrandt, T., Langenbucher, J., Carr, S., & Sanjuan, P. (2007). Modelling population heterogeneity in appearance and performance enhancing drug (APED) use: applications of mixture modeling in 400 regular APED users. *Journal of Abnormal Psychology, 116*(4): 717–733.

Hill, W. (1915). Library of Congress Prints and Photographs Division Washington, D.C. 20540 USA http://hdl.loc.gov/loc.pnp/pp.print. No known restrictions on publication.

Hillier, T. (1865). *Handbook of Skin Disease.* London: Walton and Maberly.

Hodgson, S. (2004). Cutting through the silence: a sociological construction of self-injury. *Sociological Inquiry, 74*(2): 162–179.

Holmes, W., & Slap, G. (1998). Sexual abuse of boys: definition, prevalence, correlates, sequelae and management. *American Medical Journal, 280*(21): 1855–1862.

Hood, B. (2013). *The Self Illusion: Why There is No 'You' Inside your Head.* London: Constable.

Hope-Franklin, J., & Meier, A. (1982). *Black Leaders of the Twentieth Century.* Chicago, IL: University of Illinois Press.

Hornbacher, M. (2009). *Wasted: A Memoir of Anorexia and Bulimia.* New York: HarperCollins.

Hornberger, R. (1959). The differential reduction of aggressive responses as a function of interpolated activities. *American Psychologist, 14*: 354.

Hudson, J., Hiripi, E., Pope, H., & Kessler, R. (2007). The prevalence and correlates of eating disorders in the National Comorbidity Survey replication. *Biological Psychiatry, 61*(3): 348–358.

Hughes, B., & Hertel, M. (1990). The significance of colour remains: a study of life chances, mate selection, and ethnic consciousness among Black Americans. *Social Forces, 68*(4): 1105–1120.

Hunter, J. (1991). A comparison of the psychosocial maladjustment of adult males and females sexually molested as children. *Journal of Interpersonal Violence, 6*(2): 205–217.

Hunter, M. (2002). "If you're light, you're alright": light skin colour as social capital for women of colour. *Gender & Society, 16*(2): 175–193.

Hunter, M. (2005). *Race, Gender, and the Politics of Skin Tone*. New York: Routledge.

Huxley, A. (1954). *The Doors of Perception*. London: Chatto & Windus.

Irani, N. (2012). *The Goblin and the Girl*. London: Small Fish Books.

Irwin, H. (1985). *Flight of Mind: A Psychological Study of the Out-of-Body Experience*. Metuchen, NJ: Scarecrow Press.

Isaacowitz, D., Toner, K., Goren, D., & Wilson, H. (2008). Looking while unhappy: mood congruent gaze in young adults, positive gaze in older adults. *Psychological Science, 19*: 848–853.

Isaacs, J. (1996). *An Investigation of Predictive Factors of Psychological Morbidity in Burn Injured Patients Three Months Post Burn*. Manchester: University of Manchester Press.

Ishizu, T., & Zeki, S. (2011). Towards a brain-based theory of beauty. *Public Library of Science ONE, 6*(7): 1–10.

Jaggi, M. (2004). Profile: Jeanette Winterson. *Guardian*, 29 May 2004. Available at: www.theguardian.com/books/2004/may/29/fiction. jeanettewinterson, accessed 13 February, 2016.

James, W. (1890). *The Principles of Psychology*. Cambridge, MA: Harvard University Press.

Jaynes, J. (1982). *Origin of Consciousness in the Breakdown of the Bicameral Mind*. Boston, MA: Houghton Mifflin.

Jefferson, T. (1785). Letter to Peter Carr, Paris, 19th August 1785. In: *The Letters of Thomas Jefferson*. Accessed at: http://avalon.law.yale.edu/18th_century/let31.asp on 12 July 2015.

Jeffreys, S. (2005). *Beauty and Misogyny: Harmful Cultural Practices in the West*. New York: Routledge.

Johnston, J., & Elliot, C. (2002). Healthy limb amputation: ethical and legal aspects. *Clinical Medicine, 2*: 431–435.

Johnston, V., & Franklin, M. (1993). Is beauty in the eye of the beholder? *Ethology and Sociobiology, 14*(3): 183–199.

Johnstone, L. (2000). *Users and Abusers of Psychiatry: A Critical Look at Psychiatric Practice*. London: Routledge.

Johnstone, L. (2014). *A Straight Talking Introduction to Psychiatric Diagnosis.* Ross-on-Wye: PCCS Books.

Joshi, L., Joshi, V., & Gokhale, L. (1992). Effect of short-term 'pranayama' practice on breathing rate and ventilatory functions of lung. *Indian Journal Physiological Pharmacology, 36*(2): 105–108.

Kabat-Zinn, J. (1990). *Full Catastrophe Living: Using the Wisdom of Your Body and Mind to Face Stress, Pain and Illness.* New York: Bantam Doubleday Dell.

Kaisa, A., Hakan, S., & Jari-Erik, N. (2000). Parenting styles and adolescents' achievement strategies. *Journal of Adolescence, 23*(2): 205–222.

Kalick, S., Goldwyn, R., & Noe, J. (1981). Social issues and body image concerns of port wine stain patients undergoing laser therapy. *Lasers in Surgery and Medicine, 1*(3): 205–213.

Kalsched, D. (1996). *The Inner World of Trauma: Archetypal Defences of the Personal Spirit.* London: Routledge.

Kannings, A. (2015). *Kahlil Gibran, Life and Words: Volume 6.* London: CreateSpace.

Kant, I. (2007)[1781]. *The Critique of Pure Reason*, M. Weigelt (Trans.). London: Penguin Classics.

Kearney, P., Levin, E., & Rosen, G. (2003). *SCIE Report 2: Alcohol, Drug and Mental Health Problems: Working with Families.* Social Care Institute for Excellence (SCIE). London: SCIE.

Kearney-Cooke, A., & Striegel-Moore, R. (1994). Treatment of childhood sexual abuse in anorexia nervosa and bulimia nervosa: a feminist psychodynamic approach. *International Journal of Eating Disorders, 15*(4): 305–319.

Kellett, S., & Gawkrodger, D. (1999). The psychological and emotional impact of acne and the effect of treatment with isotretinoin. *British Journal of Dermatology, 140*(2): 273–282.

Kellett, S., & Gilbert, P. (2001). Acne: a bio psychosocial and evolutionary perspective with a focus on shame. *British Journal of Health Psychology, 6*(1): 1–24.

Kelly, L. (2007). Lesbian body image perceptions: the context of body silence. *Qualitative Health Research, 17*(7): 873–883.

Kendall-Tackett, K., Williams, L., & Finkelhor, D. (1993). Impact of sexual abuse on children: a review and synthesis of recent empirical studies. *Psychological Bulletin, 113*(1): 164–180.

Kent, G. (2002). Testing a model of disfigurement: effects of a skin camouflage service on well-being and appearance anxiety. *Psychology and Heath, 17*: 377–386.

Keski-Rahkonen, A., Hoek, H. W., Linna, M. S., Raevuori, A., Sihvola, E., Bulik, C. M., Rissanen, A., & Kaprio, J. (2009). Incidence and outcomes of bulimia nervosa: a nationwide population based study. *Psychological Medicine, 39*(5): 823–831.

Kessler, R., Sonnega, A., Bromet, E., Hughes, M., & Nelson, C. (1995). Posttraumatic stress disorder in the national comorbidity survey. *Archives of General Psychiatry, 52*(12): 1048–1060.

Keys, A., Brozek, J., Henschel, A., Mickelson, O., & Taylor, H. (1950). *The Biology of Human Starvation.* Oxford: University of Minnesota Press.

Kinnell, G. (1980). Saint Francis and the sow. In: *Mortal Acts, Mortal Words* (p. 9). Boston, MA: Houghton Mifflin.

Klein, M., & Guest-Jelley, A. (2014). *Yoga and Body Image: 25 Personal Stories about Beauty, Bravery and Loving your Body.* Minnesota: Llewellyn.

Klein, R. (1997). *Eat Fat.* London: Macmillan.

Kleve, L., Rumsey, N., Wyn-Williams, M., & White, P. (2002). The effectiveness of cognitive-behavioural interventions provided at outlook: a disfigurement support unit. *Journal of Evaluation in Clinical Practice, 8*(4): 387–395.

Knauss, C., Paxton, S., & Alasker, F. (2008). Body dissatisfaction in adolescent boys and girls: objectified body consciousness, internalization of the media body ideal and perceived pressure from media. *Sex Roles, 59*: 633–643.

Kondziolka, D., & Hudak, R. (2008). Management of obsessive-compulsive disorder-related skin picking with gamma knife radiosurgical anterior capsulotomies: a case report. *Journal of Clinical Psychiatry, 69*: 1337–1340.

Kornmeier, J., & Bach, M. (2005). The Necker Cube—an ambiguous figure disambiguated in early visual processing. *Vision Research, 45*(8): 955–960.

Kottler, J. (1996). *The Language of Tears.* San Francisco, CA: Jossey-Bass.

Kraus, P. (1999). Body image, decision making, and breast cancer treatment. *Cancer Nursing, 22*(6): 196–204.

Kristeller, J., & Hallett, B. (1999). An exploratory study of a meditation-based intervention for binge eating disorder. *Journal of Health Psychology, 4*(3): 357–363.

Kuiper, A. (1991). *Transexualism: Evaluation of Sex-reassignment Treatment.* Utrecht: Elinkwijk.

Kunstman, J., Clerkin, E., Palmer, K., Peters, M., Dodd, D., & Smith, A. (2015). The power within: the experimental manipulation of power interacts with trait BDD symptoms to predict interoceptive accuracy. *Journal of Behaviour Therapy and Experimental Psychiatry, 10*(50): 178–186.

Lacan, J. (1977). The mirror-stage as formative of the I as revealed in psychoanalytic experience. In: *Ecrits: A Selection*, A. Sheridan (Trans.) New York: W. W. Norton.

Laird, J. (1974). Self-attribution of emotion: the effects of expressive behaviour on the quality of emotional experience. *Journal of Personality and Social Psychology, 29*(4): 475–486.

Laird-Birmingham, C., & Treasure, J. (2010). *Medical Management of Eating Disorders.* Cambridge: Cambridge University Press.

Langer, E., & Moldoveanu, M. (2000). The construct of mindfulness. *Journal of Social Issues, 56*(1): 1–9.

Langlois, J., Kalakanis, L., Rubenstein, A., Larson, A., Hallam, M., & Smoot, M. (2000). Maxims or myths of beauty? A meta-analytic and theoretical review. *Psychological Bulletin, 126*(3): 390–423.

Langlois, J., Roggman, L., & Rieser-Danner, L. (1990). Infants' differential social responses to attractive and unattractive faces. *Developmental Psychology, 26*(1): 153–159.

Lanigan, E., & Cotterill, J. (1989). Psychological disabilities amongst patients with port-wine stains. *British Journal of Dermatology, 121*: 209–215.

Lansdown, R., Rumsey, N., Bradbury, E., Carr, T., & Partridge, J. (1997). *Visibly Different: Coping with Disfigurement.* Oxford: Butterworth Heinemann.

Laqueur, T. (1990). *Making Sex: Body and Gender from the Greeks to Freud.* Cambridge, MA: Harvard University Press.

Laszlo, E. (1993). *The Creative Cosmos.* Edinburgh: Floris.

Latner, J., Stunkard, A., & Wilson, G. (2005). Stigmatized students: age, sex, and ethnicity effects in the stigmatization of obesity. *Obesity Research, 13*(7): 1226–1231.

Leary, M., & Kowalski, R. (1995). *Social Anxiety.* London: Guilford Press.

Lee, S., Leung, C., Wing, Y., Chiu, H., & Chen, C. (1991). Acne as a risk factor for anorexia nervosa in Chinese. *Australian and New Zealand Journal of Psychiatry, 25*(1): 134–137.

Leit, R., Pope, H., & Grey, J. (2001). Cultural expectations of muscularity in men: the evolution of Playgirl centrefolds. *International Journal of Eating Disorders, 22*: 90–93.

Lemma, A. (2015). *Minding the Body: The Body in Psychoanalysis and Beyond.* Hove: Routledge.

Lever, J., Frederick, D., & Peplau, L. (2006). Does size matter? Men's and women's views on penis size across the lifespan. *Psychology of Men and Masculinity, 7*(3): 129–143.

Libet, B., Gleason, C., Wright, E., & Pearl, D. (1983). Time of conscious intention to act in relation to onset of cerebral activity (readiness potential): the unconscious initiation of a freely voluntary act. *Brain*, *106*(3): 623–642.

Liebling, H., Chipchase, H., & Velangi, R. (1997). Why do women harm themselves? Surviving special hospitals. *Feminism & Psychology*, *7*(3): 427–437.

Little, M. (1990). *Psychotic Anxieties and Containment: A Personal Record of an Analysis with Winnicott*. Northvale, NJ: Jason Aronson.

Liu, A. (2007). *Gaining: The Truth About Life After Eating Disorders*. New York: Warner.

Loehr, J., & Migden, J. (1999). *Breathe In, Breathe Out*. Alexandra, VA: True Life Books.

Lorde, A. (2009). Burst of light. In: *I Am Your Sister* (pp. 81–150). New York: Oxford University Press.

Lowe, W., & Forster, J. (1997). Managing acne in adult women. *Patient Care*, *31*: 30–40.

Lucal, B. (1999). What it means to be gendered me: life on the boundaries of a dichotomous gender. *Gender and Society*, *13*(6): 781–797.

Lupton, D. (1995). *The Imperative of Health: Public Health and the Regulated Body*. London: Sage.

Luutonen, S. (2007). Anger and depression—theoretical and clinical considerations. *Nordic Journal of Psychiatry*, *61*(4): 246–251.

MacCormack, P. (2006). The great ephemeral tattooed skin. *Body & Society*, *12*(2): 57–82.

MacDonald, M. (Ed.) (2000). www.ukia.co.uk. Accessed on 8 May 2014.

Mahe, A., Ly, F., Aymard, G., & Dangou, J. (2003). Skin diseases associated with bleaching products in women from Dakar, Senegal. *British Journal of Dermatology*. *148*(3): 493–500.

Main, M. (1995). Attachment theory: social, developmental and clinical perspectives. In: *Recent Studies in Attachment: Overview, with Selected Implications for Clinical Work*. Hillsdale, NJ: Analytic Press.

Mainz, V., Schulte-Ruther, M., Fink, G., Herpertz-Dahlmann, B., & Konrad, K. (2012). Structural brain abnormalities in adolescent anorexia nervosa before and after weight recovery and associated hormonal changes. *Psychosomatic Medicine*, *74*(6): 574–582.

Malangu, N., & Ogubanjo, G. (2001). For the colour of me. *Jamaica Observer*, May 23. www.jamaicaobserver.com/20010422t2300000500_7342_obs_for_the_colour_of_me.as. Accessed on 20 April 2015.

Malangu, N., & Ogubanjo, G. (2006). Predictors of tropical steroid misuse among patrons of pharmacies in Pretoria. *South African Family Practices*, *48*(1): 14.

Manago, A., Graham, M., Greenfield, P., & Salimkhan, G. (2008). Self presentation and gender on MySpace. *Journal of Applied Developmental Psychology*, *29*(6): 446–458.

Mandel, L., & Shakeshaft, C. (2000). Heterosexism in middle schools. In: N. Lesko (Ed.), *Masculinities at School* (pp. 75–105). Thousand Oaks, CA: Sage.

Marino Carper, T., Negy, C., & Tantleff-Dunn, S. (2010). Relations among media influence, body image, eating concerns, and sexual orientation in men: a preliminary investigation. *Body Image*, *23*(1): 301–309.

Marlon, S. (2005). *The Black Sun: The Alchemy and Art of Darkness*. College Station, TX: A & M University Press.

Martin, J. (2010). The development of ideal body image perceptions in the United States. *Nutrition Today*, *24*: 98–110.

Martinson, A., Nangle, D., Boulard, N., & Sigmon, S. (2011). Old habits die hard: treating a woman with a 20-year severe case of skin picking. *Clinical Case Studies*, *10*(6): 411–426.

Marx, B., Forsyth, J., Gallup, G., Fuse, T., & Lexington, J. (2008). Tonic immobility as an evolved predator defence: implications for sexual assault survivors. *Clinical Psychology: Science and Practice*, *15*: 74–94.

Maslow, A. (1973). Neurosis as a failure of personal growth. In: M. Vich (Ed.), *The Farther Reaches of Human Nature* (pp. 24–39). New York: Penguin.

Maslow, A. (1997). *Motivation and Personality* (2nd edn). New York: Harper & Row.

Masuda, A., Hayes, S., Sackett, C., & Twohig, M. (2004). Cognitive defusion and self-relevant negative thoughts: examining the impact of a ninety year old technique. *Behaviour Research and Therapy*, *42*: 477–485.

Mauger, P., Perry, J., Freeman, T., Grove, D., & McKinney, K. (1992). The measurement of forgiveness: preliminary research. *Journal of Psychology and Christianity*, *11*: 170–180.

McCabe, M., & Ricciardelli, L. (2001). Parent, peer, and media influences on body image and strategies to both increase and decrease body size among adolescent boys and girls. *Adolescence*, *36*(142): 225–241.

McCreary, D., & Sasse, D. (2000). An exploration of the drive for muscularity in adolescent boys and girls. *Journal of American College Health*, *48*(6): 197–304.

McEwen, B., Eiland, L., Hunter, R., & Miller, M. (2012). Stress and anxiety: structural plasticity and epigenetic regulation as a consequence of stress. *Neuropharmacology, 62*(1): 3–12.

McIver, S., McGartland, M., & O'Halloran, P. (1999). Overeating is not about the food: women describe their experience of a yoga treatment program for binge eating. *Qualitative Heath Research, 19*(9): 1234–1245.

McKenzie, S., Williamson, D., & Cubic, B. (1993). Stable and reactive body image disturbances in bulimia nervosa. *Behaviour Therapy, 24*: 195–207.

McLaren, K. (2010). *The Language of Emotions: What Your Feelings Are Trying To Tell You*. Louisville, KY: Sounds True.

McManus, F., & Waller, G. (1995). A functional analysis of binge eating. *Clinical Psychology Review, 15*(8): 845–863.

Melzack, R. (1990). Phantom limbs and the concept of a neuromatrix. *Trends in Neurosciences, 13*(3): 88–92.

Mendelson, M., Mendelson, B., & Andrews, J. (2000). Self esteem, body-esteem, and body mass in late adolescence: is a competence-importance model needed? *Journal of Applied Developmental Psychology, 21*(3): 249–266.

Merleau-Ponty, M. (1962). *Phenomenology of Perception*. London: Routledge.

Meyer-Bahlburg, H. (2010). From mental disorder to iatrogenic hypogonadism—dilemmas in conceptualizing gender identity variants as psychiatric conditions. *Archives of Sexual Behaviour, 39*(2): 461–476.

Meyerson, M. (2001). Resiliency and success in adults with Moebius syndrome. *Cleft Palate Craniofacial Journal, 38*(3): 231–235.

Michikyan, M., Dennis, J., & Subrahmanyam, K. (2014). Can you guess who I am? Real, ideal, and false self-presentation on Facebook among emerging adults. *Emerging Adulthood*, published online 24 April 2014.

Mifflin, M. (1997). *Bodies of Subversion: A Secret History of Women and Tattoo*. New York: Juno.

Miller, D. (2005). *Women Who Hurt Themselves: A Book of Hope and Understanding*. New York: Basic Books.

Minuchin, S. (1974). *Families and Family Therapy*. Cambridge, MA: Harvard University Press.

Minuchin, S. (1985). Families and individual development: provocations from the field of family therapy. *Child Development, 56*(2): 289–302.

Mock, V. (1993). Body image in women treated for breast cancer. *Nursing Research, 42*(3): 153–157.

Mohr, C., & Blanke, O. (2005). The demystification of autoscopic phenomena: experimental propositions. *Current Psychiatry Reports, 7*(3): 189–195.

Moncrieff, J. (2009). *A Straight Talking Introduction to Psychiatric Drugs*. Monmouth: PCCS Books.

Money, J. (1985). The conceptual neutering of gender and the criminalisation of sex. *Archives of Sexual Behaviour*, 14(3): 279–291.

Mooji (2011). Satsang in Brixton, London on 28 May 2011. Video and transcript available at http://amara.org/en/videos/D5SkXAoNkfIh/en/690228/. Accessed on 3 May 2015.

Mooji (2012). *Satsang with Mooji*. www.youtube.com/user/Moojiji. Video accessed on 2 November 2014.

Mooji (2014). *Before I Am*. London: Mooji Media.

Moore, C., & Egeth, H. (1997). Perception without attention: evidence of grouping under conditions of inattention. *Journal of Experimental Psychology: Human Perception and Performance*, 23(2): 339–352.

Moore, S. (2002). Diagnosis for a straight planet: a critique of gender identity disorder for children and adolescents in the *DSM-IV*. Unpublished doctoral dissertation, The Wright Institute, Berkeley, CA.

Moradi, B., & Huang, Y. (2008). Objectification theory and psychology of women: a decade of advances and future directions. *Psychology of Women Quarterly*, 32: 377–398.

Morry, M., & Statska, S. (2001). Magazine exposure: internalisation, self-objectification, eating attitudes, and body satisfaction in male and female university students. *Canadian Journal of Behavioural Science*, 33(4): 269–279.

Muise, A., Stein, D., & Arbess, G. (2003). Eating disorders in adolescent boys: a review of the adolescent and young adult literature. *Journal of Adolescent Health*, 33(6): 427–435.

Murguia, E., & Telles, E. (1996). Phenotype and schooling among Mexican Americans. *Sociology of Education*, 69(4): 276–289.

Murray, S., & Griffiths, S. (2015). Adolescent muscle dysmorphia and family-based treatment: a case report. *Clinical Child Psychology and Psychiatry*, 20(2): 324–330.

Murray, S., & Touyz, S. (2013). Muscle dysmorphia: towards a diagnostic consensus. *Australian & New Zealand Journal of Psychiatry*, 47(3): 206–207.

Musafar, F. (1996). Body play: state of grace or sickness? In: A. Favazza (Ed.), *Bodies Under Siege: Self-mutilation and Body Modification in Culture and Psychiatry* (pp. 325–334). Baltimore, MD: Johns Hopkins University Press.

Myers, P., & Biocca, F. (1992). The elastic body image: the effect of television advertising and programming on body image distortions in young women. *Journal of Communication*, 42(3): 108–133.

National Institute for Clinical Excellence (NICE) (2004). *Core interventions in the treatment and management of ANOREXIA NERVOSA, BULIMIA NERVOSA and related EATING DISORDERS.* Clinical Guideline 9. London: NICE.

National Institute for Clinical Excellence (NICE) (2014). *OBESITY: identification, assessment and management of OVERWEIGHT and OBESITY in children, young people and adults.* Clinical Guideline 189. London: NICE.

Neff, K. (2003a). The development and validation of a scale to measure self-compassion. *Self and Identity,* 2(3): 223–250.

Neff, K. (2003b). Self-compassion: an alternative conceptualization of a healthy attitude toward oneself. *Self and Identity,* 2(2): 85–102.

Neff, K., & Germer, C. (2012). A pilot study and randomised controlled trial of the mindful self-compassion program. *Journal of Clinical Psychology,* 69(1): 28–44.

Neziroglu, F., Hickey, M., & McKay, D. (2010). Psycho-physiological and self-report components of disgust in body dysmorphic disorder: the effects of repeated exposure. *International Journal of Cognitive Therapy,* 3: 40–51.

Neziroglu, F., Khemlani-Patel, S., & Veale, D. (2008). Social learning theory and cognitive behavioural models of body dysmorphic disorder. *Body Image,* 5(1): 28–38.

Nielsen, M., Dissanayake, C., & Kashima, Y. (2003). A longitudinal investigation of self-other discrimination and the emergence of mirror self-recognition. *Infant Behaviour and Development,* 26(2): 213–226.

Ntshingila, F. (2005). Female buppies using harmful skin lighteners. *Sunday Times,* South Africa, 27 November. www.sundaytimes.co.za. Accessed on 13 April 2015.

Null, G., & Dean, M. (2003). *Death by Medicine.* New York: Nutrition Institute of America.

O'Doherty, J., Winston, J., Critchley, H., Perrett, D., Burt, D., & Dolan, R. (2003). Beauty in a smile: the role of medial orbitofrontal cortex in facial attractiveness. *Neuropsychologia,* 41(2): 147–155.

O'Kearney, R. (1996). Attachment disruption in anorexia nervosa and bulimia nervosa: a review of theory and empirical research. *International Journal of Eating Disorders,* 20(2): 115–127.

Olivardia, R., Pope, H., Jr., Mangweth, B., & Hudson, J. (1995). Eating disorders in college men. *American Journal of Psychiatry,* 152(9): 1279–1285.

Olson, D., Bell, R., & Portner, J. (1992). FACES II. St. Paul: University of Minnesota, Department of Family Social Science.

Orbach, S. (1985). *Hunger Strike: Starving Amidst Plenty.* London: Karnac.

Orobio de Castro, I. (1993). *Made to Order. Sex/Gender in a Transsexual Perspective.* Amsterdam: Het Spinhuis.

Osman, S., Cooper, M., Hackmann, A., & Veale, D. (2004). Spontaneously occurring images and early memories in people with body dysmorphic disorder. *Memory, 12*(4): 428–436.

Papadopoulos, L., & Walker, C. (2003). *Understanding Skin Problems: Acne, Eczema, Psoriasis and Related Conditions.* Hove: Wiley.

Papadopoulos, L., Bor, R., Legg, C., & Hawk, J. (1998). Impact of stressful life events on the onset of vitiligo in adults: preliminary evidence for a psychological dimension in aetiology. *Clinical and Experimental Dermatology, 23*(6): 243–248.

Parrott, L., Jacobs, G., & Roberts, D. (2008). *Stress and Resilience Factors in Parents with Mental Health Problems and their Children.* London: SCIE Research Briefing.

Partridge, J. (1990). *The Challenge of Facial Disfigurement.* London: Penguin.

Partridge, J. (2005). Survival, socialisation, and advocacy. *Journal of Burn Care Rehabilitation, 34*: 26–32.

Patanjali (2009). *Patanjali's Yoga Sutra,* S. Ranganathan (Trans.). London: Penguin Classics.

Pereda, N., Guilera, G., Forns, M., & Gomez-Benito, J. (2009). The international epidemiology of child sexual abuse: a continuation of Finkelhor (1994). *Child Abuse and Neglect, 33*(6): 331–334.

Pérez-Cotapos, M., & Cossio, M. (2006). Tattooing and piercing in teenagers. *Revista Médica de Chile, 134*(10): 1322–1329.

Perrett, D., May, K., & Yoshikawa, S. (1994) Facial shape and judgements of female attractiveness. *Nature, 368*: 239–242.

Persaud, N., McLeod, P., & Cowey, A. (2007). Post-decision wagering objectively measures awareness. *Nature Neuroscience, 10*(2): 257–261.

Pert, C. (1997). *Molecules of Emotion: Why You Feel the Way You Feel.* New York: Scribner.

Phillips, A. (2001). *Promises, Promises: Essays on Psychoanalysis and Literature.* New York: Basic Books.

Phillips, K. (2005). *The Broken Mirror: Understanding and Treating Body Dysmorphic Disorder.* New York: Oxford University Press.

Phillips, K., Grant, J., Siniscalchi, J., & Albertini, R. (2001). Surgical and nonsurgical medical treatment of patients with body dysmorphic disorder. *Psychosomatics, 42*(6): 504–510.

Phillips, K., McElroy, S., Keck, P., Pope, H., & Hudson, J. (1993). Body dysmorphic disorder: 30 cases of imagined ugliness. *American Journal of Psychiatry, 150*(2): 302–308.

Pingleton, J. (1989). The role and function of forgiveness in the psychotherapeutic process. *Journal of Psychology and Theology*, *17*(1): 27–35.

Piper, K. (2011). *Beautiful: A Beautiful Girl. An Evil Man. One Inspiring True Story of Courage*. London: Ebury Press.

Plath, S. (1982). The Fifteen Dollar Eagle. In: *Johnny Panic and the Bible of Dreams* (pp. 43–58). London: Faber and Faber.

Polk, T., & Farah, M. (1995). Late experience alters vision. *Nature*, *376*(6542): 648–649.

Pollatos, O., Kurz, A., Albrecht, J., Schreder, T., Wiesmann, M., & Schandry, R. (2008). Reduced perception of bodily signals in anorexia nervosa. *Eating Behaviours*, *9*: 381–388.

Posada, S., & Colell, M. (2007). Another gorilla recognizes himself in a mirror. *American Journal of Primatology*, *69*(5): 576–583.

Preti, A., Pinna, C., Nocco, S., Mulliri, E., Pilia, S., Petretto, D., & Masala, C. (2006). Body of evidence: tattoos, body piercing, and eating disorder symptoms among adolescents. *Journal of Psychosomatic Research*, *61*(4): 561–566.

Price, J. (1988). Alternative channels for negotiating asymmetry in social relationships. In: M. R. A. Chance (Ed.), *Social Fabrics of the Mind* (pp. 157–195). Hove: Lawrence Erlbaum.

Prichard, I., & Tiggemann, M. (2008). Relations among exercise type, self-objectification, and body image in the fitness centre environment: the role of reasons for exercise. *Psychology of Sport and Exercise*, *9*(6): 855–866.

Proust, M. (1922). *In Search of Lost Time, Vol. 2, Within a Budding Grove*. London: Chatto and Windus.

Rajendra Acharya, U., Joseph, P., Kannathal, N., Min Lim, C., & Suri, J. (2006). Heart rate variability: a review. *Medical and Biological Engineering and Computing*, *44*(12): 1031–1051.

Ramel, W., Goldin, P., Carmona, P., & McQuaid, J. (2004). The effects of mindfulness meditation on cognitive processes and affect in patients with past depression. *Cognitive Therapy and Research*, *28*(4): 433–455.

Rank, O. (1932). *Art and Artist*. New York: Agathon Press.

Rauch, S., van der Kolk, B., Fisler, R., Alpert, N., Orr, S., & Savage, C. (1996). A symptom provocation study of posttraumatic stress disorder using positron emission tomography and script-driven imagery. *Archives of General Psychiatry*, *53*(5): 380–387.

Regmi, C., Kerwin, G., Gurung, A., Khati, D., & Jha, P. (2008). Globalising beauty: attitudes towards beauty pageants among Nepali women. *Feminism and Psychology*, *18*(1): 61–86.

Reid, D. (1998). *Chi-Gung. Harnessing the Power of the Universe.* London: Simon and Schuster.

Richardson, J. (1997). Acquired Disfigurement. In: R. Landsdown, E. Rumsey, E. Bradbury, T. Carr, & J. Partridge (Eds.), *Visibly Different: Coping with Disfigurement* (pp. 79–90). Oxford: Butterworth, Heinemann.

Richins, M. (1995). Social comparisons, advertising, and consumer discontent. *American Behavioural Scientist, 38*(4): 593–607.

Ridgeway, R., & Tylka, T. (2005). College men's perceptions of ideal body composition and shape. *Psychology of Men and Masculinity, 6*(3): 209–220.

Rief, W., Buhlmann, U., Wilhelm, S., Borkenhagen, A., & Brahler, E. (2006). The prevalence of body dysmorphic disorder: a population-based survey. *Psychological Medicine, 36*(6): 877–885.

Rilke, R. M. (2011). *Selected Poems with Parallel German Text*, R. Vilain (Trans.). Oxford: Oxford University Press.

Ring, K., & Cooper, S. (1997). Near-death and out-of-body experiences in the blind: a study of apparent eyeless vision. *Journal of Near-Death Studies, 16*(12): 101–147.

Roberts, S. (2004). Female facial attractiveness increases during the fertile phase of the menstrual cycle. *Proceedings of the Royal Society of Biological Sciences, 271*(5): 270–272.

Robertson, R. (2001). *The Shadow's Gift: Find out Who You Really Are.* Newburyport, MA: Nicholas Hays.

Robinson, E. (1997). Psychological research on visible differences in adults. In: R. Lansdown, N. Rumsey, E. Bradbury, T. Carr, & J. Partridge (Eds.), *Visibly Different: Coping with Disfigurement* (pp. 102–111). Oxford: Butterworth Heinemann.

Roff, C. (2015a). From 58 pounds to thriving. www.chelsearoff.com/articles/from-58-pounds-to-thriving/. Accessed on 24 May 2015.

Roff, C. (2015b). Starving for connection. www.chelsearoff.com/articles/another-article/. Accessed on 24 June 2015.

Rogers, C. (1980). *A Way of Being.* Boston, MA: Houghton Mifflin.

Rosen, J. (1997). Cognitive-behavioural body image therapy. In: D. M. Garner & P. E. Garfinkel (Eds.), *Handbook of Treatment for Eating Disorders* (pp. 188–201). New York: Guilford Press.

Rothschild, B. (2000). *The Body Remembers: The Psychophysiology of Trauma and Trauma Treatment.* New York: W. W. Norton.

Rubin, E. (1915). *Visually Experienced Figures: Studies in Psychological Analysis. Part One.* Copenhagen: Gyldendalske Boghandel, Nordisk.

Rubin, L. (1996). *The Transcendent Child: Tales of Triumph over the Past*. New York: HarperCollins.

Rudd, N., & Lennon, S. (2000). Body image and appearance-management behaviours in college women. *Clothing and Textiles Research Journal*, *18*(3): 152–162.

Rudd, N., & Lennon, S. (2001). Body image: linking aesthetics and social psychology of appearance. *Clothing and Textiles Research Journal*, *19*(3): 120–133.

Rumi (1995). *The Essential Rumi*, R. Vilain (Trans.). New York: HarperCollins.

Rumsey, N. (2002). Body image & congenital conditions with visible differences. In: T. F. Cash & T. Pruzinsky (Eds.), *Body Image: A Handbook of Theory, Research, and Clinical Practice* (pp. 226–233). New York: Guilford Press.

Rumsey, N., & Harcourt, D. (2004). Body image and disfigurement: issues and interventions. *Body Image*, *1*(1): 83–97.

Rumsey, N., & Harcourt, D. (2014). *The Psychology of Appearance*. London: Open University Press.

Rumsey, N., Bull, R., & Gahagan, D. (1982). The effect of facial disfigurement on the proxemic behaviour of the general public. *Journal of Applied Social Psychology*, *12*(2): 137–150.

Rumsey, N., Charlton, R., Clarke, A., Harcourt, D., James, H., Jenkinson, E., & White, P. (2012). Factors associated with distress and positive adjustment in people with disfigurement: evidence from a large multi-centered study. *Body Image*, *9*(4): 455–461.

Rushton, A., & Dance, C. (2005). Health visitors, social services departments and child and adolescent mental negative parental treatment of the singled-out child: responses to the problem by health services. *Clinical Child Psychology and Psychiatry*, *10*(3): 413–428.

Sadock, B., Sadock, V., & Ruiz, P. (2009). *Kaplan & Sadock's Comprehensive Textbook of Psychiatry* (9th edn). Philadelphia, PA: Lippincott Williams and Wilkins.

Sameroff, A., Bartko, W., Baldwin, A., Baldwin, C., & Seifer, R. (1998). Family and social influences on the development of child competence. In: C. Feiring & M. Lewis (Eds.), *Families, Risk, and Competence* (pp. 161–185). Mahwah, NJ: Lawrence Erlbaum.

Sanford, M. (2006). *Waking: A Memoir of Trauma and Transcendence: A Passage into the Body*. New York: Rodale.

Sarwer, D. (2002). Awareness and identification of body dysmorphic disorder by aesthetic surgeons: results of a survey of American Society for Aesthetic Plastic Surgery members. *Aesthetic Surgery Journal*, *22*: 531–535.

Sarwer, D., & Margolis, D. (2007). Body dysmorphic disorder symptoms among patients with acne vulgaris. *Journal of American Academy of Dermatology*, *57*(2): 222–230.

Sartre, J.-P. (1943). *Being and Nothingness*. London: Methuen.

Scheff, T. (2001). *Catharsis in Healing, Ritual, and Drama*. Lincoln, NE: iUniverse.com.

Schilder, P. (1950). *The Image and Appearance of the Human Body*. New York: International Universities Press.

Schrock, L., Reid, L., & Boyd, E. (2005). Transsexuals' embodiment of womanhood. *Gender and Society*, *19*(3): 317–335.

Segal, Z., Williams, J., & Teasdale, J. (2002). *Mindfulness-Based Cognitive Therapy for Depression*. New York: Guilford Press.

Serrano, M. (1966). *C. G. Jung and Herman Hesse: A Record of Two Friendships*. London: Routledge & Kegan Paul.

Shafran, R., Lee, M., Payne, E., & Fairburn, C. (2007). An experimental analysis of body checking. *Behaviour Research and Therapy*, *45*(1): 113–121.

Shakespeare, W. (1982). *Hamlet*, H. Jenkins (Ed.). London: Methuen.

Shakespeare, W. (2002). *King Henry IV Pt 1*, D. Kastan (Ed.). London: Arden Shakespeare.

Sharkey, V. (2003). Self-wounding: a literature review. *Mental Health Practice*, *6*(7): 35–37.

Shaw, A., & Ardener, S. (2005). *Changing Sex and Bending Gender (Social Identities)*. New York: Berghahn Books.

Shek, D. (1999). Parenting characteristics and adolescent psychological well-being: a longitudinal study in a Chinese context. *Genetic, Social, and General Psychology Monographs*, *125*(1): 27–44.

Shiffrin, R., & Dumais, S. (1981). The development of automatism. In: J. Anderson (Ed.), *Cognitive Skills and their Acquisition* (pp. 111–140). Hillsdale, NJ: Lawrence Erlbaum.

Shoemaker, L., & Furman, W. (2009). Parent–adolescent relationship qualities, internal working models, and attachment styles as predictors of adolescents' interactions with friends. *Journal of Social and Personal Relationships*, *26*(5): 579–603.

Short, F., & Ward, R. (2009). Virtual limbs and body space: critical features for the distinction between body space and near-body space. *Journal of Experimental Psychology: Human Perception and Performance*, *35*(4): 102–103.

Shuster, R. (1992). Bisexuality and the quest for principled loving. In: E. R. Weise (Ed.), *Closer to Home: Bi-sexuality and Feminism*, *3*(5) (pp. 147–154). Washington, DC: Seal Press.

Sierra, M., Baker, D., Medford, N., & David, A. (2005). Unpacking the depersonalization syndrome: an exploratory factor analysis on the Cambridge depersonalization scale. *Psychological Medicine, 35*(10): 1523–1532.

Silberstein, L., Mishkind, L., Striegel-Moore, R., Timko, C., & Rodin, J. (1989). Men and their bodies: a comparison of homosexual and heterosexual men. *Psychosomatic Medicine, 51*(3): 1173–1182.

Sim, L., & Zeman, J. (2004). Emotion awareness and identification skills in adolescent girls with bulimia nervosa. *Journal of Clinical Child and Adolescent Psychology, 33*(4): 760–771.

Smith, D. (1997). Introduction: "A life of pure immanence": Deleuze's "Critique et Clinique" project. In: G. Deleuze, *Essays Critical and Clinical* (pp. 11–16). Minneapolis, MN: University of Minnesota Press.

Smith, E. (1989). Butches, femmes and feminists: the politics of lesbian sexuality. *NWSA Journal, 1*(3): 398–421.

Smolak, L., & Murnen, S. (2002). A meta-analytic examination of the relationship between child sexual abuse and eating disorders. *International Journal of Eating Disorders, 31*(2): 136–150.

Sorene, E., Heras-Palou, C., & Burke, F. (2006). Self-amputation of a healthy hand: a case of body integrity disorder. *Journal of Hand Surgery, 31*(6): 593–595.

Soul Magazine (1970). Jackson 5 Interview, Vol. 5, No. 5. August 19th, pp. 1–6.

Sparks, S. (1962). *Laugh Your Way to Grace.* Woodstock, VT: Skylight Paths.

Sri Ramana Maharshi (1988). *Be As You Are: The Teachings of Sri Ramana Maharshi,* D. Godman (Ed.). London: Penguin.

Stearns, P. (1997). *Fat History: Bodies and Beauty in the Modern West.* New York: New York University Press.

Steiner, J. (1993). *Psychic Retreats.* London: Routledge

Steinhausen, H. (2009). Outcome of eating disorders. *Child Adolescent Psychiatry Clinics of North America, 18*(1): 225–242.

Stewart, T. (2004). Light on body image treatment: acceptance through mindfulness. *Behaviour Modification, 28*(6): 783–811.

Stones, M. (2014). 'We exaggerated obesity crisis': pressure group. Foodmanufacture.co.uk, 20 January.

Strauss, R., & Pollack, H. (2003). Social marginalization of overweight children. *Archives of Pediatrics and Adolescent Medicine, 157*(8): 746–752.

Streeter, C. (2010). Effects of yoga versus walking on mood, anxiety, and brain GABA levels: a randomized controlled MRS study. *Journal of Alternative & Complementary Medicine, 16*(11): 1145–115.

Striegel-Moore, R., Rosselli, F., DeBar, N., Wilson, L., May, G., & Kraemer, A. (2009). Gender differences in the prevalence of eating disorder symptoms. *International Journal of Eating Disorders, 42*(5): 471–474.

Striegel-Moore, R., Tucker, N., & Hsu, J. (1990). Body image dissatisfaction and disordered eating in lesbians. *International Journal of Eating Disorders, 9*(5): 493–500.

Strong, M. (2005). *A Bright Red Scream: Self-Mutilation and the Language of Pain*. London: Virago.

Stylelikeu (2015). The what's underneath project. http://stylelikeu.com/the-whats-underneath-project-2/. Accessed on 25 January 2015.

Tasca, G., Szadkowski, L., Illing, V., Trinneer, A., Grenon, R., & Demidenko, N. (2009). Adult attachment, depression and eating disorder symptoms: the mediating role of affect regulation strategies. *Personality and Individual Differences, 47*: 662–667.

Telljohann, S., & Price, J. (1993). A qualitative examination of adolescent homosexuals' life experiences: ramifications for secondary school personnel. *Journal of Homosexuality, 26*(1): 41–56.

Tenconi, E., Lunardi, N., Zanetti, T., Santonastaso, P., & Favaro, A. (2006). Predictors of binge eating in restrictive anorexia nervosa patients. *Italian Journal of Nervous Mental Disorders, 194*(9): 712–715.

Teng, E., Woods, D., Twohig, M., & Marcks, B. (2002). Body focused repetitive behaviour problems: prevalence in a non-referred population and differences in perceived somatic activity. *Behaviour Modification, 26*(3): 340–360.

Teshima, H., Kubo, C., & Kihara, H. (1982). Psychosomatic aspects of skin disease from the standpoint of immunology. *Psychotherapy Psychosomatics, 37*(3): 165–175.

Tewsbury, R., & Mustaine, E. (2001). Lifestyle factors associated with sexual assault of men: a routine activity theory analysis. *Journal of Men's Studies, 9*(2): 153–182.

Thomas, M. (2012). Sick/beautiful/freak: nonmainstream body modification and the social construction of deviance. *Sage Open, 2*: 1–12.

Thompson, A. (2001). Adjusting to disfigurement: processes involved in dealing with being visibly different. *Clinical Psychology Review, 21*(5): 663–682.

Thompson, A., Kent, G., & Smith, J. (2002). Living with vitiligo: dealing with difference. *British Journal of Health Psychology, 7*(2): 213–225.

Thompson, E. (2015). *Waking, Dreaming, Being: Self and Consciousness in Neuroscience, Meditation, and Philosophy*. New York: Columbia University Press.

Thompson, J., Heinberg, L., Altabe, M., & Tantleff-Dunn, S. (1999). *Exacting Beauty: Theory, Assessment, and Treatment of Body Image Disturbance*. Washington, DC: American Psychological Association.

Thompson, L. (1995). Feminist methodology for family studies. *Journal of Marriage and the Family, 54*(1): 3–11.

Thoresen, C., Harris, A., & Luskin, F. (2000). Forgiveness and health. In: M. McCullough, K. Pargament, & C. Thoresen (Eds.), *Forgiveness: Theory, Research, and Practice* (pp. 254–280). New York: Guilford Press.

Tjaden, P., & Thoennes, N. (1998). Prevalence, incidence, and consequences of violence against women: findings from the National Violence Against Women Survey. www.ncjrs.orgltxtfiles/l72837.txt. Accessed on 23 July 2015.

Toppino, T., & Long, G. (1987). Selective adaptation with reversible figures: don't change that channel. *Perception and Psychophysics, 42*(1): 37–48.

Trevena, J., & Miller, J. (2002). Cortical movement preparation before and after a conscious decision to move. *Consciousness and Cognition, 11*(2): 162–190.

Tustin, F., Mitrani, T., & Mitrani, J. (1992). *Encounters with Autistic States*. Maryland, AL: Jason Aronson.

Tylka, T., & Hill, M. (2004). Objectification theory as it relates to disordered eating among college women. *Sex Roles, 51*(11–12): 719–730.

Uzun, O., Basoglu, C., Akar, A., Cansever, A., Ozahin, A., Cetin, M., & Ebrinc, S. (2003). Body dysmorphic disorder in patients with acne. *Comprehensive Psychiatry, 44*(5): 415–419.

Valantasis, R. (1997). *The Gospel of Thomas*. London: Routledge.

Van der Donk, J., Hunfeld, J., Passcher, J., Knegt-Junk, K., & Nieboer, C. (1994). Quality of life and maladjustment associated with hair loss in women with alopecia androgenetica. *Social Science and Medicine, 38*(1): 159–163.

Van der Kolk, B. (1987). *Psychological Trauma*. Arlington, VA: American Psychiatric Publishing.

Van der Kolk, B. (2009). Yoga and post traumatic stress disorder: an interview with Bessel van der Kolk. *Integral Yoga Magazine*: 12–13.

Van der Kolk, B. (2014). *The Body Keeps the Score: Mind, Brain and Body in the Transformation of Trauma*. London: Allen Lane.

Van Holle, A., Pinheiro, A., Thornton, L., Klump, K., Berrettini, W., & Brandt, H. (2008). Temporal patterns of recovery across eating disorder subtypes. *Australia and New Zealand Journal of Psychiatry, 42*(2): 108–117.

Van IJzendoorn, M., Schuengel, C., & Bakermans-Kranenburg, M. (1999). Disorganised attachment in early childhood: meta-analysis of precursors, concomitants, and sequelae. *Development and Psychopathology, 11*: 225–249.

Veale, D. (2000). Outcome of cosmetic surgery and "DIY" surgery in patients with body dysmorphic disorder. *Psychiatric Bulletin, 24*(6): 218–221.

Veale, D., & Gilbert, P. (2012). Body dysmorphic disorder: the function and evolutionary context in phenomenology and a compassionate mind. *Journal of Obsessive-Compulsive and Related Disorders, 3*(2): 150–160.

Veale, D., & Riley, S. (2001). Mirror, mirror on the wall, who is the ugliest of them all? The psychopathology of mirror gazing in body dysmorphic disorder. *Behaviour Research and Therapy, 39*(12): 1381–1393.

Veale, D., Gournay, K., Dryden, W., Boocock, A., Shah, F., & Willson, R. (1996). Body dysmorphic disorder: a cognitive behavioural model and pilot randomised controlled trial. *Behaviour Research and Therapy, 34*(9): 717–729.

Verna, K., & Herring, C. (1991). Skin tone and stratification in the black community. *American Journal of Sociology, 97*(3): 760–778.

Vickers, D. (1972). A cyclic decision model of perceptual alternation. *Perception, 1*(1): 31–48.

Wagner-Martin, L. (1997). *Sylvia Plath: A Biography*. London: Routledge (Collected Critical Heritage).

Walcott, D. (1962). Love after Love. In: *Collected Poems 1948–1984* (p. 328). New York: Farrar, Straus & Giroux.

Wallis Simons, J. (2015). Ink with meaning: what we can learn from the tattoos of our ancestors. *CNN Style Magazine*, 29th June.

Walt, K. (1972). *Pogo: We Have Met the Enemy and He Is Us*. New York: Simon and Schuster.

Walther, M., Flessner, C., Conelea, C., & Woods, D. (2009). The Milwaukee Inventory for the Dimensions of Adult Skin Picking (MIDAS): initial development and psychometric properties. *Journal of Behaviour Therapy and Experimental Psychiatry, 40*(1): 127–135.

Ward, A., Ramsay, R., & Treasure, J. (2000). Attachment research in eating disorders. *British Journal of Medical Psychology, 73*: 35–51.

Washburn, M. (1995). *The Ego and the Dynamic Ground: A Transpersonal Theory of Human Development*. New York: New York University Press.

Wegner, D. (2002). *The Illusion of Conscious Will*. Cambridge, MA: MIT Press.

Weins, S. (2005). Introception in emotional experience. *Current Opinion in Neurology*, *18*: 442–447.

Weins, S., Mezzacappa, E., & Katkin, E. (2000). Heartbeat detection and the experience of emotion. *Cognition and Emotion*, *14*(3): 417–427.

Weiskrantz, L. (1991). Disconnected awareness for detecting, processing, and remembering in neurological patients. *Journal of the Royal Society of Medicine*, *4*: 466–470.

Weiss, G. (1999). *Body Images: Embodiment as Intercorporeality*. New York: Routledge.

Wenninger, K., & Heiman, J. (1998). Relating body image to psychological and sexual functioning in child sexual abuse survivors. *Journal of Traumatic Stress*, *11*(3): 543–562.

Wester, K., & Trepal, H. (2005). Working with clients who self-injure: providing alternatives. *Journal of College Counselling*, *8*: 180–189.

Williams, M. (2007). *The Velveteen Rabbit*. New York: Grosset and Dunlap.

Williamson, D., Prather, C., McKenzie, S., & Blouin, D. (1990). Behavioural assessment procedures can differentiate bulimia nervosa, compulsive overeater, obese, and normal subjects. *Behavioural Assessment*, *12*: 239–252.

Williamson, M. (1996). *A Return to Love: Reflections on the Principles of 'A Course in Miracles'*. London: Thorsons.

Winnicott, D. W. (1945). Primitive emotional development. *International Journal of Psychoanalysis*, *47*: 510–516.

Winnicott, D. W. (1965). Ego distortion in terms of true and false self. In: *Maturational Processes and the Facilitating Environment* (pp. 140–157). London: Hogarth Press.

Winnicott, D. W. (1975). Withdrawal and regression. In: D. W. Winnicott, *Through Paediatrics to Psychoanalysis* (pp. 255–261). London: Karnac.

Wiseman, M., & Moradi, B. (2010). Body image and eating disorder symptoms in sexual minority men. *Journal of Counselling Psychology*, *57*(2): 154–166.

Wocjik, D. (1995). *Punk and Neo-Tribal Body Art*. Jackson, MS: University Press of Mississippi.

Wolf, N. (1991). *The Beauty Myth: How Images of Beauty Are Used Against Women*. New York: Doubleday.

Wright, J., O'Flynn, G., & Macdonald D. (2006). Being fit and looking healthy: young women's and men's constructions of health and fitness. *Sex Roles*, *54*(9–10): 707–716.

Yabiku, S., Axinn, W., & Thornton, A. (1999). Family integration and children's self-esteem. *American Journal of Sociology*, *104*(5): 1494–1524.

Yeragani, V., Rao, K., Smitha, M., Pohl, R., Balon, R., & Srinivasan, K. (2002). Diminished chaos of heart rate time series in patients with major depression. *Biological Psychiatry, 51*(9): 733–744.

Zachrisson, H., & Skarderud, F. (2010). Feelings of insecurity: review of attachment and eating disorders. *European Eating Disorders Review, 18*(2): 97–106.

Zahn-Waxler, C., Ianotti, S., Cummings, E., & Denham, S. (1990). Antecedents of problem behaviours in children of depressed mothers. *Development and Psychopathology, 2*: 271–291.

Zaitsoff, S., Geller, J., & Srikameswaran, S. (2002). Silencing the self and suppressed anger: relationship to eating disorder symptoms in adolescent females. *European Eating Disorders Review, 10*(1): 51–60.

Zucker, T., Greenberg, M., & Gevirtz, R. (2008). The effects of rhythmic breathing intervention on posttraumatic stress disorder (PTSD) symptoms and heart rate variability (HRV). Paper presented to SYTAR conference.

INDEX

INDEX 325

medicalised, 79
mixed, 89
nature, 211
objectification, 13–14, 174
Offences Act, 81
organs, 79
orientations, 80–82
potency, 79
powerful, 8
readiness, 14
traits, 17
trans-, 85–87, 251
variability, 84
victimisation, 14
violence, 80, 253
shadow, xix, 175, 181–185, 187–190,
    192, 194, 199, 206
  collective, 182, 189
  reintegration, 187
  side, xix, 48, 184, 203
Shafran, R., 28
Shah, F., 28
Shakeshaft, C., 88
Shakespeare, W., 42, 193
  Hamlet, 193
Shalita, A., 61
shame, 14, 24, 29, 33, 35–36, 40, 42,
    60–62, 64, 69–70, 77, 81, 83, 101,
    114, 136, 138–139, 141–143, 165,
    174, 176, 193–194, 209, 211, 229,
    252
Shapiro, V., 200
Sharkey, V., 70
Shaver, P., 114, 122
Shaw, A., 85
Shek, D., 121
Shiffrin, R., 150
shock, 32, 44, 47, 61, 64, 69, 78, 97,
    100, 168
Shoemaker, L., 116
Short, F., 26
Shuster, R., 217
siblings, 118, 200
  number of, 118
side effects, 48
  chemotherapy, 60

known, 78
life-threatening, 78
of APEDs, 77
of hormones
Sierra, M., 23
Sigmon, S., 69
Sihvola, E., 40
Silberstein, L., 82
silence, 89, 189–190, 209, 231
  residual, 190
  small, 231
silent, 164, 197, 212, 237, 241 *see also*:
    body
  activity, 231
silhouette techniques, 41
Sim, L., 131
Sinclair, C., 37
Singh, J., 70
singling out, 118
Siniscalchi, J., 30
Siqueland, L., 122
Skarderud, F., 116
skin, 8, 23, 27, 29–31, 35, 61–62, 65–66,
    69, 71–72, 74, 89, 96–104, 112,
    145, 167, 184, 206–207, 209–210,
    222, 230, 242
  atrophy, 100
  bleaching, 99
  colour, 22, 96, 99
  conditions, 59, 62–64, 89
  cutting, 71, 95
  disease, 59, 63, 100
    episodic nature, 59
  facial, 29
  imperfect, 21
  integrity, 64
  lesions, 74
  lightening, 99–101, 103
  obsession, 207, 209
  picking, 29, 34, 42, 63, 68–69, 128,
      169, 180, 186, 194, 198,
      205–206, 229, 250 *see also*:
      behaviour
    focused, 68–69
    severity, 68
  pigmentation, 74

Made in the USA
Monee, IL
22 April 2022

95173811R00193